CW00549211

WORRY: A MAIEUTIC ANALYSIS

Worry: A Maieutic Analysis

MICK CAMPION
Murdoch University
Western Australia

Gower

Mick Campion, 1986

Published by
Gower Publishing Company Limited,
Gower House, Croft Road, Aldershot, Hampshire, England.

Gower Publishing Company,
Old Post Road.,
Brookfield,
Vermont, 05036,
USA.

British Library Cataloguing in Publication Data

Campion, Mick
    Worry : a maieutic analysis.——(Avebury
    series in philosophy)
    1. Anxiety——Philosophy
    I. Title   II. Series
    152.4   BF575.A6

ISBN 0-566-05118-4

Printed in Great Britain by Paradigm Print, Gateshead, Tyne & Wear

Contents

Preface

This book consists of work which was submitted as a doctoral thesis through the Department of Sociology at The University of Edinburgh late in 1979 which was entitled 'On the Relationship between Philosophy and Sociology'. The only changes are: the new title which is more appropriate for a wider audience; the introduction of section headings where none existed in the original; this preface which replaces the original abstract and acknowledgements; and the correction of a few typographical errors together with the removal of a few grammatical inconsistencies.

From the very first line of the first section it will be clear that this was far from a conventional PhD thesis. I am therefore more fortunate than might normally be the case to be taking this opportunity to thank the examiners of the thesis for recommending acceptance, and to thank Gower's anonymous reader for recommending publication.

My thesis supervisor was Stanley Raffel of the University of Edinburgh's Sociology Department and I want to thank him for helping me to generate the apparent confusion out of which this work was drawn, and for the numerous stimulating suggestions which helped to get the project moving. I should add that he continues to confuse me.

At the time of writing up the thesis I was in a desperate situation economically; I am well enough aware that that situation is shared by many, but it is only by mentioning it that I can effectively express my thanks to Lynne Jamieson of the Sociology Department at Edinburgh and her friends who provided me with a place to live and work.

Thanks to Terri Ainslie in Edinburgh for her caring work on the original typescript and to Jan Bide at Murdoch University for reworking that into a wordprocessed form suitable for publication.

Sue Campion deserves my thanks for her friendship over a far longer period for without it I might not even have started studying.

It is standard practice in a preface to pass a remark or two on the extent of the author's responsibility for the work in question, however, I am not adopting that practice here for the issue of responsibility is dealt with at length and in some detail at different stages in the book.

It is also common for authors to take the opportunity a preface provides to offer explicit advice to readers on how they might approach the particular work referred to. I am not adopting that practice either, for this book is illustrative of, amongst other things, my effort to try to improve my mode of reading.

Whilst I am aware that this is in some ways a difficult book to read I hope that you will not see that as sufficient reason to put it down.

1 Personal becomes public

Dear Stan,

I trust that my recent silence has not been presumed by you to display indifference or displeasure at receiving your response to my last paper. And I think I am right in presuming that even although my manner of proceeding could be surprising you will respond to it as you have to my previous speeches. And yet, it occurs to me to say that I am happy to be proceeding in this way, indeed that proceeding in this way makes me happy for I have decided that though this manner of proceeding could appear dangerous to some, as it does to me in my weaker moments, I shall not allow my resolve to shrink by treating apparent dangers as something to avoid. For I know well enough that a good listener will always be seeking virtue/thoughtfulness through this or any speech, and so I can only do myself good when I engage in dialogue.

What I want to say here is that your response to that last paper has helped me to feel ashamed that a piece of writing so dangerous could come from my hand. And yet, it would be disgraceful if after all our conversations/work I preferred to remain silent now, when the blindness to which you refer continues to be cracked by a glimmer of the thoughtful life to which we continue to aspire. There is much to be done, and though I shall make mistakes and take wrong turns, we will not be surprised at that. But I will proceed, for I want and need our inquiry to continue for I am entirely lost outside it: indeed I cannot be myself outside of it.

One further brief remark before I explain the place of this letter which perhaps you are wondering about. Thank you for helping to bring to my attention the irony of Socrates' speech to the effect that being persuaded by one's accusers could ever be one's problem. This has reminded me that our own personal conversation seemed at the time to begin only when I was persuaded by what I took to be your accusation that I was a worrier.[1] But appearances need not deceive for whilst that could have been allowed to mark the beginning of the end of a conversation it has become a part of our collaborative attempt to pursue our examination of the place of self: to continue reconstituting ourselves through further inquiry, through further thought/speech. When we have been talking about worry we haven't been talking about me, but about an activity which itself displays, as all speeches display, our place as speakers. We use our time well when we engage in thoughtful conversation, and I'm writing now for I think our work bears that out.

However, enough of these remarks, and I'll risk the 'enough' even though as we will see later when we turn to the work of Nietzsche it (i.e. 'enough') can display a failure to resist the inclination to stop speaking when the speech needs to proceed. Here it makes reference to my desire to continue getting on with the work that I need to do, for the material we have to work with was organised by a version of self that I am no longer pretending to be; and that material is now desperately being thought through in such a way as to display our continuing resistance to the temptation to remain or become what we merely seem to be. I will be and am showing how past work is helping me to develop, how it is not baggage that becomes a burden to one who carries it only for later use, but how it provides me with the strength to work now.

It is time to say how I am using this letter, for it is certainly not the extent of my response; that would have been a grave insult. And yet, at the same time, by saying that my response extends beyond the confines of this letter, the letter does make reference to my commitment to continue. This letter is being written for whilst I could remain silent I choose not to, but the decision to respond in this particular way shows my awareness that I cannot respond in a seemingly neat and tidy way, and I know that this is not what you would want of me.

So here is the surprise, which I now think you may well have anticipated, this letter is to be used as the introduction to a larger work which will itself provide material for our continuing dialogue, the larger work will in effect be my response. I'm taking this step not because I'm well prepared, but in order to continue doing the work of paring away that which detracts from my character and instructing and improving that which is essential to it. Any response that was less than that which this work will seek to become would not be becoming for it would not have displayed my true character. It would have done justice to no one. I only do myself justice by remembering that I will always have more to do if I am to do other justice, for we only do ourselves justice by acknowledging that we haven't yet done each other justice, i.e. by seeing that we have more to do.

Well, I've broken the pause in our conversation and by doing so increase both its jaggedness and its extent, but as this letter does also provide the introduction to a less private conversation we are breaking a wider silence. As this work has become less private our task must be to display how both our desire to break that silence, and our manner of breaking it, can allow for the recollection of the pieces into a thoughtful conversation. We must illustrate how that which could have appeared as an intrusion is rather part of an inquiry in which all are already necessarily involved.

I'm not requesting a reply to this letter, though should you choose to respond to it by writing I will incorporate your reply in the body of the work as it proceeds. Whilst this may or may not seem a reasonable way to proceed, and it will of course come as no surprise to you that I have many doubts about it, on balance it is the route out of the many I've tried in the last few months, which appeals to me, and you also know that that may be reason enough. I know that you and any thoughtful reader will not be distracted by fears about conventionality and acceptability though I don't deny that I also have to contend with them: I admit that by mentioning them.

I want to enjoy writing this work as I'm enjoying writing this letter for I think there is something in what Werther in Goethe's 'The Sorrows of Young Werther' says when he says:

> Ill humour (for us worry) is like indolence, because it is a form of indolence. Our natures tend towards it. But if we can muster the strength to pull ourselves together, work can be made easy and we can find true pleasure in activity. (Goethe 1962, p46)

But is there bitter irony here? For it seems that Goethe didn't hear the words he put into Werther's mouth for Goethe's work appears to have tended towards nature, perhaps he has been misunderstood and we do him an injustice. If not, he misunderstands himself, and does himself an injustice. But no matter for the moment, for there will be more of specific speakers in the main body of this work. What we are saying is that those who are indolent i.e. those who allow themselves to fall prey to that tendency towards nature, must deeply be ill humoured/worried; for our true strength can only lie in our ability and willingness to improve our natures/our selves through speech/thought. True pleasure is always produced in thoughtful, hence social, activity and not, as Goethe and others like him accidentally tempt us to believe, in nature, that is, if nature is formulated as unthoughtful, presocial.

When Socrates says to Phaedrus that he (Socrates) was a lover of knowledge and that the men who dwelt in the city were his teachers not the trees or the country; he chooses as all men and women must choose.

But am I rambling now, as if in the country? I must own up to the fact that I do not know, and consequently I have good reason to invite those who imagine they know to join me for they perhaps can show me how to proceed. And yet, I would be surprised beyond belief if you joined me for that reason, rather I strongly expect that you will join with me in my efforts, as you have done so frequently in the past, not because you think of yourself as knowing, but because you own up to your own ignorance (as I am now owning up to mine), and seek through conversation/inquiry to become more thoughtful about what thoughtful men/women do do.

Here then is where this letter draws to a close, though of course the work continues, and will continue beyond the limits of the work of which this letter forms a part. For, given that our intent is to breathe thoughtfulness into a form of life that if left as it is strangles both self and other, we have no interest in bringing our work to a close.

I suggested earlier in this letter that I was not requesting a reply and I think I should have the courage of my convictions here and ask you more firmly not to reply, for I know that it was my hand that wrote so dangerously, and it must be my head that frees it if my speech is to illustrate the good of our inquiry. I must be showing through my writing that even the hands of the speech that strangles (i.e. worry) can be turned to the work of sustaining a thoughtful life by their user. I will do what I think is right, as I know you will, and that will ensure that our conversations continue to be worthwhile. But I have not

Alcibiades' confidence for I remember how frequently, with the help of the questions you've raised and I've heard, I've become aware of the gulf between my thoughts and the actions I've become engaged in. And yet, whilst this letter no doubt provides yet another example, it also illustrates that I am continuing to make the effort of pulling them together for I'm glad to have been offered and accepted the opportunity to do so.

But even here I'm almost forgetting the reason I had for writing, and there is humour in that, for my reason for writing was and is related to my increasing awareness of my forgetfulness: of my tendency to act as if I know that what I am doing is worth doing when I do not know. Your comments on my last paper have helped remind me how forgetful I am of what I've previously been reminded of, both in and by our previous conversations. And it is for this reason that as a response to your request that I display my willingness and ability to respond to your detailed comments I am, and will be, doing everything I can at this stage and will leave out nothing that requires to be said.

So now to the detailed work which I hope you will detect from this letter is already underway.

But wait! I shall resist that temptation, i.e. to hear your silence (if indeed you choose to remain silent) as approval, by reminding myself that as the work has been, and is, for the good I can approve of it myself, for if I have come to approve of myself/my work as seeking to be thoughtful I don't need or want to wait for others' approval.

I no longer seek your approval, though when I've written all I can I will most certainly want you to join with me in raising further issues worthy of thought, and in this way continuing our inquiry. I don't know how the work will proceed from here, but I do know that even that fact can help make for a thoughtful, lively and honest inquiry, and we'll both enjoy that.

It is time I spoke for myself and whilst this whole work could be construed as a defence, that construction would prevent the depths of its moral commitment from reaching that surface that can join speaker and listener. I'm beginning in this way for I'm reminded there is much for all to give and gain through thoughtful conversation and nothing of value to be lost.

Mick

NOTES

[1] Fortunately, this personal conversation, like all conversations can have something to say to any who choose to listen.

2 A worried reader's response

By proceeding to reform worry, an activity which may appear to make even the calmest situation trying, in such a way as to replace it on a path of action which displays a philosophical attitude of calmness in even apparently the most trying circumstances, we set ourselves a task that, though seemingly stern, is a necessary test for this and any thoughtful conversation.

Whilst we recognise that that statement is no more than a slogan (and is perhaps not even a good slogan) it can convey a hint of the task in which this work plays a part. But, the work and the worker are not external to the task as tools or observers may appear to be; they are not apart but a part. Indeed the very fact that we set out on this attempt at all displays a commitment which worry would begin by trying to deny itself.

Perhaps if we mention two characters and situations from literature the nature of our task will be made more available. On the one side we have the story of Ivan Illyich Pralinsky the 'hero' of Dostoyevsky's 'A Nasty Story', whose story ends with him sinking helplessly into his chair saying to himself that he wasn't able to stand it. (Dostoyevsky 1966, p238) On the other side we have the speech of Socrates, and in this work specific weight is likely to be laid upon his speech in the 'Apology', though, given his consistency we could draw from elsewhere equally well.

We have begun by talking of one side and another, of one character and another, but our task is to relate these two sides, to show how Ivan, had he been more thoughtful, more honest with himself and others, would have become Socrates. We relate to both Ivan and Socrates as social developments, and by doing so make the desirable speech of Socrates a real possibility for us. We do not begin by invoking and relying upon notions such as natural genius, or whatever, in such a way as to diminish our responsibilities. Socrates is social whether he is conceived of as an historical character or as a product of Plato's thought, and so, most importantly, are we. Our decision to relate to Socrates as one of us is what this work is about for we cannot take Nietzsche at his word when he says in 'The Twilight of Idols' that 'The dialectician devitalizes his opponent's intellect'. (Nietzsche 1975, p32) We choose to think of the intellect as dialectical, as not producing other as opponent but as collaborator. Nietzsche's fight with Socrates would have required Socrates' collaboration to become more than shadow boxing, for the collaboration of an opponent is necessary for wrestling to take place. Whilst we do not take Nietzsche at his word we seek to revitalise his speech and the speeches of others including ourselves, not to devitalise.

Since writing the letter reproduced in Section 1 I have decided that what I will do is to question, and take issue with this work as it proceeds, or better, to use this work to raise questions and issues as it proceeds, in the same manner that they would be raised by any thoughtful colleague. I must ask questions, and take up issues, on behalf of this thoughtful colleague, for by doing so I will be acting both on your behalf and mine, for we need and want to relate to others and to ourselves as would those who, by asking thoughtful questions, act with profound moral intent. Though these questions stretch us we need not heed any inclination to shrink away from them for we have been being reminded through our work that that would do no good; that we could not choose to do that.

That paragraph begins to remind us how although this work may have appeared to have begun in a very personal manner that does not make it private. On the contrary what it helps us to uncover is that as we become more true to our characters so we also have less need for privacy.

Still, some readers may be choosing to feel like newcomers to an ongoing conversation, for references have been made to particulars (e.g. that dangerous piece of writing) about which they have as yet no knowledge. If this situation is not comfortable for them, that will very likely not be altered by us reminding them that we have all experienced finding ourselves at a loss in situations of this kind. Neither would it alter matters if we suggested that perhaps this is one way of making reference to the place of all men and women as speakers/thinkers.

What we can question is an orientation which produces being a newcomer to an ongoing conversation as a disadvantage, for perhaps a thoughtful colleague is one who always tries to proceed as a newcomer. As we think this is so, we ask these readers to try to approach this material as newcomers for by so doing they are not at a disadvantage, rather we are the same, for it is only through our efforts to reachieve this newness that we can make good use of this material, or better make use of any material in such a way that we continue directing our conversations by considering issues worthy of our thought. It is only if we genuinely recognise and own up to the fact that we are at a loss that our inquiry can be worthwhile.

What we discern here is that a problem that this transitional section could have been delayed by i.e. that of how to write in such a way as to engage both new and old interlocutors would not have been worthy of our attention. For we have come to remember that a thoughtful interlocutor, whether speaking or listening/writing or reading, tries to remain a newcomer. That a thoughtful interlocutor resists the temptation to begin or end by stipulating that he or she knows what is best, i.e. what is for the good; for isn't it stipulations that preempt dialogue or thought, and make for empty speech?

We are saying that thoughtful colleagues, or good friends, are those who would relate to others and to their own pasts etc. in such a way as to collaborate in conversations which increased the worth of these relationships. This work represents on one level our continuing effort to befriend ourselves, on another our relationship with others who act as thoughtful colleagues or good friends towards us, and our attempt to do the same for them; and on a third level it represents the relationship between social, thoughtful action and inaction. What it represents to you the reader that we do not yet know will depend upon what you conceive yourself to be, but we choose to proceed by relating to you as we would with any thoughtful interlocutor.

The question we choose to orient to here is how can we relate to our past conversations? How would one who wanted to act thoughtfully relate to what he and others had previously said and heard? How, more deeply, does one who wants to act thoughtfully relate to anything? Perhaps we could begin by saying that the thoughtful character tends to relate through rather than to things i.e. her topics: the things about which she speaks are made by her into valuable resources both for herself and others. The topic becomes part of the collaborative effort, for it is worked with in such a way as to reachieve through conversation/thought a more worthy understanding of those relationships, and enables them to continue in a more thoughtful manner. We need to use what we come into contact with whatever it may be to remind ourselves - to exhort ourselves - to act more thoughtfully. By producing that which we come into contact with, that which we think about, as analogous to reminders, we provide strong reasons for preserving that with which we have dealt and deal. As anything can be used by a thoughtful interlocutor to continue directing attention towards issues worthy of concern, we see how by being thoughtful we need not relate to past speeches, or others' speeches as 'things' to abandon. This is not though a recipe for a collection of random objects, but for recollection. For we are not concerned simply to regurgitate what we have previously heard or said, rather we display how we can be reminded to be ourselves by the way we relate to that with which we deal. We are active and, if we are to act thoughtfully we need to keep in mind how even what might appear to some as innocuous passive activities, for instance reading, or for that matter collecting, or remaining silent, or choosing examples, call for thoughtful effort if we are truly to be engaged in them.

However, even having said this I'm still tempted to prefer what I, for reasons as yet unclear to me, perceive as the security of my current internal conversation to the insecurity of dealing with past conversations. (Perhaps this preference could help account for bad memory?) But, the raising of this issue encourages me to ask in what way the internal conversation in which I begin by perceiving myself to be engaged is mine? This assumes that I am what I appear to myself to be, when if, or rather by being honest, I have to admit that I cannot be sure about this. What we are saying is that if we approach our selves as topics to think about, we can change our minds in the strong sense of change i.e. become more thoughtful about what we are. We don't have to remain as what we may appear to be, and that in itself provides a good reason to continue thinking, conversing about what we do, what we are, what we want. However, by noticing the way we spoke there of 'that in itself' we remind ourselves that it is we who provide good reasons they are not provided for us.

I begin to doubt that this work is worthy of you, but I remind myself to continue for that doubt is no reason to stop, but is reason to continue; it should provide a spur for our continued efforts. And yet we see that I doubted it was worthy of you because I doubted it was worthy of me, for now each paragraph seems to exude more loudly the hollow ring of the speech of one who moves away from, rather than into that material with which he/she works. But I know the material I have stares me in the face whilst the clock does tick in my ears, for I also know that it is now I must deal with the inclination to remain as I appear to be i.e. the inclination to do nothing. But we might ask, to whom would doing nothing appear the most reasonable course of action? For course of action is what it is. Already we make progress for the very fact that I considered entering into doing nothing, without thinking about what sort of character would pursue that course of action, itself displays the accidentalness of that version of doing nothing. However, doing nothing could be the action of one who was not prepared to act too soon i.e. before he/she decided what was a good thing to do, but of course he/she should realise that they perceive doing nothing as a good thing to do. When we act thoughtfully we act as we think one who acted or acts thoughtfully would act; and do not need to follow our actions by asking what sort of person would have acted in that way.

So now we come to formulate a good friend or thoughtful colleague as one whose actions display his effort to act as one who thinks about what it is good to do. But we must also bear in mind that thinking does not precede action in the way that stops precede starts, or absence precedes presence. Thinking is part of action, we do not separate them in such a way that thinking needs to stop to allow action to proceed, for that reduces action to accident. So, we move into the materials with which we deal thoughtfully, but not as if we began to act after we finished thinking. Our manner of dealing with the materials around us displays our efforts to continue thinking as we do. We are not finished objects, we change as we read and write, we forget and we remember, and we imagine you might be the same, and will do well, as will we, to bear this in mind whilst proceeding. However, even the idea of bearing in mind is too static, much too static, perhaps the idea of bearing our minds, of revealing to ourselves and others what we can be is more productive? It is by not being finished objects that we can always thoughtfully change ourselves for the better: that we can choose to read in productive ways: that we can need and want, and most importantly maintain social relationships: that we can give and take in dialectical relationships. I said in the letter that I wanted to enjoy writing this work and at present I am, and by realising that we can always improve ourselves we resist the temptation to defend ourselves as we seem to be, but by doing so we recognise we always have work to do. We know, of course, that the fact I'm enjoying this work does not detract from its seriousness, on the contrary the very fact that work and pleasure seem so frequently to be separated in certain 'societies' makes reference to the separation of thought from action in the dealings of those 'societies' members.

But I suggested above that I preferred what I perceived as the security of dealing with my current internal conversation rather than with the insecurity of dealing with past conversations. It occurs to us now that this distinction is bogus, for our current internal conversations are our ways of dealing with past conversations, so what follows for us are our internal conversations. How else can we who are thinking proceed? When I wrote earlier of the material that had to be dealt with staring me in the face, I relied upon the same sort of thoughtless distinction between speaker/thinker and what he/she has to work with, that we seem to be relying on now, if we separate our selves from that earlier work. Yet now it is you, the thoughtful reader who I see staring at me, but I can take heart, for we know that you must recognise at least a bit of yourself in what you see. We also suggested earlier that we began by talking of

8

one side and the other, and what we propose to do now is to relate the views of one who considered herself to be worried, in this instance by what she has so far read of this work. You may or may not consider yourself to be worried, that is of little concern for we are adopting this strategy if such it can be called, as a way to step away from, or distance ourselves from an activity in which we could have become engaged.

What then might one who considered herself to be worried be saying to herself about what she had so far read, and we say - saying to herself - for we doubt that the one who acts worried feels close enough to others to say it to them.

That reader's response:

'Immediate problem for me is to write or speak about what has been said so far in this work given that the same uneasiness exists about writing/speaking about this as exists about writing/speaking about anything else. To put this another way, work is needed to maintain an interest in it and I can't see why I should be interested in this rather than anything else. Even if I was to try to maintain an interest in it I might be doing no more than trying to stop myself being bored. But I have to admit to myself that I'm rarely bored for there is so much to think about, so many problems, so many pitfalls and dangers.

One big problem if I was to have been forced to write or speak about what I've read arises because I have to admit I haven't really read it, at least not closely, and I suppose this is because it is obvious that its author is trying to save his own skin i.e. it sounds like a forced confession, and I suspect that if pressed its author would say quite the opposite if he thought that would help him. Given that I haven't read it closely, and that I can't really see why I should it isn't surprising that I can't bring myself to deal with the details.

However, given the specific circumstances surrounding my reading of this work I'm almost certain to be asked about it and I'll have to say something intelligent in order to keep face; so what should I do? What shall I say? What comes to mind? Well, its author certainly seems enthusiastic, but then so are numerous others e.g. academics, 'Lets study this, lets study that, perhaps we'll get a grant etc.' And yet I suppose this author's apparent enthusiasm is less surprising given the pressure he is under.
Oh, even these thoughts on it don't seem worth having, but I will admit it seems a strange way to begin a thesis!

I guess I'll have to hope for the best and wait and see what happens, with a bit of luck, now I think about it, I won't have to say anything much because no-one else will take it seriously or read it closely anyway.'

Now the first remark we can make is that if any readers, not you of course, did have thoughts that ran somewhere along these lines and they also are thinking that with luck they won't have to reveal this, we know that the work that follows could help them to become less reliant upon chance. For if one relies upon chance i.e. upon what may happen there is always plenty of space for worry and little room for any other activity. For instance, I could have sat here and hoped that the next sentence would come to me, when in fact I need to remember that I must and will be producing it. If I had treated the

9

sentences as merely coming to me I would have been reducing my person to the status of my pencil, and whilst things can and do happen to pencils, pencils cannot choose to act. If I treat myself as a pencil that is my choice and I must be making it because I prefer being a thing to being a thinker: one who admits to himself that he can and does choose what he wants to do, to be.

In the same way that the distinction between current and past conversations came to be bogus so now does the strategy of differentiating between us and them, or between worry and thoughtfulness in the manner which would have been necessary to continue writing as if the dialogue were between disparate individuals. For it is modes of speech that we are using and referring through and these do not separate out in such a way as to allow us to proceed with two entirely different characters. Indeed if the characters were entirely different no dialogue could take place. As speakers/thinkers we are in a manner of speaking always in the middle and we do well if we realise our place and act in it or through it. So we'll spend no more time on strategies but will use the time available to us at this stage to discuss the material at hand in the light of how this conversation proceeds. If this is not to your liking then it is yourselves or at least what you produce us to be, that you must think about and instruct, for we in no way disown our work or separate ourselves from it. Like all work it is not merely something that has been done, but it displays the author's characters, it displays what we are.

As always the question arises of how to proceed from here? And yet to speak of questions arising is an instance of what we are continually improving upon for we asked that question, we do the questioning, it doesn't simply happen to us. We play a part in the production of questions and need to take responsibility for them by showing how they are specific responses to the way the situation has been formulated which could have been otherwise. That is, we don't have to begin with a question, or at least not with this question, and not by treating questions as if they arise from nowhere. So we need to think about why we did begin this paragraph in the way we did. For instance, I could have stopped at the end of the previous paragraph, or I could have asked how you or another might proceed. This resonates with earlier ideas and may be more productive, for what sort of character begins with questions? This reminds us of the beginning of that reader's response i.e. 'Immediate problem for me ... etc.' and it also reminds us of Socrates' response to what he was told of the Oracle's remark i.e. 'When I heard the answer, I said to myself what can the God mean?' (Plato 1970, p63) Both speeches begin with questions, so perhaps the immediate desire to question is an aspect of our dialectical character. This desire to question can make writing seem far too static, for questions are produced before sentences are finished, and yet this can be good as it enables us to move through those early sentences. Frequently when we leave situations we wish we'd said or done something else, something better, but what we need to remember about this is that it doesn't provide a reason to regret having done what we did, but rather can help us remember our ability to be improving upon what we do by thinking. We should not stifle questions or thoughts and hold them back, and this we dare to say is very common in a 'society' such as the one in which we have lived. All too frequently people have avoided asking questions of themselves, and others, and they have done this merely to maintain relationships at a level at which they know they were not making as much as they could out of them.

(A remark to my supervisor, when I look at past work I see how frequently I refused to say I didn't understand what you were saying simply because I did not want to appear inadequate. It is clear that by not asking thoughtful questions I revealed my inadequacy. But, by making reference to my inadequacy I reveal several other inadequacies e.g. a failure to resist the inclination to dwell upon what I have imagined is myself, and upon what I have imagined are my bad points. But, is it really bad to dwell on them? Perhaps it is only bad if nothing is done about them i.e. it is good to get to notice them, but noticing must be noticed to be not enough, we must do something about them. We are not simply trying to bring matters to our attention, but to attend to them by writing/thinking about them).

However we are learning that good intentions, such as these seem to be, are by no means enough, for the naive can and do have good intentions, and it is these that end in tragedy. We are reminded of Ivan Illyich Pralinsky but also of the following stanza:

Then Old Age and Experience, hand in hand
Lead him to death, and make him understand,
After a search so painful and long,
That all his life he has been in the wrong. (Goethe 1962, p143)

What we are saying is that naivety is not the newness or freshness that it might seem to be, for those conventionally recognised as naive are those who have been previously persuaded that they know what it is good to do. Perhaps naivety is a product of being too ready to listen to others' recommendations uncritically, unthoughtfully. Throughout this work we are trying to retrieve newness but not in a naive way. Perhaps the writer of the above stanza did continue to wait for Old Age and Experience to make him understand, but should we be made to understand? Do we want to be made to understand? What room would this leave for our thoughtful good intentions? We think that the fact that the writer wrote those lines displays his/her refusal to wait for Old Age and Experience to lead him/her. The stanza displays for us that we choose to act now even though we do not and cannot know whether our actions are right or wrong and our actions are all the better for that. Realising that we do not begin, or end by knowing what is right or wrong/good or bad enables us to continue thoughtfully producing our social relationships and to allow ourselves not to be reduced to subjects that have to be told what is right or wrong. Where would the morality be in that? And who would do the telling?

Naivety has listened to, in the manner of having been leaned upon. We have no desire to lean upon others with our writing i.e. to force others to hear what is said in a certain way for we need others' collaboration, not their submissive agreement. We don't begin speaking by knowing what it is to speak honestly, but we seek to relate honestly through our continuing efforts to speak. Each sentence, and each word requires further thought, and we know that they always will. But, we also know that it is sentences and words that enable us to further our efforts, and we don't seek effortless lives but seek to free our efforts, our lives, from current constraints through our use of the very sentences and words that can bind us and blind us. Let us work in some detail now with that reader's response:

The first sentence was as follows:

'Immediate problem for me is to write or speak about what has been said so far in this work given that the same uneasiness exists about writing/speaking about this as exists about writing/speaking about anything else. ...

Let us proceed by saying that this first sentence of the 'worrier's' response might have been our last if we could have allowed ourselves to be ruled by the usage of worry; for we, like worry are uneasy about what we write. Yet we are remembering that this uneasiness is a feature of all speech, it is a feature of speech that issues forth from the speaker's intermediate position.

However, worry appears to go so far as to own up here to feeling uneasy about speaking or writing to other and by doing so seems to produce a difference between self and other, such that its speech isn't good enough for other to hear but is good enough for itself. We are reminded by this that we also feel uneasy talking to ourselves. What we are saying is that worry seems to be being allowed to conceal from that sentence's speaker the fact that the speaker/thinker is not one: that when we converse with ourselves, when we think, we ought to treat ourselves with the same respect that we treat other. We are being reminded that as thoughtful interlocutors, we value the uneasiness of the speaker's position, for through it is maintained the source of, and for, lively, thoughtful, moral, social activity.

We are concerned to remind ourselves that if we were convinced by the usage of worry to wait for uneasiness to go before we begin to speak, we would be waiting for ever. Deeply we all know this, and this is why worry's speech can only almost convince us. What we are expressing here is that we doubt that anyone actually ever is wholly committed to worry i.e. we are committed to displaying that worry is impossible as a course of action.

However, if we are to respond to other as a thoughtful interlocutor we cannot set out by 'accepting' that other i.e. the writer of that sentence, begins with a distinction between speaking/writing and thinking (i.e. talking with one's self), for how could we know other does this? So whilst we could have read 'Immediate problem for me is to write or speak about ... etc.' as indicating an erroneous omission of thought, i.e. whilst we could have said it would have been better if what had been written had been 'Immediate problem for me is to write, or speak, or think about ... etc.' we choose to read the clause as indicating its author's awareness that thought is writing/speaking, that to have included it would have been to treat us like dummies who need to be told the obvious. Furthermore, by saying 'Immediate problem for me ... etc.' this speaker displays her commitment not to leave her 'problems' for others to solve and we must do the same. We, like she do not delegate our work to others for we know that the 'Immediate problem ...' is for us in the strong sense of good for us. The 'Immediate problem ...' enables us to proceed, as it enables that speaker to proceed. It is 'for' her/us in the sense of with her/us, as in - are you for or against us - and not in the weak sense of indicating potential ownership i.e. that is mine not yours.

Through making the choice to read that clause in that way we are reminded that we always do choose how we read 'things' that our readings are our responses, that we produce or present ourselves through them. That we always choose is another way of referring to immediacy, for we do not separate ourselves from our choices by screening ourselves from them; by placing something between us and them, for whether we act or don't act, act in this way or in that, as thinkers/speakers choosing is what we do.

But what of beginning with a problem? Our reading need not be slovenly, for whilst if we were lazy we might rely upon a version of problems as analogous to blemishes, i.e. as something we wished to be without, we know that for the thinker saying she has a problem is emblemising her place, for a problem is like a mark on her behalf. The thinker plays a part in producing the problem. This notion of problem could seem contrived, but what that helps us to remember is that conventional usage is no less contrived and we are seeking to achieve more thoughtful conventions.

The notion of immediacy also requires work for it need not mean urgent, or without delay, especially if thought is seen to delay, rather it makes reference to the place of self as being in mediacy, as neither god nor beast. Recognition of our immediacy is recognition of our place as intermediate. So, whilst the immediate 'Immediate' could have misled us into seeing its author as wanting to treat beginnings as not following and preceding: as not intermediate, we show that a more thoughtful reading was and is possible. Had that author begun with the less thoughtful version of beginnings as immediate i.e. as not intermediate, we can understand how beginning would have been beyond her. A beginning would have had to have been like a miracle for she would have feared that writing about something would have been intermediate, for she wouldn't have acknowledged that this - uneasiness about - makes uneasiness intermediate. That author would have forgotten that being uneasy about writing or speaking was contingent upon the specific versions of writing/speaking and beginning that were being relied upon. Neither would that author have remembered that her uneasiness with uneasiness was the same as her uneasiness with intermediacy; that is that uneasiness is intermediacy.

But as we have said, we are concerned to preserve the author's thoughtfulness not to proceed by differentiating as if we knew she was different from us. For how could we know that, and how could we work at understanding her speech if that was what we claimed?

So, the author of that sentence is working even although she has participated in producing the formulation of writing/speaking/thinking/working as always being enveloped in uneasiness (i.e. uneasiness about). That author can refer to this uneasiness as given, for she is, by so doing, making reference to the fact that she chose to provide or give this honest speech about speaking, rather than to dishonestly remain silent on the issue of the uneasiness that does accompany all thoughtful speeches. And can an unthoughtful speech even be called a speech? Speeches are utterances alright but they are by no means complete or total in the sense that utter could denote if it were forgetfully used in this context in the manner it is used when, for instance, we might speak of 'utter' dejection.

The 'worrier' continued as follows:

... To put this another way work is needed to maintain an interest in it, and I can't see why I should be interested in this rather than anything else ...

What is going on here? Well, we read how that author treats her own speech as also something to be uneasy about; this is why she chooses to try to put what she was saying in another way. To want to put something in another way is to not be contented with impulse or convention, it is to want to improve upon what has been said. But we must not forget that the 'worrier' was speaking to herself so this sentence can also remind us that we always have to offer speeches which we don't completely understand ourselves, to say this another way our intermediate place as speakers is such that we do not completely understand ourselves, though we seek understanding.

Furthermore, through the author's remark that ' ... work is needed to maintain an interest in it' we see displayed her decision that topics do not generate interest by themselves, that interest is a product of the choices, the preferences of the speaker/thinker. That author is deeply aware that by

13

generating a notion of topics such that they cannot generate interest by themselves we leave space, or make space, for our own active participation. So, when she says she can't see why she should be interested in this rather than anything else, that author reminds us that by producing ourselves as merely seeing or observing things we would be leaving ourselves without reason to be interested in those things. We would be 'leaving ourselves' in the deeper sense of abandoning ourselves. In other words, if we had chosen to blind ourselves to our participation in the production of the 'things' we observe we should not then be surprised that we cannot retain or regain an interest in them. We do play a major part in producing what we are in, and by continuing to direct our productions we give ourselves less to worry about and more to think about.

Through reminding ourselves in this way that we are all responsible for the direction of our own productions we bring ourselves to ask whether we consider the manner in which we have been proceeding pedantic. Whether we consider ourselves to have been simply following the 'worrier's' response step by step rather than risking catching up with her and entering more fully into a lively and productive dialogue. And yet, given that we have committed ourselves to responding to other as we would to a thoughtful interlocutor perhaps we do well, at the outset, to lay behind a little and to try to get the measure of her and ourselves before we decide to approach. We console ourselves here by remembering that to ask whether we are proceeding pedantically or not is one way of expressing that we are not satisfied with, or by what we have done, but this is good for we seek to sustain, and be sustained by our work, not to finish or be finished by it. So we will risk turning yet again to read the 'worrier's' response:

> ... Even if I was to try to maintain an interest in it I might be doing no more than trying to stop myself being bored. But, I have to admit to myself that I'm rarely bored for there is so much to think about, so many problems, so many pitfalls and dangers.

We are mildly amused now for whilst we were only a moment ago commenting upon the fact that we were not satisfied with what we've done we see now that the 'worrier' also was expressing her desire to do more than simply anything: her desire to stretch herself further than the entertainment/boredom continuum allows. For she, like we, knows that entertainments, attractions, are like side shows, and whilst side shows do deserve a place they do not readily call forth the committed responses that we as thinkers/speakers do not stifle. And yet, the 'worrier's' sentence also expresses her awareness of her own ignorance for her 'might' is her way of telling herself and us that she does not and cannot know whether by trying to maintain an interest she is doing any more, or no more than trying to stop herself being bored. Similarly we did not know if our manner of proceeding was pedantic, as if some external measure exists: we, by proposing that we are not, and cannot be, committed to standards as if they are external, i.e. as if we had not created them, produce our freedom to proceed in the manner that pleases us, in a thoughtful, moral and social manner.

However, as we read on we hear that the 'worrier' was rarely bored and that she was prepared to offer herself a reason for this; but we must work to enable ourselves to speak here, as elsewhere, for one of the pitfalls and dangers to which the 'worrier' here refers might be that of beginning by assuming we know what other means. For if we had done this we would have felt no need to inquire in such a way as to discover what was meant. We have, as will be remembered, committed ourselves to orienting to other, in this instance the author of the 'worrier's' response, as we would to any thoughtful interlocutor, and by doing this we have come to remember that by so many pitfalls and dangers she must be referring to the fact that we could have been persuaded to treat pitfalls and dangers as something to avoid and not as something to think about, i.e. to show our willingness and ability to face up to. So, whilst the honourable character will treat acting dishonourably as the danger or pitfall, the dishonourable see dangers to lie in what might happen to them rather than in what they do.

What of the second paragraph?

One big problem if I was to have been forced to write or speak about what I've read arises because I have to admit I haven't really read it, at least not closely and I suppose this is because it is obvious that its author is trying to save his own skin i.e. it sounds like a forced confession, and I suspect that if pressed its author would say quite the opposite if he thought that would help him. Given that I haven't read it closely, and that I can't really see why I should it isn't surprising that I can't bring myself to deal with the details.

We will proceed here by saying that by referring to surface features we make reference to the relationship between reader and author, so we formulate surface as interface, and by so doing remind ourselves that we are relating to, and through it. Now which features are surface features, and which, so to speak, must be retrieved by expeditions beneath the surface depend in a very real way upon the place the reader has, from which he/she relates to that author's speech, or any speech. We see the surface of that paragraph as strewn with ironic reflectors and profound insights. For, is its author joking with herself? She refers to the speech she has been reading as being akin to a forced confession, but seems only prepared to say this when she reflects upon what she would say if she were forced to speak. That is, when she seems to force herself to speak under threat of being revealed at a later time. However, we must overcome any urge to jump to conclusions, for the author of that speech does say 'if' and we ought not to be too ready to assume that she could be forced to write or speak about what she has read, for our readiness would perhaps indicate our untrustworthiness. However, what we are saying here is that whether she did succumb to force or not, she would still be doing more or less than writing or speaking about what she had read, for the nature of speech is such that it always says more about the speaker than the topic about which he/she speaks. She then goes on to say that she hasn't really read it, at least not closely, and what we are saying is that to read something closely would be to read it closedly i.e. it would be to be constrained by it. Using our place as thinkers/speakers we know that option is neither desirable nor available to us for we always read and write openly, i.e. we always read in such a way as to reveal the interface to which we have previously referred.

The author proceeds to offer a reason for why she did not read closely/closedly i.e. 'I suppose this is because it is obvious that its author is trying to save his own skin ...'. What is obvious to us here is that she could not have meant skin in the sense of skin on one's bones, for she is a thoughtful speaker and must be using skin as a metaphor for integrity; for how else could her speech be referring to a moral, social actor? The idea of the author trying to save his own skin makes reference to the thinker's/speaker's efforts to maintain his integration and not to be reduced to parts.

'... It sounds like a forced confession, and I suspect that if pressed its author would say quite the opposite if he thought that would help him.' By saying 'It sounds like ...' the author warns us to remember our place in producing our

15

hearings, and by doing so we can remember that to '... say quite the opposite if he thought that would help him', whether pressed or not, would be a good thing for a thinker/speaker to do. For the thinker conceives of what would help him as being to act in a social, moral way, and so helping himself would be helping others. By saying the opposite of what he said before he would be developing rather than degenerating. Any who begin or end by relying upon an opposition, a distinction, between helping themselves and helping others can never do the work of integrating - of acting with integrity. However, fortunately, we can only choose to work at integrating and do so through conversation.

> Given that I haven't read it closely, and that I can't really see why I should it isn't surprising that I can't bring myself to deal with the details.

Not too much news here, for though this could have been read as a speech that doesn't hear what it itself says, i.e. 'I haven't read it too closely' could have meant I haven't brought myself to deal with the details: that is, if it is read as circular; we choose to read it as pointing to a prior thoughtful decision not to be taken in by the persuasive nature of some talk i.e. as an effort to retain a degree of autonomy by not dealing with details but with how they were and are produced.

By formulating the speaker who speaks with integrity as one who is working at integrating we provide for our own efforts; which are enabling us to continue involving ourselves with the 'worrier's response; and by so doing we have been helping ourselves to remember our place as speakers. Whilst we still have the choice of whether to stay with the worrier's response or to break away we exercise this choice by staying with the 'worrier's' response for we can only involve ourselves through worry by working with the usage it provides for us.

The third paragraph ran as follows:

> However, given the specific circumstances surrounding my reading of this work I'm almost certain to be asked about it and I'll have to say something intelligent in order to keep face; so what should I do? What should I say? What comes to mind? Well, its author certainly seems enthusiastic, but then so are numerous others e.g. academics. 'Let's study this, let's study that, perhaps we'll get a grant etc. etc.' And yet I suppose this author's apparent enthusiasm is less surprising given the pressure he's under.

What would specific circumstances be that would surround a thoughtful interlocutor's reading such that she would be almost certain to be asked about her reading? Could it be that she knows that the choice is between attempting to respond as a thoughtful interlocutor and/or being tempted to turn away, to ignore what she is thinking? So the specific circumstances are not specific to this particular situation but to the situation of speakers/thinkers in the world. Even if no other asked that author to speak upon the matter of what she read, she has to speak/think about the issues it raises if she is to respect herself i.e. to keep face. We speak of keeping face here but we must remind ourselves that keeping face frequently involves losing face (in the sense of sur-face), for by keeping face we do not mean hiding behind appearances, but allowing our true faces to appear in what we do. We need not be surprised that the author sees saying something intelligent as necessary to keep face, for our version of keeping face is speaking intelligently/thoughtfully: that is what we mean by face.

Furthermore when that author says she will 'have to' say something we do not

16

take this to mean it is difficult for her i.e. to mean she has to be forced, for having to speak thoughtfully is no hardship for one who recognises her place as a thoughtful actor. On the contrary she would not choose to act otherwise.

Then come the questions and we notice that she doesn't rest content with the first question but tries to improve upon it. Indeed the rest of the paragraph takes on the form of a question for us when she suggests that the author certainly seems enthusiastic; it is as if she calls out for our help in reaching a decision about enthusiasm. That is, she owns up to the fact that she isn't sure whether other is enthusiastic and then she proceeds, through the example she uses, to show the good of enthusiasm for she takes for granted that enthusiasm is related to pressure. And there is much in what she says provided we remember that the pressure to which she refers does not push down but draws up.

It occurs to me to say that we are moving at a fairly break neck pace but perhaps that can be illustrative of our enthusiasm to get on with what we are doing, and not to be paralysed by fear for our necks. Let us continue for we have the momentum to stay with the 'worrier's' response, for all that remains is the concluding section:

> Oh, even these thoughts on it don't seem worth having, but I will admit it seems a strange way to begin a thesis!
> I guess I'll have to hope for the best, and wait and see what happens,, with a bit of luck, now I think about it, I won't have to say anything much because no one else will take it seriously, or read it closely anyway.

When the speaker says that even these thoughts on it don't seem worth having she reminds us that thoughts aren't worth having, if by having is meant possessing as property; and private property at that. They, thoughts, do provide the way for conversation to progress, but to relate to our thoughts as we would to commodities makes them worthless. Thinking is worth doing, thoughts aren't worth having. If we did forgetfully treat our thoughts as worth having in the sense of possessing, not doing, we would be allowing ourselves to be possessed by facts the value or virtue of which we had not inquired about.

So by bringing into question her own thoughts the 'worrier' helps us to make the progress that could not be made by non-reflexive members, and of course, we do not accept non-reflexive members as a human possibility.

But what could that author be suggesting by admitting that it is a strange way to begin a thesis, for, as a matter of fact, it is a very ordinary piece of writing? What this leads us to say is that perhaps we should be more ready to bring into question, to look at, the value of PhD's that are not so ordinary (perhaps the majority), i.e. PhD's and any works or speeches for that matter, that lay claim to be based upon beginnings the value of which does not require to be questioned. They could, and can be good, of course, but we need to think about them if we are to relate to them as more than mindless exercises.

Now in the final paragraph, by saying she is guessing that author makes reference to the fact that she takes a risk, makes a choice, even although the knowledge upon which it is based is inadequate. It is an informed guess, but informed by her thoughtful good intention rather than by a complete array of facts. And so, 'hoping for the best' is not an expression of hopelessness, i.e. of throwing up one's arms, for this thoughtful character knows that the best isn't what happens to her but what she does, and hoping isn't hopeless as a result.

17

Rather it is an expression of faith in her own potential. So, now the '... and wait and see', becomes 'whilst waiting to see', for though she doesn't fantasise that she can do everything, i.e. things will happen that she cannot control, waiting is no longer conceived of as a passive activity.

But, what do we make of the final section? Here the 'worrier' says that when she thinks about what will/may happen she assumes that others will not respond to the work in a closed way, that others will not take it seriously in the sense of being brought down by it. For if they are thoughtful about it they will have plenty to speak about, plenty of issues to raise, and so, whilst she will be happy to play a part in this conversation/inquiry she will not have to say anything much, in the sense of give a lengthy speech to others who have nothing to say.

We are not now going to be drawn into summing up what has been said so far, for to have done that could have been to forget what we have been saying about proceeding by thinking, and not orienting to our thoughts as possessions. We cannot, and do not desire to set them out neatly like a museum display, but what we can do is to display our effort to listen thoughtfully to what we have been, and are saying as we continue writing.

We acknowledge that the reading so far offered of that response is not the only reading that could have been given, but what we are proposing is that this reading is possible and, that it in no way reduces the speaker to the status of one not worth conversing with.

3 A worrier's self portrait

But the speaker persisted in arguing by claiming that we were moving too quickly here, and that she hadn't been given space to offer a speech on her own account. Rather than join with us in our attempts to produce an engaging and lively reading of her speech we expected that she would at this stage disclaim responsibility for that speech. She did disclaim responsibility, as we will show, by saying that she didn't know her speech was going to provide subject matter for our analysis, and that she could have offered a much fuller self portrait provided she could trust us. Furthermore, she asked for the opportunity to offer this self portrait, and requested that we did not interrupt her until she had said all she could say. We anticipated that this would delay us, but whilst we were impatient, for we suspected we would be required to respond to it in a lengthy manner (i.e. in a manner to which we are not accustomed) we decided to allow her to proceed. But we said to ourselves that we did not take kindly to our speech being referred to as interruption, and also resolved not to allow the worrier space to make any further lengthy speeches. For whilst we will continue to listen to worry, our manner of listening calls upon us to speak and raise questions as our conversation proceeds. Furthermore, whilst we have included this self portrait, for we have placed it complete in an appendix, we can say here that we know that the very idea of a self portrait betrays the conceit of knowledge that we are intent upon revealing. The speaker's portrayal of herself acts as a betrayal of worry as it is, but not as it could be, and not of its speaker. By working with her upon her speech we can be productive, we can remind ourselves of how we can choose to act more thoughtfully. We have been fortunate in succeeding in cajoling the speaker to offer the portrait of worry, even although it is a lengthier speech than we would have liked, for through it we provide ourselves with more material with which we continue reconstituting ourselves as actors who seek to act thoughtfully, who actively seek society.

However, before we work with the transcript of her speech we can make a few remarks about our reworking of it. We began by acceding to the speaker's request and allowing her to say all she could, but by doing so we reduced ourselves to the status of observers, or rather tried to; for only in this way could we try to observe our idea of her speech's notion of itself as a self portrait, i.e. as an instance of 'realism'; only in this way could we try to restrict ourselves to its usage. By allowing that speech to continue unquestioned we necessarily prevented ourselves offering formulations that would enrich and enliven. No doubt the speaker might, for a moment or two, have been pleased by our passivity, for she came to us, as she is as worrier, as she comes to everyone, i.e. seeking shelter from her storm, but in this section our reworking of her speech will offer her what might appear a rude, but what is a necessary awakening. We do not need to emphasise to you i.e. to thoughtful readers, that restricting ourselves to the usage of worry will not come easily to us, but we proceed in this manner, for we assumed that the worrier was likely to begin by viewing our formulations as doing violence to her speech, to her self. And yet we also assumed that she was likely to begin by resisting remembering that her speech and her self were not the same; that it is her speech that does violence to herself. We think of thoughtful speakers as those who are willing and able to reflect upon their speech in a manner that is not possible to nonreflexive members, and that our reflections, our thoughts, can make possible, and need to make possible, more than mere imitation.

Well, as soon as, or almost as soon as, she began to speak we began to doubt the wisdom of our decision to allow her to say all she could, but we did as we said we would, and we did not 'interrupt' even although each and every word, when taken as worry would have itself taken, impinged upon us and delayed us. But what now? How shall we proceed? For, as we have said we are unaccustomed to making and hearing lengthy speeches. And yet, we must proceed thoughtfully here, as elsewhere, for whilst we want to leave ourselves in no doubt about the damaging though persuasive nature of worry's speech, if it is taken as it would have itself taken, we also want to draw out its rich potential.

We have included that speech in the appendix, not because we approve of it as it is, but in order that we can show our ability and willingness to respond to it; not by ignoring it, but by working with it in such a way as to show not only that it needs to be changed, and can be changed, but also that it is we who can change it, and be changed by our work with it. We are determined to drive home, in this section, the need for, and the good of our work by revealing what we could have been reduced to if we had chosen not to continue thinking about what we can be.

In effect, we have chosen not to orient to that speech as a portrait of self, but as an effort to portray worry, i.e. as a still picture of an activity which we might have allowed to interrupt our productive work. We produce this seemingly still picture as startling us, and as encouraging us to continue engaging in our productive work with even more resolve. In the remainder of this section we keep ourselves moving, developing, by working with that speech in the only way we can. And whilst we offer no excuses for our manner of proceeding, for why should we excuse the manner which we think is for the best; what we will say is that we have presented the lengthy speech as a whole in appendix (a) in order that you are able to read it without interruptions, questions, as the speaker requested. Perhaps you want to read the portrait of worry in order that you can work with us, with it, and for this reason we have placed the appendix here.

APPENDIX A

Para. 1   Your manner of proceeding has surprised me for I never expected my earlier views to be taken up in that way. So whilst I offer this self portrait, I admit that I am often distracted by topics which appear attractive, although at this moment I can say that when I am distracted I do forget what I wanted, i.e. I forget what I am. So much is this the case that I am beginning to see that all of my work, if it is not merely to provide either a distraction, or drudgery for my reader, must express this struggle, and by doing so must help to remind the reader that I am not the only one who is involved in a struggle of this kind. My struggle can be considered, to begin with, to be with a version of myself as a worrier, and you who are reading will be well advised to keep the idea of struggle in mind for all too often, I fear that I shall succumb, and shall write as a worrier rather than (loosely) as a human about the worrier. Now lest you should judge this to be a strangely self centred and hence unworthy enterprise, I would ask you firstly to consider why you wish to charge me in this way, and secondly if you do still wish to charge me, that you at least delay your judgement until you have some evidence upon which to base it, i.e. until you have heard what I want to say. Already you should see worry at work here i.e. I'm worried about the fact that you may choose to read no further and I try to forestall this eventuality by pleading with you rather than by offering a different (perhaps more attractive) beginning. It is as if I know that there is nothing I can do to prevent this, i.e. your choosing not to read on, and this version of the relationship between me and you is, in itself, a good example of how I produce the situation as beyond my control, i.e. as one to worry about.

Para 2   My struggle will be well illustrated by the problems which you may see to arise concerning the person(s) in which this work is written, for at times, the worrier will appear as a distant and perhaps distinct person, whilst at the same time it must also be apparent that I only know the worrier so well or intimately because at times I am her. What I am suggesting here is that what may appear to be a technical problem of rhetoric, for example should I write a dialogue or a monologue, is illustrative in a weak way of the struggle in which I am involved, and perhaps involved is a good word for it! To put this another way the problem of the person in which I write i.e. first person, second person or third person, is illustrative of the complex nature of my relationship to myself, and of how my version of myself relates to my version of others etc.. When I say, for example, that - what I think I want may not be what I want - and then look for ways to deal with this statement or state of affairs, this is not a matter of marginal or peripheral interest, and it is only when its centrality is felt that I feel involved in the struggle I am commending. This can be further illustrated (and again the illustration seems weak) by the fact that the very sentences which I write, including this one, have only been written if they have in some way attracted me. The illustration

21

is weak because some 'things' are difficult to illustrate or describe, and a good example of this might be our senses, i.e. the fact that they can be treated as mediating between 'our selves' and 'the world' doesn't make them any easier to describe. For the moment then it might be useful to think of worry as mediating in this manner between the worrier's self and the world. However, I was speaking about the fact that the sentences which I write must have attracted me, but I can already see how even this sentence draws my, and perhaps your, attention away from that which is attracted, i.e. their subject, me, which as I have already indicated, is the crucial problem area at present. What I am trying to say here is that it is versions of the self that are attracted by things. For example, only the worrier would be attracted by the doubts raised by this version of attraction. More deeply it is the version of myself as a worrier that attracts me, for it, as will become apparent, offers one way in which I allow myself to imagine I make things easier for myself. So, by generating a version of what attracts me I shall be generating a version of the me that is attracted, and may as a consequence be better equipped to struggle with the version of myself which I can all too easily become. The inference I draw from this is that I must produce an analysis of worry if I am to see how what I think I want relates to what I want. Authenticity then is by no means tranquil or easy, for it will only be in this struggle that I can show or be what I am.

Para. 3   I am trying to throw some light upon one of my problems of action i.e. upon how what I think I want relates to what I want and it may help to hear again the words attraction,, distraction and action. How do I, as the worrier, think about attraction?

Para. 4   When something attracts me it promises to give me something I think I want, in effect I am induced to take what I think I want by what I see or hear etc. Attraction works quickly then, for it leads me to forget to ask myself why I might think I want what I think I want, i.e. it leads me to forget to think about whether I know what I want. The attractive encourages me to take what it promises. (How quickly I rush on here away from the question which asks me to think about whether I know what I want, for perhaps what I want will prove to be to give not to take! Yet in my rush I think I will reveal why I rush so I will go on!)

Para. 5   It may help you to understand my idea of attraction, and hence action, if you begin by considering giving, for if you cannot understand what it is to give something it is highly unlikely that you will be able to understand what it is to promise to give something (cf., idea of attraction above) i.e. for me to find something attractive. Furthermore you cannot understand giving until you draw it into a relation with taking, and for the moment, the relationship to which I refer is not simply that something needs to be given to be taken, on the contrary, it is that something needs to be taken if it is to be given, and there are different ways of taking. My point here then is that we need to acquire things if we are to divest ourselves of them. We need to generate things if we are to be generous with them. The philanthropist, as gift giver, if such he is, would begin to come more clearly into focus, and consequent scrutiny, beside his gift.

Para. 6   Now this could alert both of us to the fact that I began the last paragraph by offering you my help in the form of my understanding of attraction, in effect then I was acting as a philanthropist, and so you should demand from me an explanation of how I have achieved or taken this understanding and from where, and furthermore, why I think it will help you. At first sight my apparent unwillingness or inability to answer your demands may seem strange, but as we continue, the philanthropist's silence will begin to emerge as a necessary result of his version of himself and his relations to others i.e. as a natural rather than an unnatural (strange) consequence of his own self conception (which may indeed prove to be unnatural!)

Para. 7   We can see by now that initially I have limited the attractive to the gift i.e. that which is given, and have then gone on to transform gifts into pieces of evidence, and perhaps this can account for my reticence about receiving them for (a) if I accept and consume the gifts I will in effect be destroying the evidence and (b) if I accept and do not consume the gifts I could reduce my desire to testify by viewing myself as a receiver of stolen goods or bribes. If then I view those who offer me gifts as philanthropists I will do my best not to accept what they are offering. If you listened to me then, and treated this speech so far as a gift you would reject it for the reasons I have so far offered, and yet I will show that you could have refused merely to listen to me without rejecting my offer. I am making reference here to the fact that I could, and later I will, make substitutions and initially replace the philanthropist with the teacher and the poor with the student, but later we will replace the philanthropist with the student and the poor with the teacher!

Para. 8   By transforming the gift in the way that I have, I raise the question of acceptance as the problem that the gift presents to its possible recipient. For it seems that I should refuse all gifts if by being gifts they transform their givers into philanthropists. That is, I am faced with a decision 'should I accept or not? In this way I see a problem i.e. that of the decision coming to mediate between me and the gift, perhaps the world. I then proceed by trying to argue the case for acceptance or non-acceptance, taking or leaving, as a way to reach a decision. The fact that I do this persuades me that I am not merely impulsive/animalistic and that I have some commitment to reason. And yet you can see that my commitment to reason here is only skin deep, for I only use reason as one means to fulfil my impulses i.e. what I think I want, and I do not, as I have said think (reason) about that! My impulsiveness is shown by the fact that I treat the problem of decision as something which faces me, rather than as something which I have produced, or at least had a part in producing. I forget that I am the one who is treating decisions as having a gift like nature, and most importantly as being problems as a result. I am forever forgetting that whilst the fact that we can do the right thing or the wrong thing in any situation can be construed as a problem or a blight this is the wrong thing to do, for were it not possible for us to do the right thing or the wrong thing, good intentions would not be possible. That is, the worrier has a tendency to transform blessings into blights! Furthermore, it is worth pointing out that by using this version of myself as someone who is forever forgetting, or losing sight of things, I produce a version of myself as not being the sort of person to make decisions. But, you should be able to see what an easy way out this might seem to be by noticing how I also choose to ignore the fact that I must have known or seen things in order to forget or lose sight of them. This is further evidence of a misconceived attempt to free myself of what I allow myself to think oppresses me. The ability to know that I forget and lose sight of things however, could go some way to raising me above the animalistic!

Para. 9   I must slow down now if I am not to lose sight of other matters, for I was arguing with myself about whether or not I should accept or take a gift, and the point here is that I wanted the argument to relieve me of the need to decide in this case, as I often do in others. I tend then to treat decisions as something I would be better off without, for I find myself treating decisions as cutting off possibilities, i.e. as reducing my freedom. But when I do this I must be forgetting that the freedom I ought to sustain must be the freedom to make decisions. I ought to acknowledge that not making decisions, (perhaps not changing my mind) is deciding not to make them (or change it) i.e. that this can also be a method for cutting off possibilities i.e. of reducing my freedom. In effect, I allow myself to act as if I treat decisions as essentially arbitrary when I know that if this were so I would have no reason to make this decision. However, by my inaction i.e. the action of treating decisions as something to avoid I indicate both to you and to myself that I do think it matters what I do, that I do think I can make bad decisions, and hence that I am not as convinced by the idea of arbitrariness as I sometimes allow myself to think, or perhaps want you to think. I am trying tentatively to suggest here that worry, perhaps like other things, can never act as a successful mediator between self and the world i.e. that because of its nature it can never totally subjugate its subject, and that whilst this could be treated as something to worry about we ought to see it as a virtue.

Para.10   But, what is it that I as worrier, prefer to think of myself as, even if I can never quite do it? I think I want to think of myself as not being responsible for anything that goes wrong, and to this end as being prepared to pay the price of never being responsible for anything, even that which goes right, as a way of minimising that risk. My idea of me doing good then is limited to that of not doing harm. That is, I produce paradoxically a version of myself as unproductive. I prefer to think I prefer being mastered by the situation rather than being the situation's master. When, as we will see, this turns out to be my way of mastering the situation which isn't to say it is a good thing for as we will discover worry has a misconceived notion of mastery. To say this another way, I act when I worry as if I find possibility (cf., the making of decisions) more worrying than necessity, and this is because I conceive of necessity as relieving me of responsibility for what goes wrong.

Para.11   The notion of responsibility begins to hang very heavily over this part of the discussion for I am beginning to feel how actively I, as worrier, try to avoid facing up to, or better grasping, the fact that I have the gift of decision making i.e. the one gift which, as we shall see, the philanthropist would not or could not offer. Furthermore, the fact is that I must accept this gift because of my nature, I can no more be the worrier than I can be any other version of myself. For though I may act like a worrier, when I do so it is always by accident i.e. unintentionally.

Para.12   Goodness! the worrier does seem to be a slippery character for now I feel that it is he who is saying that when he does act it is not his fault because it is an accident i.e. because it is unintentional.

Para.13   By now you, as reader, may be beginning to wonder what happened to the struggle, for it seems that worry is not even lifting a finger in opposition to what is being said i.e. it seems it has nothing to say. Yet whilst in one sense I think this is true, in another I think that we have been listening to nothing but worry so far, for by unintentionally resorting to a device of treating worry as a version of myself and referring to the distance between this version and myself, I have in effect been treating it as another person (cf., original problem of style of writing). I have been, in effect, relieving myself of responsibility for its action or inaction, when I know all too well that this is simply me succumbing yet again to a version of myself as someone with something to worry about. That is, I have allowed the struggle I was initially engaged in to become yet another instance of worry. What I am saying here is that if you are to see any suffering, and hence any struggle, in this speech I must show you not how distant and distinct I am from this version of myself as the worrier, but, how I have become in most of my speech constrained and limited by its rules!

Para.14   Even if for the moment we allow the separation of myself from the version of myself as a worrier, which the preceding paragraph brings into much doubt, I still feel that the worrier's apparent lack of resistance is by no means uncharacteristic, for I do tend to accept the bad reading of myself as a worrier, i.e. as trying to shirk my responsibilities by saying in effect that I am not response-able; by accepting that I am not authentic. Yet strangely it is by accepting this reading that I allow myself to think that I gain a sense of relief; for I allow myself to feel even more convinced that I am not the sort of person who should be making decisions. Furthermore, I ought to point out that 'decision' is being treated throughout this speech as a prerequisite for action and so we can see that a much stronger (or weaker!) claim is being made. For in effect, the acceptance of the idea that the worrier is not the type of person to make decisions is an acceptance of the worrier as inactive. That is, it is a version of worries as something to be got out of the way before you can begin to act. Now it should be plain how this analysis has a bearing on the problem of action mentioned at the outset, for if we can begin to see how relief from worry comes to be integrated with action we can see how I as the worrier produce an even greater distance between worry/thought and action. The point is then that I formulate myself as non actor, for I reduce my own actions to the status of inaction by treating them as merely reactions to, for example, dangers or exigencies. So we can begin to see now how I produced attraction as inducement for this placed me in an essentially passive inactive role! (By treating myself as being attracted to the version of myself as a worrier I am exemplifying this form of passivity!)

Para.15   (As an example of how I as a worrier produce a distance between action and worry I would refer to my own writing, for whenever I reread what I have written I tend to see it as inauthentic, i.e. as not really expressing how I feel i.e. as the product of lack of concern, and whilst you may view this as mildly crazy I'm sure you can imagine that it does not appear to aid productivity!)

Para.16   By now you might expect that I, the worrier, would be feeling pretty bad, and in a way you would be right, but, perhaps not too surprisingly it is now that I, as the worrier, start to take the offensive. For as if this wasn't bad enough, I go on to treat all action, including the supposed criticism of me as the worrier, as being the result of a lack of concern because of the distance between worry and action, or conversely, because of the integration of lack of concern with action. That is, I produce others, in this instance my supposed critic, as icons of myself. It is this that helps me to feel just in my state of inaction for by allowing the argument to persuade me that action is always the result of a lack of concern its consequences whether apparently good or bad are treated as accidents. That is I reduce others to the status of the mechanical, the unintentional or the unthinking, the inauthentic.

Para.17   Perhaps I could clear the air here by returning to the idea of the gift, for if we treat gift giving as accidental i.e. as being the result of a lack of concern, we can begin to see why I would be suspicious of the giver's motives, for by producing the gift as an accident I treat myself, its possible receiver, as undeserving. It is just a matter of chance that I am offered it. As a receiver (or possible receiver) of a gift from a philanthropist I am not deserving in the strong sense, but merely lucky, for I have not earnt what I get, I am simply lucky to meet or know a rich and generous man! This could be why I am reticent about receiving gifts i.e. because I think I haven't earnt them I fear that they may be taken away as soon as either my undeserving character, or a more deserving character is brought to light. By treating myself as undeserving i.e. by treating myself as an accidental receiver, i.e. a receiver of charity, I remove myself from the productive process, I act as if I am relaxing. For when we relax we just let things happen i.e. we produce the situation as being one in which accidents (bad accidents) are certainly excluded, and the result is that the most we could expect to receive would be pleasant surprises; gifts. I think I remove the possibility of a bad accident by producing myself as unproductive, for, as I have said, what I, as the worrier, think I fear is being responsible for something that goes wrong. Hence my version of a bad accident is something I am responsible for, and so I go on to allow myself to think that if I am unproductive i.e. if I produce nothing, I cannot be responsible for anything bad. I forget that I still consume and hence that even if I produce nothing else I produce needs!

Para.18   But isn't something worrying happening here for at first glance worrying and relaxing would seem to be very different social forms? After raising this question doubts immediately arise however, for it is apparent that worrying and relaxing do share one important characteristic, both are conceived of as making it difficult to proceed with your work.

Para.19   This problem is raised by relaxation in the form of the Monday morning feeling. For like a surprise relaxation cannot last, and it cannot last because it relies upon a version of work as something which has to be done but which would be better avoided. When work is seen as drudgery relaxation becomes important, and also the problem it creates (cf., the Monday morning feeling) becomes heightened. (This suggests that as we proceed our attention should not merely be directed to the worry, in this instance the Monday morning feeling, but to that which creates it, in this instance the creation of drudgery.) However, in ordinary usage relaxation has to stop if we are to start work.

Para.20   Similarly our ordinary usage of worry is as of something which has to stop before we can start work, e.g. 'Stop worrying and get on with it'. But we can see here how work is treated as drudgery, and we will come to see how drudgery is a form of relaxation, for it is what I am involved in when I worry, if I really conceive of myself as not being responsible for anything i.e. as not being productive!

Para.21   But, aren't I at least responsible for pointing to the obstructions and hence in a sense responsible for their removal, i.e. isn't this the sort of work in which worry is involved? So whilst not being directly involved in the production of anything, perhaps I am indirectly involved, for by pointing to problems, I allow production to continue to run smoothly. Yet this is even worse than being unproductive, for now I appear as a member of the Human Relations Movement whose only interest is in continued production, i.e. it seems that I relax when the real questions are asked!

Para.22   But this is too malicious, for I know that it is I who would begrudge myself even this moment of relaxation by worrying about why I was no longer worrying i.e. by thinking that I was, or had been, acting irresponsibly, for as we have seen I tend to see all actions as irresponsible especially my own! In this way, I transform solutions into problems, and smooth running into uneasiness. That is I can only work or feel I am working, when I am vexed or troubled.

Para.23   So I do think I work after all! Yes, but I never manage to produce anything, and hence am always dissatisfied. It is because of this feeling of lack of productivity that I can see myself as being involved in merely a difficult form of relaxation! My point here is that when I think I am working I am involved (cf., paragraph 2) but it is a weak involvement, for whilst I do have a version of work as investing myself, I restrict this idea of investing myself to that of investigating.

Para.24   This, like much else, isn't too clear to me, but I think I think of the work of worry as investigating i.e. as looking into; which is in fact only a special case of looking at, or on; which is in turn what relaxation does. Whilst relaxing is analogous to spectating, worrying is analogous to inspecting or investigating and this begins to suggest that whilst worrying appears to be work because it isn't easy, it now seems more like a difficult form of relaxing. The point being that the difficulty for worry is the energy expended in trying to remain separate i.e. in trying not to be responsible for anything i.e. in not getting involved.

Para.25   This idea of separation is a powerful one and underlies Paragraph 15, which refers to my problem with re-reading, for so strongly do I want to refuse to accept responsibility that I even forget how I write what I write, and then treat it as an accident i.e. as inauthentic. So now my dissatisfaction with my own work comes to be a source of ease not of unease. That is, this is the means by which I remove myself from this productive process.

Para.26   Goodness, this is getting complicated for earlier, i.e. in a previous draft of this speech I wrote that:

> The worrier is dissatisfied with her work because she doesn't see it as producing rewards, satisfaction, and yet she teaches us by her dissatisfaction with gifts that she knows that satisfaction or ease is the problem rather than work. The danger for the worrier is that she can become satisfied with her work (i.e. that she can feel delighted when she points out problems) when becoming satisfied is leaving herself no more work to do. She needs to keep in mind that relieving her own frustration or hunger, i.e. killing those sensations isn't enough to produce a good human life, and hence isn't enough to deal with worry, indeed it may not be enough to introduce it.

Para.27   Now it seems that dissatisfaction is her (my) problem, for it is the source from which I relieve my own frustration or hunger. Perhaps we get a hint here of the fact that I seem to require myself to be involved in a specific type of social situation. A desperate one at that, for on the one side I don't think I can produce anything because I worry, whilst on the other side I see products to be the result of a lack of concern. It is this version of myself as unproductive which leaves me dependent upon the philanthropist for my sustenance, and given the chance nature of philanthropy, which I have already referred to, it is no wonder that I worry! Indeed to construe a situation as desperate is to construe it as having to stop if danger is to be removed, for it holds no hope. Desperation then, like relaxation and worry relies upon an idea of having to stop i.e. they all treat possibility as lying outside of them i.e. beyond their grasp. So as a worrier, the only solution I can see to my own situation lies outside it i.e. my only future is seen to lie in my changing from something I am to something I am not. (There is no sense of movement it is simply one thing or the other!)

Para.28　　One way in which I tend to produce the situation as desperate is by treating raising problems as raising the stakes, and it is worth remembering that raising problems is about all the worrier can do with her 'yes but'. In this way I reduce the situation to one of desperation i.e. of decision in its worst sense, and if we can think about a decision in these circumstances we can understand why earlier I thought of decisions as arbitrary, i.e. you jump or you don't jump! But once I treat the situation in this way the most I can do is save my own skin even if I have raised the stakes in the process, and as a consequence all of my actions do take on the character of self defence i.e. I do only react and then think as a result I need not feel responsible. I forget very easily that I am responsible for what I don't do i.e. that not responding is my response.

Para.29　　It is in this way that I, as worrier, use a sense of desperation as a way of reducing my responsibility, for I come to consider survival as the goal, and then if I do survive, I treat my survival as what I have profited from the situation. I am pleased to have got through but still treat this outcome as fortuitous, i.e. not as anything I have produced.

Para.30　　This can perhaps help explain why as a worrier, I find writing so difficult; it is because I think I am totally dependent upon my reader's reaction, and I tend to see this reaction as a product of arbitrary considerations, e.g. his work load etc! I tend to see my reader's reaction as a product of arbitrary considerations but not of my speech, (cf., the idea of treating other as inauthentic Paragraph 16.) The worrier in me seems to have a one track mind though, for she could have used the same view of the situation to produce writing as easy for me, for if it doesn't matter what I say I could surely say anything! But of course even that isn't an easy situation for the worrier as it involves choosing.

Para.31　　This note raises the problem of distancing again, for whilst I do tend to react in this way I also feel that I could not say I did unless I treat it as a tendency, i.e. as something I slip into rather than am. The point is though that I do react this way, although when I think, I think I ought not to!

Para.32   We have seen here how I tend to produce the situation as desperate and to move from this to a concern for safety, i.e. a concern to avoid accidents (memories of relaxation again), but we can also see that the only sure way of avoiding the risk that attends writing for example, is to not write; but, as you can see I do write. However, as a worrier, I even construe my writing as being a way to avoid the risk attached to not writing, and its possible painful consequences, and by doing this I again feel myself relieved of some of the responsibility for what I write. By producing a version of my own work as analogous to a forced confession I can begin to see how I would feel that I do not deserve any approval or reward for this product. (For me a product is transformed into a prod-uct!) Yet as we've also seen it is precisely as a result of my view of myself as unproductive that I need even more the approval or reward which does sustain me, for as I am unable to give it to myself (or produce it myself) I become totally dependent upon other.

Para.33   Whilst on the one hand then I have been trying to show how an orientation towards gifts of mere acceptance must lead to dissatisfaction I, at the same time, show that it is I, because of my view of myself as unproductive, who needs to accept them to stay alive.

Para.34   By now, the fact that I saw the attractive as something to take, rather than as something to give to, begins to sound more plausible, but its increased plausibility is apparently being gained at my increased cost.

Para.35   By writing then, I see myself as escaping the dangers of not writing (N.B. perhaps this helps account for the rush mentioned in Paragraph 4), but am immediately plunged into another worriesome situation for now I must look on whilst you read what I write. Thus I have changed nothing, my work is still the same in the way that drudgery is the same. All I can do, as a worrier, is worry whilst I wait. If we think of stopping temporarily just beyond the danger mark we can feel how precarious the worrier's life is, but, obviously if we just look on, i.e. if we just observe him, we will be in an equally dangerous situation, and can feel how we are no safer than he is. One way of proceeding here will be to ask myself why I am tempted to stop here, why I don't want to go any further, why I limit myself to reacting to dangers and in a way produce them by failing to address how they are produced. This will be to ask why I have a problem giving as well as taking/accepting, i.e. it will be to begin the scrutiny of the philanthropist which earlier I intimated would follow. This scrutiny must however take a more active form i.e. it must be more than simply looking on yet again; it must involve a response, or be a response to the social situation which treats it as what it is, i.e. as a situation within which the worrier places himself and the philanthropist, and this response must by its very nature begin to change the relationship.

Para.36   One way of accounting for my failure to move any further than just beyond the danger mark is by seeing that, as yet, it has only been danger and fear that has moved me, i.e. once this is removed I stop moving. This fact can help us to understand the philanthropist as soon as we see that he is worried too! He only gives enough to alleviate his fears, whether these fears be of his own sense of guilt or perhaps more forcibly of the discontent of the poor. More dramatically I can deepen my understanding here by realising that it isn't only that I don't want to go any further, but that I don't want, i.e. I am moved by fears, and not by desires.

Para.37   Perhaps we begin to see now why I didn't and don't willingly accept gifts, or better why the only gifts I think I can accept are generous ones, i.e. ones given out of charity! It is because I don't know what I want, I only think I know what I don't want. This may become clearer as we remember the earlier remarks about giving being dependent upon taking, for from these we can see that the philanthropist was only a euphemism for the benevolent despot, and he in turn for the master in the master/slave relationship and it is from this relationship that we must move if we are to proceed.

Para.38   How have I reacted then to being called, and in a sense being a slave? For a slave is surely one who is dominated by fear to such an extent that he forgets he had desires. My reaction has indeed been a slavish one, for after in some sense feeling some surprise that I of all people should be seen as a slave, I react by mumbling to myself that at least I am free to think as I please, and that this is better than acting unintentionally, which is what my accuser or master must be doing. For, by his action of accusation he shows me that he isn't thinking, i.e. that he is unintentional. I humour him then, but don't help him. My reaction is the same, again it is a 'Yes but.'

Para.39   If we think of what has been said so far we will remember that a constant theme has been my failure to accept responsibilities, frequently by simply accepting that I am not a responsible type i.e. that I don't have the ability to respond. So successfully do I do this, that I produce a version of myself as not being the kind of person to make decisions. (Worse than the deferential voter I become the deferential non-voter!) In effect I persuade myself that I am suited to be a slave. I allow myself to be mastered by the idea that I would find the freedom involved in making decisions oppressive. I said above that I, as worrier, am moved by fears and not by desires, and now we can remember that whereas fear is a reaction, i.e. it is impulsive, desires are responses, they do involve self in a way that impulses do not.

Para.40   What work does a slave do then? I pursue my master's business which, because (a) it is a result of the master's nature i.e. thoughtlessness, and (b) because it is not my own business (concern), becomes drudgery; and the thing about drudgery is that it does, or can, provide a strong sense of knowing where you are, in the sense of knowing you aren't there. (With this writing, however, my struggle is that I'm unsure where I am in it and consequently it is anything but drudgery though this has not prevented it hurting.) My point here is that when I'm involved in drudgery I find a home in my thoughts, worries, and see these as separating me from, and raising me above, the unworried i.e. he who I think of as my master. (This is how I conceived of myself as being master of the situation Paragraph 10.)

Para.41   I become the proud silent type then, but need to wake up to the fact that this reaction gives the master just what he wants as a master i.e. compliance, subservience, but certainly not what he needs. This silence in turn allows the master to remain silent about the fact that decisions don't come easily to him either, that mastery and ease need not and do not go hand in hand. (I think that because I find work difficult I haven't mastered it, but the only sort of easy work there is is drudgery!) Why do I refuse to admit that the master might not be relaxing? Why, because I, as slave, rely upon my idea of my private life, my thoughts, my worries, as being free in order to generate a version of mastery as freedom. I think that thinking is easy, and this is why I want to think that I want what I think I want, this is why I cannot answer if I am asked to discipline myself by deciding what I want. I transform this into a question that asks me whether I know what I want.

Para.42   When I worry then I treat my thinking as a form of relaxation for I do not commit myself to any course of action, I treat my thinking as free for it seems to be the only thing that cannot be taken from me, that is my thoughts are free of other's demands. As a worrier, I think of my thinking as just looking on and as not participating, and I go on to transpose this idea of freedom onto the master, for I see the master as making demands but as having none made on him.

Para.43   So now we can see how I, as a slave, treat my own thoughts or worries as all I own and as the symbol of my freedom, but I need to keep constantly in mind how this is just a reaction for it fails to address the question of the social and in this case unnatural nature of this set of social relationships. For, far from symbolising my freedom, my worries merely point to my oppressor: they need to show me that it is my that is, the slave's version of my freedom as my worries which contributes to, and sustains the presence of my oppression.

Para.44   But again I must slow down for whilst I may be making some progress here I would certainly not have made enough if I thought that this supposedly new knowledge would be enough, or ought to make me a master. But even whilst I write I know that my excitement must show, and that the danger that this could occur is ever present. So now I need to clear the air for myself and perhaps one way of doing this will be to return to the question of substitutions mentioned in Paragraph 7, i.e. firstly the philanthropist by the teacher and the poor by the student and latterly the philanthropist by the student and the poor by the teacher. What can this mean?

Para.45   The first substitution need not delay us very long for we should see by now that the sort of gifts offered by the philanthropist do little if anything to teach the poor, in fact they hinder the learning of the poor, and leave the philanthropist in a blissful state of ignorance to boot. I am not commending that the philanthropist gives less here, far from it, I am demanding that the worrier, in this instance the philanthropist, begins to give i.e. that the philanthropist gives much more.

Para.46 On to the second, what have the poor to teach the philanthropist? They need to teach him that his gift, though it may appear generous, is only a bribe, and that whilst both he and they refuse to speak to each other it will remain so. It is the refusal of both the philanthropist and the poor to address the social nature of their relationship which makes room for bribery and hence corruption.

Para.47 But now I must remember that it isn't simply a question of slowing down for I am not involved in a public debate i.e. my clarity of diction is not the issue. What I must remember is that I am these characters, I am involved in bribery and corruption for I, as worrier, help to produce it. By thinking of my thoughts as free and my actions/speech as unfree I make reference to the fact that I think I need to be induced to speak, and it is in this way that I come to produce everything I react to as an inducement, as an attempt to silence my thought. Every call to action becomes a threat or a bribe, and as a result when I do act or write, I begin by seeing my action or writing as at best irresponsible and at worst as the corrupt silence of the receiver of a bribe. I see then that worry begins and sticks with a conception of social relationships as corrupt, i.e. that worry produces corruption. (In fact worry is always a producer of bribes for they are seen to remove a danger, or risk, at least temporarily!)

Para.48 I begin to remember then, as a result of this speech how deeply my mode of thinking and of acting, and hence of thinking about the relationship between the two, is imbued by the grammar of worry, but this should remind me that I will not free myself of it in the way I might discard an empty ballpoint pen. Rather, I must remember that social relationships are not static, and that it is only by using and working with what I have got, i.e. what I am, that I can produce something better. My task then, as my struggle continues, must be to make these words less empty.

Having read the speech, and tried in a variety of ways to come to grips with it, we begin to see how arrogant our approach to it was. For in the same way that we only began to learn/remember in the latter part of section 2 when we suspended our tendency to imagine we understood the speech before we worked upon it, so also now do we remember that it is ourselves who need to do the work, for this speech, like all speeches, requires us to stretch ourselves if we are even to begin to do it, and ourselves justice. We will work with it paragraph by paragraph, for only in this way can we begin to get to grips with ourselves through it.

But before we do, we want to draw attention to the similarity between our naive but arrogant manner at the beginning of this section, and the speech of

Ivan Illyich Pralinsky who, in his drunken ramblings, comes out with the following:

> The main thing is that I'm convinced, convinced with all my heart. Humanity ... love for mankind. Restoring a man to himself ... reviving his self respect and then ... set to work with finished materials. It seems clear enough! Yes, Sir! Allow me, Your Excellency, to take the syllogism: we meet, for example, government clerk, a poor downtrodden government clerk. All right, a clerk; next: what sort of a clerk are you? answer: this or that sort of clerk. Are you employed? Yes, I am! Do you want to be happy? Yes. What is necessary for your happiness? This and that. Why? because ... And the man understands me, you see, at a word: the man is caught, so to speak, in my snare, and I can do anything I want with him, for his own good, I mean. (Dostoyevsky 1966, p192)

Ivan's failure to be reminded by this that it was himself he should have questioned, was paralleled by our failure at the beginning of this section to treat the speech with sufficient respect. For, as soon as we do this, and not before, we begin to grasp how it can help us to help ourselves much more perhaps than we ever imagined.

ANALYSIS OF LENGTHY SPEECH

Analysis of Paragraph 1

We need to read carefully, for as always with thoughtful effort we can uncover a great deal which will be of mutual benefit.

> Your manner of proceeding has surprised me for I never expected my earlier views to be taken up in that way. So whilst I offer this self portrait, I admit that I am often distracted by topics which appear attractive, although at this moment I can say that when I am distracted I do forget what I wanted, i.e. I forget what I am. So much is this the case that I am beginning to see that all of my work, if it is not merely to provide either a distraction or drudgery for my reader, must express this struggle, and by doing so must help to remind the reader that I am not the only one who is involved in a struggle of this kind. My struggle can be considered, to begin with, to be with a version of myself as a worrier, and you who are reading will be well advised to keep the idea of struggle in mind for all too often, I fear that I shall succumb, and shall write as a worrier rather than (loosely) as a human about the worrier. Now lest you should judge this to be a strangely self centred and hence unworthy enterprise, I would ask you firstly to consider why you wish to charge me in this way, and secondly if you do still wish to charge me, that you at least delay your judgement until you have some evidence upon which to base it, i.e. until you have heard what I want to say. Already you should see worry at work here i.e. I'm worried about the fact that you may choose to read no further and I try to forestall this eventuality by pleading with you rather than by offering a different (perhaps more attractive) beginning. It is as if I know that there is nothing I can do to prevent this i.e. your choosing not to read on, and this version of the relationship between me and you is, in itself, a good example of how I produce the situation as beyond my control, i.e. as one to worry about.

Response:

The speaker begins in a manner that we overlook at our peril, for as soon as she has said that she will offer a self portrait she goes on to say that she is often distracted and forgets what she is. In effect she warns us here to take care, for what she portrays may not be herself. We are reminded by this that we are not prepared to speak of ourselves as 'I's for by doing so we could be led to conceive of ourselves as one, when we know full well, that our place as thinkers/speakers makes it necessary for us to remain aware of our dialectical characters. Furthermore the temptation to speak of our selves as 'I's could also lead us to imagine we know what we are, what our 'I' is, but we consider that the thoughtful social actor is always prepared to bring this in to question, and not to rely upon it. When that speaker spoke of forgetting what she is, she was referring to situations when she acts as if she knows what her 'I' is.

We must either work at removing 'I' from our discourse, or commit ourselves to continually formulating 'I' as representing self as that which does not know what it is. When we speak in this work we will opt for the former, when we listen we will hear the usage of 'I' as alerting us to the speakers continuing attempt to reconstitute self.

But, to return to the speech, she says she is often distracted by topics which appear attractive, and by saying this she reminds us how easily we could have been drawn to reduce all attractions to distractions. How easily we can fetishise attraction and see it as standing outside of ourselves i.e. as appearing as appearance, when we know that our dialectical, productive characters enable us to decide to produce what attracts us. And, what really attracts us are attractive acts, thoughtful social acts, not things; for attractive acts encourage us to work at improving ourselves.

So now we remember that we produce all of our work, our thoughtful lives, as part of our quest to continue reconstituting and re-enlivening our dialectical characters, and by producing our work as our work, i.e. as for us, we enable ourselves not to be distracted, not to engage in drudgery, in effect we ennoble our work by reminding ourselves that we choose what we do.

But we must discipline ourselves and keep working with the speech at hand, for as we have said, there is much we can teach ourselves with its help. We already know that the speaker isn't sure who, or what, she is talking about when she talks about 'I', so we must not be too ready to assume that the 'I' in her speech is speaking as non worrier, for as she goes on to tell us this is not always the case. So what she draws out of us is the fact that simply because a speech is about worry, it does not follow that it is not another instance of worry. It may or may not be. We are reminded by this that we must think about how we are writing/speaking, listening and not imagine that our speech is in some miraculous way separate and beyond, or above, the grammatical constraints of the speech we study. If our speech is different, it will be so by our thoughtful efforts to make it so.

This work is difficult, but whether it is difficult or not we need to do it, and we know that our work asks no more from others than it asks from ourselves. So, when in the above paragraph the speaker says that she must express this struggle and by doing so must help remind the reader ... etc., we know that she is herself a reader, and that she is expressing her awareness that others share her place with her. The struggle is of course to express ourselves, and so she is not speaking like a recruiting officer who, by occupying himself in this fashion at home avoids being on the front. She expresses the struggle by choosing to engage in it, by setting a good example. How else can we show the depth of our commitments? By showing us in her speech what could happen if we chose to worry, that writer risks being misunderstood. But by struggling for ourselves through this work we hear how it reminds us of the irrationality of settling for a version of ourselves, or others, as worried. Speakers' speeches are always misunderstood if they are assumed by other or self to be easily understood; we have to, and want to, work to understand each other better.

We read on and find again that the worrier issues a warning to the reader, but we know when she does this she is warning herself, in effect she is saying to herself that unless she keeps the idea of struggle in mind she will succumb, she indicates that she realises we worry if we aren't thoughtful enough about what we are, not when we are thoughtful.

At this stage she moves on to taunt herself in the name of other as charging her speech with being self centred and hence unworthy. Again she stretches us, for she reminds us that we know that our work is not self centred, if by 'self centred', is meant oriented to the interests of an already known self. For, we do not know ourselves. But, if 'self centred' means work oriented to achieving more thoughtful selves, we do not deny our work is self centred, why should we? Also, if we produce our work as self centred in the latter sense, we certainly have no reason to judge it to be an unworthy enterprise, indeed if we knew of any more worthy enterprise we would be engaged in it. Furthermore, once we treat work as an orientation to achieve, to improve i.e. to change, we see the limitations of judging/charging, for these only have relevance when the possibility for change has been forgotten.

In section 2 (P.16) we produced the notion that those who rely upon an opposition between their own interests and others interests could not act with integrity; what we are saying here is that those, if any, who conceive of an interest in self as unworthy, are operating with versions of self that are unworthy of them, and we ask them to join us in our inquiry.

But what of the notion of evidence, isn't this a very positivist idea, and doesn't this betray that speaker's unthoughtful nature? If we had assumed so, we would have been mistaken, for she does not treat what she says as evidence, but calls upon us, and herself, to make the effort to hear what she wants to say, not what she says. She reminds us that if we are drawn into judging, we should remember to concentrate upon intentions not appearances.

However, now she starts to play with us for she says that ' ... Already you should see worry at work here ... etc.', and she says this after reminding us not to attend to appearances. So whilst we may have started i.e. begun by (hence 'already') seeing worry at work, our good work is to move ourselves beyond this production of ourselves as observers, or for that matter worriers. She reminds us how to move on by (a) describing what we would have seen if we left ourselves and observed worry, and (b) by reminding us that we could not leave ourselves in this way. We have no need to worry about the fact that certain 'readers' may choose to read no further, for we write for ourselves as well as for others. Even if no others read what we are writing, by writing/thinking in this manner we are improving ourselves. Furthermore, unlike those who worry, we do not begin with a conception of our reader as untrustworthy i.e. as liable to stop. We are reminded by that speaker that we have no need to plead with you, for we know that we write both to help and be helped by you as well as to help ourselves. That is, we orient to you as one of ourselves, and given this, why would you stop?

We do not then conceive of our relationship with you as something to worry about, but as that which we are enhancing by trying better to get to be ourselves. Neither are we relating to the speech of worry as something to worry about.

Before we move on to the second paragraph a couple of further reminders have helped us (a) the speaker starts the final sentence 'It is as if I know ...' this is taken by us as indicating her playful attitude with us, for it warns us not to proceed by assuming she thinks she does know this, but by producing her as not knowing but as speaking about what would have happened if she had known. So whilst we began by finding her usage of 'good example' misleading, (for how could such a weak failure to resist worry be a good example?) we propose that what she is saying is a good example is what she says, i.e. that she produced the situation as such and such. For by grasping how we, like she, are producers we show, as she shows, how our productions need not be externalised in such a way as to subordinate our selves.

Reading and working in a productive and thoughtful way, as we are doing here, is so much more enjoyable and so much better for us and others than is reading as consumption, but let us ensure in this work that we respect our partner in this dialogue, i.e. the speaker who tries to capture the nature of worry for us.
Analysis of Paragraph 2

My struggle will be well illustrated by the problems which you may see to arise concerning the person(s) in which this work is written, for at times, the worrier will appear as a distant and perhaps distinct person, whilst at the same time it must also be apparent that I only know the worrier so well or intimately because at times I am her. What I am suggesting here is that what may appear to be a technical problem of rhetoric, for example should I write a dialogue or a monologue, is illustrative in a weak way of the struggle in which I am involved, and perhaps involved is a good word for it! To put this another way the problem of the person in which I write i.e. first person, second person or third person, is illustrative of the complex nature of my relationship to myself, and of how my version of myself relates to my version of others etc. When I say for example, that - what I think I want may not be what I want - and then look for ways to deal with this statement or state of affairs, this is not a matter of marginal or peripheral interest, and it is only when its centrality is felt that I feel involved in the struggle I am commending. This can be further illustrated (and again the illustration seems weak) by the fact that the very sentences which I write, including this one, have only been written if they have in some way attracted me. The illustration is weak because some 'things' are difficult to illustrate or describe, and a good example of this might be our senses, i.e. the fact that they can be treated as mediating between 'our selves' and 'the world' doesn't make them any easier to describe. For the moment then it might be useful to think of worry as mediating in this manner between the worrier's self and the world. However, I was speaking about the fact that the sentences which I write must have attracted me, but I can already see how even this sentence draws my, and perhaps your, attention away from that which is attracted, i.e. their subject, me, which as I have already indicated, is the crucial problem area at present. What I am trying to say here is that it is versions of the self that are attracted by things. For example, only the worrier would be attracted by the doubts raised by this version of attraction. More deeply it is the version of myself as a worrier that attracts me, for it, as will become apparent, offers one way in which I allow myself to imagine I make things easier for myself. So, by generating a version of what attracts me I shall be generating a version of the me that is attracted, and may as a consequence be better equipped to struggle with the version of myself which I can all too easily become. The inference I draw from this is that I must produce an analysis of worry if I am to see how what I think I want relates to what I want. Authenticity then is by no means tranquil or easy, for it will only be in this struggle that I can show or be what I am.

Response:

The speaker has already alerted us to the fact that we need not see problems as arising for us, but that we raise the problems, and so her 'may see' tells us that she does not force us to read productively. She allows us to choose to read productively. That is, we choose not to see the struggle as hers as we may have done, but to take our place in the struggle. For our struggle is well illustrated for us by the problems we produce concerning the person(s) in which all works are written and read. For example, in the worrier's self portrait the worrier seems distant and distinct, and yet close and indistinct, and this illustrates for us the perplexities that are produced by, and for, speakers who are ruled by conceit of knowledge. For when she says that ' ... it must be apparent that I only know the worrier so well or intimately because at times I am her' she reminds us not to concern ourselves with the apparent, for we think of that which we are as being what we do not and cannot know, but that which we decide to become.

What we are suggesting is that if we were asked how we would approach a seemingly technical problem of rhetoric i.e. should we write dialogues or monologues, our answer i.e. that monologues are not a human possibility, illustrates in a strong way our commitment to the struggle in which we choose to be involved. 'Involved' is a good word, if it means involvement/commitment but not if it is read as enmeshment. We do not produce writing dialogue as problematic (in the bad sense), on the contrary we see writing or speaking in the first person, as we have said above, as unnecessarily complicating our relationships with ourselves and others.

Ourselves become complex if we have become perplexed by imagined differences between self and other, and between different others i.e. our lives become more complicated the more we hide what we are in common with others from ourselves and each other.

What can the speaker be referring us to by her example i.e. 'When I say, for example, that - what I think I want may not be what I want ...' Again we must stretch ourselves so as to reach a better reading, for whilst the lazy, effortless reading, i.e. that of the reader that doesn't want to think, would have read this as asking how to move from what she thinks she wants, to what she wants, we begin by reversing this direction. That is by showing the movement desired to be from unthoughtful wants (i.e. impulses) to thoughtful wants (i.e. socially and morally desirable choices). Indeed we show that the thoughtful character is one who wants what she thinks she wants, and of course nothing could be more worthy of effort i.e. more central.

We will say this once more, we are not concerned to transform what we think

38

we want into what we want, and we view any who set themselves this task as having matters backwards, not least because we do not begin by knowing what we think we want. To suggest that we do, would be to reduce thought to impulse, it would be to reduce conversation, dialectical development, thought, to a waste of time. Whilst the speaker says she looks for ways to deal with her state of affairs we know that she and we are doing the work of thinking about what we want, rather than looking for ways, as if we might find them ready laid out. That would be to lay ourselves out. To imagine we desire to move from what we think we want to what we want is self destructive and why would any thoughtful character join that struggle?

What of the speaker's illustration regarding the sentences she writes? Of course they have only been written because they attract, this is what speech or discourse is for i.e. trying to improve our selves, and whilst she suggests the illustration is weak, by doing so she encourages us to offer a strong reading of it.

But what now, for the next section is demanding, for we know that our senses do not mediate between ourselves and the world for we produce ourselves as social i.e. as thoughtful, and by so doing produce our thoughts as mediating and moderating our senses. By doing so we resist sliding in an unthoughtful manner by subordinating self to unthoughtful feelings and then modelling thoughts, perhaps worry, in that mould, i.e. as impulsive. We reveal, with the help of this speech, the moving pathway to irrationalism that we refuse to place ourselves upon. By revealing this damaging impulse to rest with a view of ourselves as merely sensual, we provide for our thoughtful efforts to produce social sensuality. The speaker states that 'For the moment then it might be useful to think of worry as mediating in this manner between the worrier's self and the world'. The speaker hints here at the irrational nature of worry which is frequently in conventional usage treated as a feeling, but also when she says 'for a moment' she shows the impulsiveness or unthoughtfulness of that sentence for to think of worry as mediating etc. is self contradictory, for by thinking it we show worry doesn't mediate in the manner suggested. That she begins the next sentence with 'However - ' and returns to the question of what attracts, further indicates that she chose not to think of worry as mediating in that way for more than a moment.

We are tempted to censure the speaker here for making things too difficult for us, but we resist this impulse by (a) acknowledging the effort she is making (b) remembering that by stretching ourselves we do improve ourselves, and (c) by remembering that it is we who choose to stretch our selves; she is not forcing us.

The speaker helps us more than a little in the next section by saying she ' ... was speaking about the fact that ...' for we are reminded by this that thinkers/social producers are not constrained by the facts, rather we produce facts as artifacts and by so doing remind ourselves of our potential not to relate to our histories as determining facts. The speaker shows her effort to encourage us to do more than stick with or in the so called facts by saying 'What I am trying to say ...' she wants us to join her in making the effort to say what she isn't yet saying, but is trying to say, and we need to make this effort for if we don't we do her speech violence. For instance, we must work to produce the irony and profundity of her remark that 'More deeply it is the version of myself as a worrier that attracts me for it, as will become apparent, offers one way in which I allow myself to imagine I can make things easier for myself'. The irony is that this will only be apparent to those who want to make things easier for themselves before thinking about whether ease is necessarily good. A stronger reading recognises that the speaker is describing what need not happen, what she will not let happen, for being a thoughtful interlocutor she would never opt to allow herself to make things easy for herself in this unthoughtful way. For this would not be easy for her, thinkers/speakers do not find thoughtlessness easy.

What we are reminded of by reading this speech is that it is versions of self that are attracted by things, but we do not orient to versions of self as attractions: at least not whilst attractions are being produced as acting upon us, for we think of our versions of ourselves as what we produce, as products of our thoughtful actions. This may not make things easier for ourselves in the manner that some may pretend they want, but as we are thoughtful actors we want to be at ease in our activity not pursuing activities in order to put ourselves at ease, for that is intellectual suicide.

At first sight the speaker may appear to produce her work as generating a version of what attracts her in order to generate a version of the self that is attracted, in order to know better what she is struggling against. But we know her better, for we know she is helping us to grasp that that is not the activity we would engage in, if indeed it can be called an engagement. What we are engaged in is the generation of that which attracts us i.e. more thoughtful selves, not that which distracts us. So whilst the speaker says that she produces the analysis of worry as being necessary for her to see how what she thinks she wants relates to what she wants, we know that what she means is that she is doing the analysis for we do not produce analysis as something we need but aren't yet doing, (perhaps an unthoughtful worrier would have worried that she would never produce an analysis!). We produce our work as analytic and as what we are doing not what we are waiting for.

When the speaker concludes this paragraph she says 'Authenticity then is ...' and we must be careful not to forget the 'then' for this indicates that this version of authenticity is the version that would be drawn from the easy reading of that which preceded it. It could seem that the speaker is expressing surprise that authenticity is not easy or tranquil. However, we know that it is tranquil and easy but, not still, it is continually surprising ourselves, reminding ourselves that we do not know what we are, and by so doing, startling ourselves, and moving ourselves into thoughtful action.

Analysis of Paragraph 3

> I am trying to throw some light upon one of my problems of action i.e. upon how what I think I want relates to what I want and it may help to hear again the words attraction, distraction and action. How do I, as the worrier, think about attraction?

Response:

When the speaker says she is trying to throw light upon her problems we know that she is not saying she is doing so in order to gain sympathy, her 'trying to' should not be read as an appeal to us, as if she even needs help to gain our sympathy. She is saying she is trying i.e. that she at least is working at thinking with problems common to each and all of us, and that she is becoming more not less social, more not less thoughtful through her work. She decides to take a real risk here and to speak as she imagines a worrier would speak, this is a risk because she does not really know what worry is, but also because she may get enmeshed in and persuaded by the grammar of worry in such a way that she cannot get out. However, we see the wisdom of her action, for by thinking about, i.e. really getting inside worry, she does diminish the likelihood of engaging in the activity unintentionally. The brevity of this paragraph suggests to us that it is analogous to setting the scene for a new act in a play. She will be adopting a new role, and has prepared us for it. Perhaps also she, like we, needed to rest a while at the end of a demanding first act.

Analysis of Paragraphs 4, 5 and 6

When something attracts me it promises to give me something I think I want, in effect I am induced to take what I think I want by what I see or hear etc. Attraction works quickly then, for it leads me to forget to ask myself why I might think I want what I think I want, i.e. it leads me to forget to think about whether I know what I want. The attractive encourages me to take what it promises. (How quickly I rush on here away from the question which asks me to think about whether I know what I want, for perhaps what I want will prove to be to give not to take! Yet in my rush I think I will reveal why I rush so I will go on!)

It may help you to understand my idea of attraction, and hence action, if you begin by considering giving, for if you cannot understand what it is to give something it is highly unlikely that you will be able to understand what it is to promise to give something (cf., idea of attraction above) i.e. for me to find something attractive. Furthermore you cannot understand giving until you draw it into a relation with taking, and for the moment, the relationship to which I refer is not simply that something needs to be given to be taken, on the contrary, it is that something needs to be taken if it is to be given, and there are different ways of taking. My point here then is that we need to acquire things if we are to divest ourselves of them. We need to generate things if we are to be generous with them. The philanthropist, as gift giver, if such he is, would begin to come more clearly into focus, and consequent scrutiny, beside his gift.

Now this could alert both of us to the fact that I began the last paragraph by offering you my help in the form of my understanding of attraction, in effect then I was acting as a philanthropist, and so you should demand from me an explanation of how I have achieved or taken this understanding and from where, and furthermore, why I think it will help you. At first sight my apparent unwillingness or inability to answer your demands may seem strange, but as we continue, the philanthropist's silence will begin to emerge as a necessary result of his version of himself and his relations to others i.e. as a natural rather than an unnatural (strange) consequence of his own self conception (which may indeed prove to be unnatural!)

Response:

We have been warned that the speech we are now hearing is the speaker's version of the speech of worry, and we need to remind ourselves that the speaker has settled to offer a speech that reveals worry as she imagines it is conventionally heard. We want in the remainder of the section, with the assistance of the speaker's version of conventional worry, to display how both we and that speaker would differentiate ourselves from the speech of worry as we imagine it is conventionally understood, but we could not do this adequately without thinking about it, getting inside it; we have to work through it and not ignore it. We will not offer enlivening formulations as we have been doing so far, instead we will tend to offer an alternative speech on the same themes, that is a product of our work with that speech. So whilst we are grateful to the speaker for the account she offers, we do her the service of not recognising it as an honest account of herself, i.e. we do not forget that she is speaking as if she were a worrier, which she is not. She leads us through this detailed account in a skilful manner not to mislead us, but to collaborate with us in our desire through our work to take the risk of being more honest, and by so doing coming to understand that being honest is no real risk at all, but it isn't easy for the dishonest to realise this. Those, if any, who remain worried would lose everything for nothing, but we cannot show them this they will have to show themselves.

What attracts us are thoughtful social actions for these encourage us to do what we think is good to do. Attractive actions do work quickly for they startle us, encourage us, and remind us to ask ourselves to think about what we want to do. They help us to remember to think about, and decide even although we do not and cannot know. Attractive actions are those that display their author's commitment to producing a more thoughtful society. They are those that are engaged in by those who do not rush away from the question which they ask themselves about what a thoughtful character would want to do. They do not leave it to chance in the manner that this speech suggests worry would. Worry leaves everything for other to do, other must search/work while it rushes on.

We do not need to help each other to understand our idea of attraction for it is ours. By saying this we acknowledge that the most our writing can do is remind us of what we already know we do not, and cannot, know.

The version of attraction that worry produces in paragraphs 4, 5 and 6 relies upon differences between givers and takers, have-nots and haves, self and other. Hence its reduction of the student/teacher relationship to that of the philanthropist/poor. But we know that this version of attraction is unattractive because of its refusal to reach beyond differences. Giving and taking are different sides of the same activity, and a dialectical involvement, as is a social relationship, requires an understanding of what we share, through which can be generated less static relationships between self and other. To reduce social relationships to giving or taking in the manner that the speech of worry does is to refuse to remember that truly social relationships are give and take, not give or take.

As the speech of worry continues we read that it views helping other to understand as philanthropy, (memories of Ivan Illyich Pralinsky!). Such a weak notion of the relationship between teaching and learning could only be proposed by worry which has not yet grasped that good teaching, good teachers, is that, and are those, that learn from their own activities. This is why their words, unlike the words of worry as conventionally understood, sound empty neither to others nor to themselves. But, this is not to say that others will always choose to join the inquiry i.e. to instruct themselves, for they may well prematurely decide that learning is too dangerous, and active an activity for them. But if they do they are not only digging their own graves but also, and more importantly, they are helping to dig the grave of the society they live in. And, they are doing so when they could be using their efforts to thoughtfully enliven both.

Whilst worry is in reality necessarily incapable of meeting our demands for an explanation of why it acts as it does, it irrationally prefers to continue worrying, and pretends that its necessary incapability is at worst unwillingness, or an inability of the type that at some later time will be overcome. It persuades those it subjects that they are not yet ready to act. It produces this necessary incapability as its subjects unwillingness and inability to meet their own demands, but it could and should have reminded them to proceed more honestly and thoughtfully by stopping worrying because they had no reason to continue. Which is not, of course, to say they should have stopped thinking, or inquiring into how to act more thoughtfully for, on the contrary, until worry can teach its subjects that they are stopping short in an anti social/self destructive way, they will not bring themselves to think about how they are already engaged in our inquiry.

Analysis of Paragraph 7

> We can see by now that initially I have limited the attractive to the gift i.e. that which is given, and have then gone on to transform gifts into pieces of evidence, and perhaps this can account for my reticence about receiving them for (a) if I accept and consume the gifts I will in effect be destroying the evidence and (b) if I accept and do not consume the gifts I could reduce my desire to testify by viewing myself as a receiver of stolen goods or bribes. If then I view those who offer me gifts as philanthropists I will do my best not to accept what they are offering. If you listened to me then, and treated this speech so far as a gift you would reject it for the reasons I have so far offered, and yet I will show that you could have refused merely to listen to me without rejecting my offer. I am making reference here to the fact that I could, and later I will, make substitutions and initially replace the philanthropist with the teacher and the poor with the student, but later we will replace the philanthropist with the student and the poor with the teacher!

Response:

The speaker does well to convey worry's unruliness here as the speech moves lackadaisically from the giver, in its terms the philanthropist, to the gift, and similarly conveys the irrationality of worry, as conventionally understood, by allowing worry to proceed by limiting gifts to evidence of bribery and corruption, for anyone who blindly accepts this view of gifts and givers would indeed have something to worry about, if that is, he or she wanted social relationships. But, of course all of this is irrational, for why on earth should we transform the attractive (a) into gifts and then gifts into bribes? Worry offers no reasons. Worry is not only dragging itself down, but others also, and we see this as a product of its too ready acceptance of its own speech. We produce its speech as no more than a rationalisation for its unthoughtful refusal to accept what it refers to as gifts. It allows itself to be persuaded not to engage in further thoughtful inquiry into why it does not want to accept. But we know that its reticence about receiving is a product of its awareness that in its version of the past it has been encouraged to accept passively what it did not want. It persuaded those it subjected that they were not, and are not, strong enough, perhaps like children, to stand up against their parents and teachers and to challenge them when they acted as if they knew the virtue/value of what they were doing, when always they did not. Had the children been encouraged to let others know what they thought, they could have much more quickly uncovered either with or without others' willing help that the others did not know, and at best decided to act even though they did not know, or at worst did not know that they did not know.

We begin to uncover how worry is produced and how it prevents those it subjects from getting to produce better versions of themselves and from getting closer to other. It is a product of and a producer of resentful silence on the part of students and lazy dishonest speech on the part of teachers. The speech of worry is helping us here, but it would help itself if it also would choose to recognise how the version of the gift that it relies upon is a product of this kind of lazy authoritarian relationship: that it can do, and needs to do something about working, in fact it needs to recognise that it is already doing something, and by doing so will realise it can do much more.

It chooses to advise the reader about what they can do rather than to do it itself; while it asks other to act i.e. to refuse to merely listen to its speech, it persuades itself that by speaking it is doing enough. It recognises that as it speaks it reveals what it is but foolishly considers that what it is is good enough. Throughout its speech we find it strangling and restraining its speaker when it could be improving itself by deciding to listen to its own speech in a productive way. It does not do what it commends we ought to do. It thinks it is telling others something they do not know, but it knows, and yet whilst its speech does remind us of important issues it resists remembering these through its conceit, its satisfaction with what it perceives as its knowledge of itself. The good of our work is to remind ourselves that we can produce versions of ourselves which are better than this, better than we seem at present to be.

Analysis of Paragraph 8

By transforming the gift in the way that I have, I raise the question of acceptance as the problem that the gift presents to its possible recipient. For it seems that I should refuse all gifts if by being gifts they transform their givers into philanthropists. That is, I am faced with a decision 'should I accept or not? In this way I see a problem i.e. that of the decision coming to mediate between me and the gift, perhaps the world. I then proceed by trying to argue the case for acceptance or non-acceptance, taking or leaving, as a way to reach a decision. The fact that I do this persuades me that I am not merely impulsive/animalistic and that I have some commitment to reason. And yet you can see that my commitment to reason here is only skin deep, for I only use reason as one means to fulfil my impulses i.e. what I think I want, and I do not, as I have said think (reason) about that! My impulsiveness is shown by the fact that I treat the problem of decision as something which faces me, rather than as something which I have produced, or at least had a part in producing. I forget that I am the one who is treating decisions as having a gift like nature, and most importantly as being problems as a result. I am forever forgetting that whilst the fact that we can do the right thing or the wrong thing in any situation can be construed as a problem or a blight this is the wrong thing to do, for were it not possible for us to do the right thing or the wrong thing, good intentions would not be possible. That is, the worrier has a tendency to transform blessings into blights! Furthermore, it is worth pointing out that by using this version of myself as someone who is forever forgetting, or losing sight of things, I produce a version of myself as not being the sort of person to make decisions. But, you should be able to see what an easy way out this might seem to be by noticing how I also choose to ignore the fact that I must have known or seen things in order to forget or lose sight of them. This is further evidence of a misconceived attempt to free myself of what I allow myself to think oppresses me. The ability to know that I forget and lose sight of things however, could go some way to raising me above the animalistic!

Response:

After seemingly already having convinced itself that gifts are bribes or stolen goods, it now decides to raise the question of acceptance of gifts as the problem that gifts present, but of course if gifts were bribes or stolen goods we have reason enough to accept none: i.e. there is no problem for the incorrupt character. But worry is aware that there is something wrong, but it doesn't think about what it is, and so let us see how it runs from this rather than dealing with it.

It begins by producing the decision of whether to accept or not as a problem (and we restrict it to its ordinary usage, here i.e. problems as something to be rid of), rather than as expressing its subjects place as a thoughtful actor: that is one who is able to make decisions for the good. But, by placing an argument, or rather what it itself refers to as an inadequate argument between itself and the decision, it produces its subject as moving a step further back from response-ability. And then it has the affrontary to admit to us that it should be clear that its commitment is only skin deep for it is subordinated to its impulses. It does as we imagined it would, for it reduces thought to impulse. It acts as if it believes being impulsive is what it must be, when we know that it need not be and must not be if it is to become social. It has to decide for itself to treat decisions as its products and not as problems in the weak sense, for by doing so it can come to befriend itself and be worth talking with.

Unlike it, we are forever remembering that the fact we can choose to decide for the good makes our thoughtful good intentions possible. Thoughtful/social actors realise that whatever the situation by their response they are able to make it an occasion for social activity.

Unlike the speech of worry we remember that by referring to a version of self as forever remembering, we produce ourselves as being able to make decisions. We do not limit ourselves to pointing, as it did in that paragraph, we do not take what worry refers to as the easy way out, for how could we?

More importantly we do not produce a version of the worrier as one who is suffering from a misconceived attempt to free herself from what she allows herself to think oppresses her: we produce her as failing to resist the temptation to hide from herself behind rationalisations of a blatantly irrational nature. We don't see it as better than the animalistic for the animal has no choice, it is either the same as the animal or worse, for it turns its back upon its ability to decide. It allows its speech to oppress its subjects and it is not deserving of sympathy.

Analysis of Paragraph 9

> I must slow down now if I am not to lose sight of other matters, for I was arguing with myself about whether or not I should accept or take a gift, and the point here is that I wanted the argument to relieve me of the need to decide in this case, as I often do in others. I tend then to treat decisions as something I would be better off without, for I find myself treating decisions as cutting off possibilities, i.e. as reducing my freedom. But when I do this I must be forgetting that the freedom I ought to sustain must be the freedom to make decisions. I ought to acknowledge that not making decisions, (perhaps not changing my mind) is deciding not to make them (or change it) i.e. that this can also

45

be a method for cutting off possibilities i.e. of reducing my freeaom. In effect, I allow myself to act as if I treat decisions as essentially arbitrary when I know that if this were so I would have no reason to make this decision. However, by my inaction i.e. the action of treating decisions as something to avoid I indicate both to you and to myself that I do think it matters what I do, that I do think I can make bad decisions, and hence that I am not as convinced by the idea of arbitrariness as I sometimes allow myself to think, or perhaps want you to think. I am trying tentatively to suggest here that worry, perhaps like other things, can never act as a successful mediator between self and the world i.e. that because of its nature it can never totally subjugate its subject, and that whilst this could be treated as something to worry about we ought to see it as a virtue.

Response:

This paragraph is depressingly weak, for after having shown us, and itself, that it knows it has potential it chooses to turn its back upon the possibilities it opens up. Indeed when at the end of this paragraph it says it is 'Trying tentatively to suggest ... etc.' it shows us that it is worse than the animal for it does know it could act in a virtuous manner but doesn't, even although it can offer no reason why it should not. Its speech tells us that it would prefer it if it was totally subjugated and had no choice; it is worrying about the fact that worry doesn't totally subjugate it and by so doing it is subjugating itself to worry when it need not.

Analysis of Paragraph 10

But, what is it that I as worrier, prefer to think of myself as, even if I can never quite do it? I think I want to think of myself as not being responsible for anything that goes wrong, and to this end as being prepared to pay the price of never being responsible for anything, even that which goes right, as a way of minimising that risk. My idea of me doing good then is limited to that of not doing harm. That is, I produce paradoxically a version of myself as unproductive. I prefer to think I prefer being mastered by the situation rather than being the situation's master. When, as we will see, this turns out to be my way of mastering the situation which isn't to say it is a good thing for as we will discover worry has a misconceived notion of mastery. To say this another way, I act when I worry as if I find possibility (cf., the making of decisions) more worrying than necessity, and this is because I conceive of necessity as relieving me of responsibility for what goes wrong.

Response:

We have to admire the speaker's skills here for she continues to express so well in these transitions from one topic to another the way worry refuses to 'see' reason.   How could anyone prefer to think of themselves as never being responsible for anything! The speech of worry revels in submission as if submission were its mission, and we are pleased to be engaged in subversion i.e. in subverting submissiveness. This paragraph is crucial to our understanding of worry as conventionally understood, as an activity that strangles self and other, for by submitting to what it conceives of as necessity, worry does produce the continuance of corruption, and its reasoning is so weak, for it is its conception of necessity. Worry forgets that it produces the possibility of what it conceives of as necessary, whilst we are showing the necessity for humans of our possibility. Worry sees its potential, but by refusing to seize it throws it all away.

Analysis of Paragraphs 11, 12

The notion of responsibility begins to hang very heavily over this part of the discussion for I am beginning to feel how actively I, as worrier, try to avoid facing up to, or better grasping, the fact that I have the gift of decision making i.e. the one gift which, as we shall see, the philanthropist would not or could not offer. Furthermore, the fact is that I must accept this gift because of my nature, I can no more be the worrier than I can be any other version of myself. For though I may act like a worrier, when I do so it is always by accident i.e. unintentionally.

Goodness! the worrier does seem to be a slippery character for now I feel that it is he who is saying that when he does act it is not his fault because it is an accident i.e. because it is unintentional.

Response:

Responsibility as pressing down on the speech here is the way pressure for good is subverted, for the desire for response-ability raises our heads. We seek to be more response-able through our conversations, our lives. We do not accept worry's irrational notion that we can no more be worriers than we can be other versions of ourselves, for that is unnecessarily hopeless. We can be other versions of ourselves for we produce our willingness and ability to seek to make thoughtful decisions as a version of ourselves that is a possible course of action where worry is not. We do not wish to hide behind accident, unintentionality, in the way that worry commends, for we have no desire to display slipperiness in the manner that the speech of worry does for that could never be becoming.

Analysis of Paragraph 13

By now you, as reader, may be beginning to wonder what happened to the struggle, for it seems that worry is not even lifting a finger in opposition to what is being said i.e. it seems it has nothing to say. Yet whilst in one sense I think this is true, in another I think that we have been listening to nothing but worry so far, for by unintentionally resorting to a device of treating worry as a version of myself and referring to the distance between this version and myself, I have in effect been treating it as another person (cf., original problem of style of writing). I have been, in effect, relieving myself of responsibility for its action or inaction, when I know all too well that this is simply me succumbing yet again to a version of myself as someone with something to worry about. That is, I have allowed the struggle I was initially engaged in to become yet another instance of worry. What I am saying here is that if you are to see any suffering, and hence any struggle, in this speech I must show you not how distant and distinct I am from this version of myself as the worrier, but, how I have become in most of my speech constrained and limited by its rules!

Response

But we are startled and reawakened here for we are reminded that the speaker was intending to contend with, struggle against, worry, and that her speech has, as a result of its commitment to the usage of a weak notion of 'I', become confused. For she says here that it seems that worry is not even lifting a finger in opposition, but we remember that at the end of paragraph 3 she decided to speak 'as if' she was the worrier. We know that it was not worry that weakened but herself, and now it is clear to us that it has been for this reason that we could no longer maintain our commitment to enriching and enlivening her speech in this section. She has become so enmeshed in the usage of worry, as we hinted she might, that we decided to demonstrate how differently she could have spoken by differentiating ourselves and her from the speech she offers, rather than offering formulations of it. We have intended to demonstrate in our analysis of these paragraphs i.e. from the end of paragraph 3 how we/she are much stronger than her speech suggests.

For example in this paragraph (i.e. 13) she is persuaded to produce the device of treating the worrier as a version of herself and then distancing herself from it as unintentional, and as relieving her of responsibility; when we would produce her attempt to distance herself from worry as her morally courageous effort to take hold of her response-ability for her actions. She draws the burden of worry upon herself in order to display how she can contend with it, and with the help of reasonable arguments, conversations, moderates worry and puts it in its place. She, like we, is showing how by engaging with ourselves, by bringing versions of ourselves into our inquiry, we are able to continue to stretch the rules of forms of speech/life that could, if we settled with consuming them, have limited and constrained us.

But whilst in this section of our work we have been demonstrating our distance from worry, and that we do need to do, we know that this is not enough for we are dissatisfied with the way our discourse has tended to appear as the speech of one against the other. We want to remind ourselves at this juncture that we would have reason to worry if one against the other came to represent one speaker against another rather than reasoned argument, dialogue against silence, i.e. the decision not to make the effort to think any more about our speech, our lives. So let us not forget that whilst in this section we are concerned in the main with differentiation, this is in order to make reparation rather than continued separation possible. We are not choosing to relieve ourselves of response-ability.

Analysis of Paragraph 14

Even if for the moment we allow the separation of myself from the version of myself as a worrier, which the preceding paragraph brings into much doubt, I still feel that the worrier's apparent lack of resistance is by no means uncharacteristic, for I do tend to accept the bad reading of myself as a worrier, i.e. as trying to shirk my responsibilities by saying in effect that I am not response-able; by accepting that I am not authentic. Yet strangely it is by accepting this reading that I allow myself to think that I gain a sense of relief; for I allow myself to feel even more convinced that I am not the sort of person who should be making decisions. Furthermore, I ought to point out that 'decision' is being treated throughout this speech as a prerequisite for action and so we can see that a much stronger (or weaker!) claim is being made. For in effect, the acceptance of the idea that the worrier is not the type of person to make decisions is an acceptance of the worrier as inactive. That is, it is a version of worries as something to be got out of the way before you can begin to act. Now it should be plain how this analysis has a bearing on the problem of action mentioned at the outset, for if we can begin to see how relief from worry comes to be integrated with action we can see how I as the worrier produce an even greater distance between worry/thought and action. The point is then that I formulate myself as non actor, for I reduce my own actions to the status of inaction by treating them as merely reactions to, for example, dangers or exigencies. So we can begin to see now how I produced attraction as inducement for this placed me in an essentially passive inactive role! (By treating myself as being attracted to the version of myself as a worrier I am exemplifying this form of passivity!

Response:

The speaker through this paragraph helps remind us of how separation is not good enough, and we can begin to grasp this by more diligently producing the 'I' as a problem as we earlier proposed we would. What we are saying is that any who conceive of themselves as 'I's have chosen to remain with worry; that the author of this self portrait of worry, being herself a thoughtful social actor, could not intend her self when she speaks of 'I' but is speaking of 'I's i.e. of that which we are not.

She begins by stating that she has started to have doubts about separation and we read this paragraph as an argument against treating ourselves as 'I's (in the weak sense) for an 'I' would very likely act as she says, for an 'I' has no ability to relate, to learn or act thoughtfully. We read the paragraph as continuing in the following manner: ... an 'I' would still feel that the worrier's apparent lack of resistance is by no means uncharacteristic of it, for an 'I' by being an 'I' is tending to produce and accept a bad reading of itself as a worrier, i.e. as trying to shirk the response-ability of being social/thoughtful by saying in effect that 'I's are not response-able; by producing 'I's as acknowledging their inauthenticity. (Of course by their speaking we produce them as revealing their non 'I' ness!) Whilst 'I's, because in fact they are not 'I's, find it difficult to accept this reading of themselves, they still pretend that it is something they accept, not produce, so as to allow themselves to pretend they are convinced; content with versions of their selves as not the sort of persons to make decisions, to think. That they are not content with this condition is revealed by their difficulty making their decision appear to themselves as a non-decision, that is why they say it is strange. Furthermore an 'I' would say that it ought to point out (as if pointing was enough! This is fact-fetishism i.e. subordinating self to appearances) that decision is being treated throughout as a prerequisite for social/thoughtful action. Here the speaker reminds us of the anti social nature of all 'I' talk, for how could a thoughtful social character want to lead the dead life that deformulating self as inactive must produce. If 'I' talk is to be preserved we must produce a thoughtful formulation of 'I'.

We do have to get worry out of our way before we act, but we do this by becoming more thoughtful, more social. Relief from worry as we imagine it (worry) is conventionally conceived, is not thoughtlessness but is thoughtfulness, social activity, but an 'I' cannot grasp this because it has no need or desire for action. An 'I' if it were possible, which fortunately for us it is not, would have nothing to say. An 'I' really does become merely a pawn in the game. By helping remind us of this the author of the speech of worry helps us to proceed to work through this essentially passive, inactive, irrational role.

Analysis of Paragraph 15

(As an example of how I as a worrier produce a distance between action and worry I would refer to my own writing, for whenever I reread what I have written I tend to see it as inauthentic, i.e. as not really expressing how I feel i.e. as the product of lack of concern, and whilst you may view this as mildly crazy I'm sure you can imagine that it does not appear to aid productivity!)

Response:

Again the author produces very well here the spirit of worry, for if we viewed writing as needing to express what we feel in order to be authentic, we would all merely gabble. However, we are concerned to change ourselves for the better through our thoughtful, inquiring writing/speech and not merely to express what we feel. Feelings, as impulses alone, could provide no incentive for the reader, or writer, and this is why diary writing, if it is formulated as simply recording feelings, is such a bore. Of course we do not view the 'worrier's' position as mildly crazy we produce it, as it is, as downright degenerate, and we are pleased if it does not aid its productivity, if its products are inauthentic, as it says, for what need have we of them?

Analysis of Paragraph 16

By now you might expect that I, the worrier, would be feeling pretty bad, and in a way you would be right, but, perhaps not too surprisingly it is now that I, as the worrier, start to take the offensive. For as if this wasn't bad enough, I go on to treat all action, including the supposed criticism of me as the worrier, as being the result of a lack of concern because of the distance between worry and action, or conversely, because of the integration of lack of concern with action. That is, I produce others, in this instance my supposed critic, as icons of myself. It is this that helps me to feel just in my state of inaction for by allowing the argument to persuade me that action is always the result of a lack of concern its consequences whether apparently good or bad are treated as accidents. That is I reduce others to the status of the mechanical, the unintentional or the unthinking, the inauthentic.

Response:

Speaking about self makes worry feel bad for it decides not to notice how speech can provide means for improving self. So instead of moving from bad to better, which a thoughtful, social character would have tried to do, and by trying have done, the 'I' as worrier does surprise us, for it moves from bad to worse. Rather than decide to work with itself upon itself, it directs its attention, and tries to direct ours, towards others by producing the worst version of other's actions, and by so doing considers it raises itself in comparison. Others actions are produced as the unconcerned criticism that issues forth from unthoughtful others who fail to consider how the criticism applies to themselves.

This helps us to remember how we could never reduce others to the status of the mechanical, the unintentional etc., for by so doing we would be reducing ourselves. By producing versions of actions/speeches as thoughtful/social, we provide reminders for ourselves of how our actions are integrated with concern/thought. Our intent is not to criticise those who worry, not to reduce them, but to work with them and their speech to show how we can make more of it by stretching ourselves. Healthy criticism is always from the inside, it always calls upon self as well as other to improve, but ironically if it was to be read by 'I's, that is those who reduce self and other to the status of the mechanical etc., its profound social and moral character is missed. However, we know what we are saying is that we are not and cannot be 'I's and it is by calling ourselves to work at achieving thoughtful/social readings of speeches that we are reminding ourselves that we will only achieve a society with our own thoughtful efforts.

Analysis of Paragraph 17

> Perhaps I could clear the air here by returning to the idea of the gift, for if we treat gift giving as accidental i.e. as being the result of a lack of concern, we can begin to see why I would be suspicious of the giver's motives, for by producing the gift as an accident I treat myself, its possible receiver, as undeserving. It is just a matter of chance that I am offered it. As a receiver (or possible receiver) of a gift from a philanthropist I am not deserving in the strong sense, but merely lucky, for I have not earnt what I get, I am simply lucky to meet or know a rich and generous man! This could be why I am reticent about receiving gifts i.e. because I think I haven't earnt them I fear that they may be taken away as soon as either my undeserving character, or a more deserving character is brought to light. By treating myself as undeserving i.e. by treating myself as an accidental receiver, i.e. a receiver of charity, I remove myself from the productive process, I act as if I am relaxing. For when we relax we just let things happen i.e. we produce the situation as being one in which accidents (bad accidents) are certainly excluded, and the result is that the most we could expect to receive would be pleasant surprises; gifts. I think I remove the possibility of a bad accident by producing myself as unproductive, for, as I have said, what I, as the worrier, think I fear is being responsible for something that goes wrong. Hence my version of a bad accident is something I am responsible for, and so I go on to allow myself to think that if I am unproductive i.e. if I produce nothing, I cannot be responsible for anything bad. I forget that I still consume and hence that even if I produce nothing else I produce needs!

Response:

Worry spoke of reducing other to the mechanical etc. and now rather than stopping doing this, says it will occupy itself with clearing the air. Its survival orientation surfaces all too quickly, for after stating how it corrupts and reduces, it turns its attention to fumigation rather than reforming itself.

It tells us what would happen if we treat gift giving as accidental, but we produce this treatment of gift giving as accidental for if gift giving had been produced as intentional the following paragraph would have been possible:

> ... by treating gift giving as intentional i.e. as being the result of concern, we can begin to produce why we would not be suspicious of the giver's motives for, by producing gifts as non accidental we treat ourselves, their possible givers and receivers, as deserving. It is not simply a matter of chance if we are offered them. As receivers, or possible receivers of gifts from thoughtful characters we produce ourselves as deserving in the strong sense, and not merely lucky, for we must have related to others in such a way as to deserve their friendship. We are not then reticent about accepting gifts from thoughtful others, for we know we must have earnt them. Furthermore, we know that they will not be drawn back by their givers for their givers, in their giving, give to themselves also. By treating ourselves as deserving, i.e. by treating ourselves as earning what we get, we place ourselves in the productive process and prevent ourselves being dependent upon charity. We do this by becoming producers. By being productive we have something to give and because our productions are for others as well as self we can relax in our work,

i.e. we do have nothing to fear from it. We relax when we are acting thoughtfully/socially, when we are working, for we produce social situations as being those occasions in which intentions are displayed and happenings are responded to in a thoughtful way. By being intent upon our intentions, rather than by observing what happens to us, we pleasantly surprise ourselves with how much we can make happen. We remove bad accidents from the realm of possibility by producing ourselves as the thoughtful producers of good and bad. Our version of a bad accident is what would happen if we chose not to thoughtfully work at producing what we do. But an 'I' by producing itself as unable or unwilling to respond socially/thoughtfully has 'reasons' to imagine it is better for it to be unproductive for it is aware that its productions are, because of its nature, irresponsible and bound to cause things to go wrong. We are reminding ourselves that we do not consume in an unproductive, lazy manner for we produce that which we work with including ourselves, as enhanced by our work, our interaction.

The final sentence of this paragraph reminds us why worry is corrupt, for it accepts what it has conceptualised as bribes or stolen goods to meet its needs, but it refuses to ask itself whether its needs i.e. the 'I's needs, ought really to be met. It assumes itself is good and subordinates other to serving it, and in this way refuses to be reminded that a more attractive version of self isn't self as good but self as for good.

Analysis of Paragraphs 18, 19 and 20

But isn't something worrying happening here for at first glance worrying and relaxing would seem to be very different social forms? After raising this question doubts immediately arise however, for it is apparent that worrying and relaxing do share one important characteristic, both are conceived of as making it difficult to proceed with your work.

This problem is raised by relaxation in the form of the Monday morning feeling. For like a surprise relaxation cannot last, and it cannot last because it relies upon a version of work as something which has to be done but which would be better avoided. When work is seen as drudgery relaxation becomes important, and also the problem it creates (cf., the Monday morning feeling) becomes heightened. (This suggests that as we proceed our attention should not merely be directed to the worry, in this instance the Monday morning feeling, but to that which creates it, in this instance the creation of drudgery.) However, in ordinary usage relaxation has to stop if we are to start work.

Similarly our ordinary usage of worry is as of something which has to stop before we can start work, e.g. 'Stop worrying and get on with it'. But we can see how work is treated as drudgery, and we will come to see how drudgery is a form of relaxation, for it is what I am involved in when I worry, if I really conceive of myself as not being responsible for anything i.e. as not being productive!

Response:

'But isn't something worrying happening here ... etc.' we are better able to read this for as we have said it is happenings that worry, but only when both worry and happenings are not well placed, are not thought about. At first glance, worry takes the appearances of worrying and relaxing as things, and does not mention or think about how they are its products, how if they seem the same or different, this is through what it makes them be. We raise doubts about the thoughtfulness, trustworthiness of a speech that refuses to think about itself, that assumes that what is 'apparent' to it is apparent to others.

The whole discussion of the relations between work, relaxation and worry here is confined to, and by, what worry conceives of as conventional usage, i.e. its usage, without those confines being brought into question. We would say that usage, lazily consumed as it seems it is in those paragraphs, has to be stopped before we can relax in our work. Imagine a society that creates a version of relaxation/enjoyment as that which is limited to when its members are too tired to be engaged in drudgery. We are reminded by our reading that that kind of society (or better anti society) could not last because we have the ability to reflect upon, think about speech, through speech, and to move beyond mere imitation of what worry conceives of as ordinary usage. If the ordinary usage of worry is as of something which has to stop before work can start, we must work in an unworried way to move beyond that usage.

Of course relaxing, if conceived of in an unthoughtful fashion, may stop work but we can get a grip on ourselves and act response-ably by producing work as that which does not threaten us, our active efforts to do this begin to remove drudgery from the realms of human possibility.

Analysis of Paragraphs 21, 22

> But, aren't I at least responsible for pointing to the obstructions and hence in a sense responsible for their removal, i.e. isn't this the sort of work in which worry is involved? So whilst not being directly involved in the production of anything, perhaps I am indirectly involved, for by pointing to problems, I allow production to continue to run smoothly. Yet this is even worse than being unproductive, for now I appear as a member of the Human Relations Movement whose only interest is in continued production, i.e. it seems that I relax when the real questions are asked!
> But this is too malicious, for I know that it is I who would begrudge myself even this moment of relaxation by worrying about why I was no longer worrying i.e. by thinking that I was, or had been, acting irresponsibly, for as we have seen I tend to see all actions as irresponsible especially my own! In this way, I transform solutions into problems, and smooth running into uneasiness. That is I can only work or feel I am working, when I am vexed or troubled.

Response:

In the transition from paragraphs 20 to 21 the corrupt nature of worry, as it is, is revealed yet again, for having made itself aware of what it produces (not we) as its lack of production, it deeply realises that by telling us, it is endangering itself. That is, if we realise it contributes nothing, as it imagines, we may decide to stop bothering with or for it, and so instead of trying to change and become productive it begins to claim that it does contribute and hence does deserve a place as it is i.e. that it does not need to change. But how could pointing to obstructions remove them? Pointing can itself be obstructive if it persuades its subject that it is enough, for pointing can lack involvement/commitment.

We are reminded at this stage that it is by lacking involvement that worry refuses to come to grips with the deeper problem of production which it recognises but refuses to ask. Worry shows its awareness of the fact that so much so called production in certain 'societies' is destructive of human self by refusing to join in. But its subjects should join in the destruction of corrupt systems that produce limited selves of that type. Why would any thoughtful character relax when the real questions are asked? We are able to see that this is in fact the only place for real relaxation, for real work, but worry's 'seems' suggests it hasn't grasped that.

Once again (and that it is once again, shows us how worry holds itself back) we produce worry as hiding behind its own screen of feigned irresponsibility for it is aware that it is acting irresponsibly and is able to do something about that, but by not doing so chooses to act irresponsibly. To transform solutions into problems, and smooth running into uneasiness could be good, if the solutions and smooth running were mere surface and concealed corruption and conflict, but worry does not risk saying this. Our work takes the trouble to deal with vexation, for vexation is the product of malicious speech, and we want none of that, not even a little. To speak strongly against corruption is not malicious, but not to do so is.

Analysis of Paragraphs 23, 24

So I do think I work after all! Yes, but I never manage to produce anything, and hence am always dissatisfied. It is because of this feeling of lack of productivity that I can see myself as being involved in merely a difficult form of relaxation! My point here is that when I think I am working I am involved (cf., paragraph 2) but it is a weak involvement, for whilst I do have a version of work as investing myself, I restrict this idea of investing myself to that of investigating.
This, like much else, isn't too clear to me, but I think I think of the work of worry as investigating i.e. as looking into; which is in fact only a special case of looking at, or on; which is in turn what relaxation does. Whilst relaxing is analogous to spectating, worrying is analogous to inspecting or investigating and this begins to suggest that whilst worrying appears to be work because it isn't easy, it now seems more like a difficult form of relaxing. The point being that the difficulty for worry is the energy expended in trying to remain separate i.e. in trying not to be responsible for anything i.e. in not getting involved.

Response

At last it seems that worry recognises that it does act, but then impulsively it wraps itself up in what it mistakenly considers the protective clothing of its ordinary usage, for it says it is dissatisfied because it never produces any things. However we know that it has this backwards, for producing any things is a good reason not to be satisfied. We sustain ourselves by producing thoughtful social relationships not any things, for it is when anythings are produced that their producers have 'reason' to worry. Worry views itself as involved in merely a difficult form of relaxation, but we can relax in our work for we know it is worthwhile. Worry's idea of investing itself as investigating could have been good yet it chooses to treat it as restrictive, constraining, weak, by refusing to produce the good of investigating, inquiry, thoughtful production.

Worry continues in the next paragraph to remind us that clarity is not something we can wait for, it is produced by continuing conversation. We produce our thoughtful lives as inquiry, as investigating how we can be more thoughtful, more social, and whilst we produce this activity as good for us we

do not rely upon a conventional notion of what is good for us as being leisure
i.e. non work. Our work may or may not be easy, but it is not a difficult form
of relaxing, for we, unlike worry, are concerned to integrate, to take on
response-ability. Worry's temptation to relieve itself of response-ability is
analogous to pissing into the wind and its consequences are far more tragic.

Analysis of Paragraph 25, 26, 27

This idea of separation is a powerful one and underlies paragraph 15,
which refers to my problem with re-reading, for so strongly do I want
to refuse to accept responsibility that I even forget how I write what I
write, and then treat it as an accident i.e. as inauthentic. So now my
dissatisfaction with my own work comes to be a source of ease not of
unease. That is, this is the means by which I remove myself from this
productive process.

Goodness, this is getting complicated for earlier, i.e. in a previous
draft of this speech I wrote that:

> "The worrier is dissatisfied with her work because
> she doesn't see it as producing rewards, satisfaction,
> and yet she teaches us by her dissatisfaction with
> gifts that she knows that satisfaction or ease is the
> problem rather than work. The danger for the
> worrier is that she can become satisfied with her
> work (i.e. that she can feel delighted when she
> points out problems) when becoming satisfied is
> leaving herself no more work to do. She needs to
> keep in mind that relieving her own frustration or
> hunger, i.e. killing those sensations isn't enough to
> produce a good human life, and hence isn't enough to
> deal with worry, indeed it may not be enough to
> introduce it."

Now it seems that dissatisfaction is her (my) problem, for it is the
source from which I relieve my own frustration or hunger. Perhaps we
get a hint here of the fact that I seem to require myself to be involved
in a specific type of social situation. A desperate one at that, for on
the one side I don't think I can produce anything because I worry,
whilst on the other side I see products to be the result of a lack of
concern. It is this version of myself as unproductive which leaves me
dependent upon the philanthropist for my sustenance, and given the
chance nature of philanthropy, which I have already referred to, it is
no wonder that I worry! Indeed to construe a situation as desperate is
to construe it as having to stop if danger is to be removed, for it holds
no hope. Desperation then, like relaxation and worry relies upon an
idea of having to stop i.e. they all treat possibility as lying outside of
them i.e. beyond their grasp. So as a worrier, the only solution I can
see to my own situation lies outside it i.e. my only future is seen to lie
in my changing from something I am to something I am not. (There is
no sense of movement it is simply one thing or the other!)

Response

The issue of rereading that is raised by worry here reminds us that rereading is
work, but that only by it can we remind ourselves of how we write i.e. of what
forms of speech acted as grounds for our writing. We produce rereading as

continuing to thoughtfully search for greater authenticity, and we are making the effort to display how our speech was and is becoming more thoughtful through our work with it.

But worry provides us with a useful corrective here, for if we related to our previous speeches as it does to its earlier draft, we would come to produce our work as accidental. By including a paragraph from an earlier draft worry shows that it can change its mind, that it is complicated, but it does not do the hard work of displaying how what was previously written could have been written. By not taking on response-ability for what it said or says it shows us worry's lack of discipline, lack of direction, it is as if worry mistakes being complicated, clever and intricate for being good, when we know that cleverness all too often can merely be a sign of protectiveness. Whilst we take heed of worry's advice and remember that our work does sustain us, but not satisfy us, worry produces no middle way, and then goes on to produce dissatisfaction as a way of gaining relief i.e. satisfaction. No doubt it may be being factually correct about what it does, but we want to sustain our thoughtful conversation and we will not sustain it by deformulating it as either satisfying or dissatisfying, unless we produce versions of either that provide reasons for continuing and not finishing or leaving the conversation. Worry's speech reminds us that all social situations are desperate, that we are always in an intermediate position, but we produce this as bounded on the one side by the thoughtless, lazy production of any things and being opened up on the other by our efforts to seek to achieve, to seek to produce thoughtful social actions.

However, worry then refers back to its version of the relationship between the philanthropist and the poor as if this was a secure datum, and then moves from it to explain why this relationship makes it desperate. But yet again, it uses its 'formulations' to restrict its subjects efforts. Instead of producing a desperate situation as one in which action is called for it produces a desperate situation as hopeless, it places possibility out of reach. It makes possibility impossible in order to save itself effort when it has no reason to do so, when it has every reason not to do so. Worry sees solutions as lying outside problems, it refuses to produce problems as containing but also as possibly exposing solutions (solutions as improvements not conclusions). It has no notion of movement as it indeed recognises, but we know this is a product of its undialectical mode of speech i.e. one thing or the other, and we also know, as we are displaying through our work, that what worry recognises as itself is not the speaker's self at all. By refusing to orient to ourselves as 'I's we are able to move and improve and in this way to show that improvement is possible for us. We want to help ourselves and that speaker to move from something we are not i.e. worry towards what we produce ourselves as becoming.

Analysis of Paragraphs 28, 29, 30, 31

One way in which I tend to produce the situation as desperate is by treating raising problems as raising the stakes, and it is worth remembering that raising problems is about all the worrier can do with her 'yes but'. In this way I reduce the situation to one of desperation i.e. of decision in its worst sense, and if we can think about a decision in these circumstances we can understand why earlier I thought of decisions as arbitrary, i.e. you jump or you don't jump! But once I treat the situation in this way the most I can do is save my own skin even if I have raised the stakes in the process, and as a consequence all of my actions do take on the character of self defence i.e. I do only react and then think as a result I need not feel responsible. I forget very easily that I am responsible for what I don't do i.e. that not responding is my response.

It is in this way that I, as worrier, use a sense of desperation as a way of reducing my responsibility, for I come to consider survival as the goal, and then if I do survive, I treat my survival as what I have profited from the situation. I am pleased to have got through but still treat this outcome as fortuitous, i.e. not as anything I have produced.

This can perhaps help explain why as a worrier, I find writing so difficult; it is because I think I am totally dependent upon my reader's reaction, and I tend to see this reaction as a product of arbitrary considerations, e.g. his work load etc! I tend to see my reader's reaction as a product of arbitrary considerations but not of my speech, (cf., the idea of treating other as inauthentic paragraph 16.) The worrier in me seems to have a one track mind though, for she could have used the same view of the situation to produce writing as easy for me, for if it doesn't matter what I say I could surely say anything! But of course even that isn't an easy situation for the worrier as it involves choosing.

This note raises the problem of distancing again, for whilst I do tend to react in this way I also feel that I could not say I did unless I treat it as a tendency, i.e. as something I slip into rather than am. The point is though that I do react this way, although when I think, I think I ought not to!

Response

Unlike worry the one way we choose to produce situations as desperate is by raising the issue for ourselves of whether we are responding in a thoughtful, moral, social manner. We know that not raising questions, not responding to the speech of others and ourselves about which we have doubts with the question 'Yes, but what is the good of that?' is to fail to produce the situations social possibility for thoughtful conversation. It is to arbitrarily oppress ourselves and others.

By asking profound and searching questions of our selves we make the situation desperate in the best sense of making the choice between thinking/conversing about what it is good to do, and not thinking possible for ourselves. By producing social occasions in this way we refuse to become engaged in the irrational convolutions of worry, as conventionally understood by those who worry, who on the one hand want not to be response-able for any thing, but who also want, at the same time to save their skins. If they really believed they were unproductive, if they were totally convinced by worry's arguments, they would have to admit that saving their skins was not worth their effort.

The speech of worry reminds us that we choose to act response-ably by reminding ourselves that self defence might not always be a good response. Indeed worry's commitment to protecting itself, as it is, prevents those it subjects from developing. It prevents them from remembering that we are all always response-able for our actions and our inactions; that self defence is not necessarily thoughtful. Indeed frequently as we are discovering it is worry's commitment to ill considered self defence which constrains its subjects to produce other as attacking or accusing rather than perhaps as encouraging or befriending.

Worry is committed to the survival of an 'I' that has not yet even considered what it is, what it can be for, and it shows this by even reducing its success at surviving to being a product of chance. Which, though perhaps factually correct given worry's reduction of thought to impulse, reveals its irrational commitment to an irrational notion of self. But self can be, and is, produced as other than impulsive by thoughtful interlocutors, by social actors.

Having reduced its survival to a matter of chance worry proceeds to offer an example to strengthen its case, but by so doing merely reveals the weakness of a commitment to a notion of example as correct representation, rather than as something to seek to achieve. Worry refuses to acknowledge that the original argument, irrational though it was, was at least its own production, and that by using the example worry simply forces the irrationality it introduced further into its actions. For why does worry begin by assuming that it is totally dependent upon its reader? Why does it produce its reader as merely reacting to arbitrary considerations? We can remember that this is a result of worry's unthoughtful commitment to the removal of itself, which, tragically, its subjects come to believe is the same as stopping thinking. Whereas, as we have it, stopping worrying, as it is, is necessary for us to continue thinking, indeed it is continuing to think.

Now our decision to allow worry to speak at length can better be understood, for by allowing it to speak, and then showing our efforts to take it on i.e. to continue thinking about it, struggling with it, we make the situation desperate for those who might otherwise be subjugated by an activity they had chosen not to think about. And you are no doubt aware by now who they are - i.e. that they are us: who else? If it was not us, how could we have commented upon the speaker's skills at conveying worry as it is?

But we will not back off now, for though the speech of worry starts to plead for sympathy again in paragraph 31 we know that we must extend ourselves, that unlike worry, we cannot opt to react in an unthoughtful way for that would be to contradict our version of ourselves as thinkers, as social, and worry can provide us with no reasons to do that. In fact worry is not an option that is open to us, we cannot choose to worry without denying our characters as those that are free to choose how they respond.

Analysis of Paragraphs 32, 33, 34, 35

We have seen here how I tend to produce the situation as desperate and to move from this to a concern for safety, i.e. a concern to avoid accidents (memories of relaxation again), but we can also see that the only sure way of avoiding the risk that attends writing for example, is to not write; but, as you can see I do write. However, as a worrier, I even construe my writing as being a way to avoid the risk attached to not writing, and its possible painful consequences, and by doing this I again feel myself relieved of some of the responsibility for what I write. By producing a version of my own work as analogous to a forced confession I can begin to see how I would feel that I do not deserve any approval or reward for this product. (For me a product is transformed into a prod-uct!) Yet as we've also seen it is precisely as a result of my view of myself as unproductive that I need even more the approval or reward which does sustain me, for as I am unable to give it to myself (or produce it myself) I become totally dependent upon other.

58

Whilst on the one hand then I have been trying to show how an orientation towards gifts of mere acceptance must lead to dissatisfaction I, at the same time, show that it is I, because of my view of myself as unproductive, who needs to accept them to stay alive.

By now, the fact that I saw the attractive as something to take, rather than as something to give to, begins to sound more plausible, but its increased plausibility is apparently being gained at my increased cost.

By writing then, I see myself as escaping the dangers of not writing (N.B. perhaps this helps account for the rush mentioned in paragraph 4), but am immediately plunged into another worriesome situation for now I must look on whilst you read what I write. Thus I have changed nothing, my work is still the same in the way that drudgery is the same. All I can do, as a worrier, is worry whilst I wait. If we think of stopping temporarily just beyond the danger mark we can feel how precarious the worrier's life is, but, obviously if we just look on, i.e. if we just observe him, we will be in an equally dangerous situation, and can feel how we are no safer than he is. One way of proceeding here will be to ask myself why I am tempted to stop here, why I don't want to go any further, why I limit myself to reacting to dangers and in a way produce them by failing to address how they are produced. This will be to ask why I have a problem giving as well as taking/accepting, i.e. it will be to begin the scrutiny of the philanthropist which earlier I intimated would follow. This scrutiny must however take a more active form i.e. it must be more than simply looking on yet again; it must involve a response, or be a response to the social situation which treats it as what it is, i.e. as a situation within which the worrier places himself and the philanthropist, and this response must by its very nature begin to change the relationship.

Response:

Having unthoughtfully produced a desperate situation as one in which self orients to self defence, worry turns yet again to the issue of writing and instead of producing a version of its subject's decision to write about worry as a thoughtful and courageous effort to do something about it, it construes its subject's writing as merely a means of avoiding the painful consequences which it assumes are associated with not writing. Worry reduces courage to cowardice, and by doing so tries to persuade those it subjects not to courageously work to change it. We do not relieve ourselves of response-ability for our own speech by pretending it is forced for we know it is not. We know that worry is afraid to speak/write because it fears that its mistakes will be revealed: this is what it chooses to consider as painful consequences. But we know that a thoughtful interlocutor, i.e. a social actor, is one who is committed in such a way that he can improve, and will be grateful to those who risk collaborating with him by thinking about his speech.

Worry's notion of forced confession is weak for confession has no notion of process, change as movement, but restricts change or non change to salvation or damnation, one thing or the other. Our work isn't forced confession it is movement, it is the thoughtful production of ourselves as never needing to be forced to do what we decide is good to do.

Worry's deformed notion of product as prod-uct shows worry, as it understands itself, as thoroughly irresponsible for it jokes about its baseness as if it could hide its baseness from us behind a joke. Ironically by pretending that the joke is a fact, worry produces itself as a finished product that can never do anything freely for itself or other. Having shown us how its notion of itself as unproductive is contingent upon its version of desperation it moves on to forgetfully treat its need of approval or reward as simply there. It refuses to say that not only has it produced its inability to meet its needs, but that it also produced those needs, for approval and reward aren't necessarily good.

We are reminded that earlier when we produced the movement we seek as being from wants to thoughtful wants, we did not stress that even the initial wants are products of thought, society, but less thought; and that it is by their being such that we can change them. We are not trying to overcome or constrain 'natural' impulses but to show that our impulses can never be natural: that we are speakers/thinkers and produce our own natures, and that this is good, whereas nature as impulse is neither good nor bad.

Worry's speech about dependence could sound like repetition but we are reminded by it that worry is, in its work, seeking to deceive other, for it seeks the approval it imagines it needs for work which it itself considers valueless/virtueless. To receive reward/approval it must sell the product it itself produces as a non product to other. By producing the relationship between self and other in this way it displays to us that by producing other as that which it is dependent upon it does not raise other i.e. respect other, but reduces other to the status of a commodity necessary for its survival: other becomes that which needs to be consumed.

Having made itself more aware of the contradictory nature of its production of its relationship to other, worry proceeds by reifying the argument, for 'sounds like' for worry means 'comes from outside', must be listened to, in a submissive way. So, if worry sticks with appearances it treats the argument as making gains at its subject's expense, when it could have displayed how, by producing the argument, its subject is gaining, improving.

In paragraph 35 worry speaks of being 'immediately plunged ...' not of immediately plunging, and we can almost see the hand of force pushing its subject under, and yet we know it is her own hand. She forces herself down and appeals to us for sympathy but why should we approve of her act? Worry has to look on whilst we read because it never considered us in its writings, it imagines that it has offered us nothing and waits to see if we notice that. By admitting it has changed nothing it tells us its speech isn't worth hearing, that it is drudgery for us, if we leave it as it would have itself left.

But we do not read what it writes, we write what we read: how we read displays ourselves as other than mere consumers and whilst worry for a moment raised our hopes at the beginning of this paragraph, for it suggests that it will do something other than observe worry, and whilst we also recognise how quickly it dashed its own hopes, by our productive reading we know we don't have to rely upon what we are presented with. Worry dashed its own hopes by speaking not about possibility i.e. how it could change for the better, but by sticking with what it perceives to be the case. Instead of asking how it could improve it asks why it stops where it does. It speaks of how it produces the dangers by refusing to address how they are produced, but it is only words, it does nothing, and this is because it imagines it is what it appears to itself to be, when we know that what self can be is not what it is, but what it thinks it could be.

But, in this paragraph worry chose to continue speaking, i.e. it chose to do more, or less, than simply wait; whilst it waits, it does worry, for it starts to offer the reader advice which it does not itself take. It argues that for the reader looking on, observing, isn't good enough, and it is right, but having said this it turns its back once more and chooses to speak about how it is as worry, when it could, and should, have stopped. It is as if it thinks we will lose interest in it if it stops: when we know the reverse is the case, or rather we know it can only be interested in itself when it stops.

Worry's discussion of the facts of why it doesn't go any further is limited to questions which it raises and then chooses not to make the effort of answering, thinking about. It recognises what it does but stops there, it shows us the weakness of reflection as imitation.

Worry claims that its scrutiny of the philanthropist, i.e. its scrutiny of itself, must take a more active form, but by saying it 'must' it reveals to us that it does not take this form. By saying 'more active form' worry suggests that looking on is action though not very active. In this context we choose to produce looking on as inaction of the worst kind, and we further propose that through its manner of setting up the parameters of that which it chooses to scrutinise worry prevents itself from changing. Worry speaks of 'the situation within which' when we know that we can only produce better relationships by understanding our active role in the production of the situation. Our inquiries produce our responses as our ways of situating ourselves.

Analysis of Paragraph 36

> One way of accounting for my failure to move any further than just beyond the danger mark is by seeing that, as yet, it has only been danger and fear that has moved me, i.e. once this is removed I stop moving. This fact can help us to understand the philanthropist as soon as we see that he is worried too! He only gives enough to alleviate his fears, whether these fears be of his own sense of guilt or perhaps more forcibly of the discontent of the poor. More dramatically I can deepen my understanding here by realising that it isn't only that I don't want to go any further, but that I don't want, i.e. I am moved by fears, and not by desires.

Response:

We would not account for failure by merely recounting it, for that is to fail again, we settle our account for past failures by not doing them again, by accounting for them in such a way that we change. By displaying how dangers and fears no longer move us we start moving in a thoughtful manner and remove dangers and fears to their rightful place as matters for us to respond to in a thoughtful manner, for why should we be ruled by fears we haven't even thought about?

Worry goes on to produce the philanthropist as an icon of itself, i.e. as worried, and by doing so reduces his actions to products of fear. Again factually in some instances worry may be correct but why reduce philanthropy in this way? Perhaps it could be preserved and improved, i.e. made more thoughtful rather than abandoned in favour of doing nothing which is what worry, as it conceives of itself, does. However philanthropy is really neither here nor there in this discussion as worry is speaking about itself. It proceeds to claim that it deepens its understanding of itself by realising (in the weak sense of seeing) that it is moved by fears not desires. But we are showing how real deepening of understanding can only be achieved through desire, that worry stays in the shallows here, as elsewhere, because it fears the deep, i.e. what it doesn't know. When, precisely because it doesn't know the deep, it has no reason to fear it. It reifies understanding by treating it as drama, as happening out there and by doing so suppresses its desire to join in.

Analysis of Paragraph 37

> Perhaps we begin to see now why I didn't and don't willingly accept gifts, or better why the only gifts I think I can accept are generous ones, i.e. ones given out of charity! It is because I don't know what I want, I only think I know what I don't want. This may become clearer as we remember the earlier remarks about giving being dependent upon taking, for from these we can see that the philanthropist was only a euphemism for the benevolent despot, and he in turn for the master in the master/slave relationship and it is from this relationship that we must move if we are to proceed.

Response:

Having become aware in our response to the previous paragraph of worry's choice to remain in the shallows - to remain shallow, we can say that by continually harping back to what it can see, to appearances, to what it imagines it knows, worry continually returns to what it does and reveals that in the shallows there is no direction only avoidance, i.e. only the effort to avoid the deep. Worry does not know what it wants but imagines it knows what it doesn't want, and instead of seeing its not knowing as a reason for inquiring about what it wants, it chooses to view not knowing as something to hide from.

'This may become clearer' equals the worrier dragging deep, profound issues into the shallows and treating them in a shallow manner rather than risking going into the deep and by so doing deepening and strengthening itself. Worry can speak about the master/slave relationship in this cool dispassionate fashion because it is not aware of the depths of speech.

Analysis of Paragraph 38

> How have I reacted then to being called, and in a sense being a slave? For a slave is surely one who is dominated by fear to such an extent that he forgets he had desires. My reaction has indeed been a slavish one, for after in some sense feeling some surprise that I of all people should be seen as a slave, I react by mumbling to myself that at least I am free to think as I please, and that this is better than acting unintentionally, which is what my accuser or master must be doing. For, by his action of accusation he shows me that he isn't thinking, i.e. that he is unintentional. I humour him then, but don't help him. My reaction is the same, again it is a "Yes but."

Response:

Having helped to bring a deep issue to the surface worry then reduces it to a matter of its personal self defence. It raises questions and then produces the questions' call as accusation rather than as encouragement to improve. The version of the slave worry produces is a slur upon those who are enslaved, for it produces them as forgetful, when we know the slave is far better produced as the one who remembers his desires and will work to overthrow that which he is enslaved by. The thoughtful slave is educated by speech that refuses to be silenced by domination, he does not forgetfully turn away from it and try to defend himself as he is (appears), he does not choose to remain the same. The thoughtful slave would not respond to encouragement in a slavish manner, though he might well be surprised to receive it.

Whilst worry mumbles about its freedom to think as it pleases, we are showing in this work how unfree, unthoughtful speech can invade our thinking. How producing speech as constrained when compared with thought is an unthoughtful production for it refuses to be reminded that our speech can rule our thought, and does so as soon as we choose not to speak any more about how we think. Worry's reaction to what it produces as an accusation is a 'Yes but' that relies upon a version of freedom as arbitrary, as doing anything, as thinking wildly, randomly. Whereas we produce our freedom as our ability to think about what we do, what pleases us, and to improve ourselves by doing so, to become more social by doing so.

Worry is too ready to produce other as accusing, because by always refusing to engage in conversations with others worry silently accuses others of not being worth talking to, and then views others actions as products of the same refusal.

Analysis of Paragraph 39

If we think of what has been said so far we will remember that a constant theme has been my failure to accept responsibilities, frequently by simply accepting that I am not a responsible type i.e. that I don't have the ability to respond. So successfully do I do this, that I produce a version of myself as not being the kind of person to make decisions. (Worse than the deferential voter I become the deferential non-voter!) In effect I persuade myself that I am suited to be a slave. I allow myself to be mastered by the idea that I would find the freedom involved in making decisions oppressive. I said above that I, as worrier, am moved by fears and not by desires, and now we can remember that whereas fear is a reaction, i.e. it is impulsive, desires are responses, they do involve self in a way that impulses do not.

Response

'If we think of what has been said so far ...' here we produce worry as subordinating itself to prior speech, i.e. speech first then thoughts about it, we choose to think through and assist what was said before rather than perceive of ourselves simply as receiving its assistance. Worry produces reminding as saying what we were, not what we can possibly be. And once again worry's joke is tragic for worry is happy to say how bad it is and not to do anything about it. Imagine persuading ourselves to be slaves! Imagine producing a version of freedom as a problem, freedom as that which oppresses when we know that oppression is lack of freedom, lack of thought, lack of conversation.

Worry goes on to justify itself by arguing that fears, i.e. that which move it, are impulsive, but we know that this means it thinks they aren't free, i.e. that when it reacts fearfully it isn't responsible. And yet we know that fears are as much our response-ability as are desires, or lack of desires. Fears are no more impulsive, and that is why we need not, and ought not, to enslave ourselves to and by them. We must have thoughtful fears as we must have thoughtful desires, if we are to be achieving a society.

Worry produces desires as involving self but itself as not having desires and this reveals to us the weakness of its notion of the self it seeks irrationally to protect. By revealing worry's weak version of self we display our commitment not to settle for weak versions of ourselves.

Analysis of Paragraph 40

> What work does a slave do then? I pursue my master's business which, because (a) it is a result of the master's nature i.e. thoughtlessness, and (b) because it is not my own business (concern), becomes drudgery; and the thing about drudgery is that it does, or can, provide a strong sense of knowing where you are, in the sense of knowing you aren't there. (With this writing, however, my struggle is that I'm unsure where I am in it and consequently it is anything but drudgery though this has not prevented it hurting.) My point here is that when I'm involved in drudgery I find a home in my thoughts, worries, and see these as separating me from, and raising me above, the unworried i.e. he who I think of as my master. (This is how I conceived of myself as being master of the situation paragraph 10.)

Response:

After wandering thoughtlessly into the slavery topic worry chooses to concentrate on what the slave does, on convention, on the master's usage of the slave, when it could and should have directed its efforts to what is to be done. By doing so worry produces the slave as pursuing his master's business and not as rebelling. So we rebel against worry's usage, for what kind of home would we have in our own thoughts? Whilst for worry home is randomness, survival, no need to be afraid, no need or reliance upon other; we know that we could not be at home there. We know that to have no need of other, and to be of no use to other, is to have lost a sense of our dialectical selves, it would be to reveal a wish for separation and comparison with other rather than a desire for the form of collaboration with other which raises both by deepening the relationship, by producing a less shallow society: a less shallow sociology. The restriction to undialectical oppositions slave/master, slave becoming master and enslaving past master etc. reduces thought either to the drudgery of being a master with nothing to think about, or to being a slave and being unable to do anything.

When worry points out for the reader that its writing is hurting it, we know it asks for sympathy yet again, that it is trying to protect itself by pointing to its wounds. But we know they are only superficial wounds and that if worry was truly involved in work that was not drudgery it would not be hurt at all, for thoughtful work whether difficult or easy is good for other and self. Worry informs other that its work hurts itself but shows in this remark its total lack of interest in other, for if it had been interested in other it would have been concerned not about its own aches and pains but about what its writing was inflicting upon other i.e. upon all of us, and by concerning itself with this it would have come to understand why it could not expect sympathy.

Analysis of Paragraph 41

> I become the proud silent type then, but need to wake up to the fact that this reaction gives the master just what he wants as a master i.e. compliance, subservience, but certainly not what he needs. This silence in turn allows the master to remain silent about the fact that decisions don't come easily to him either, that mastery and ease need not and do not go hand in hand. (I think that because I find work

difficult I haven't mastered it, but the only sort of easy work there is is drudgery!) Why do I refuse to admit that the master might not be relaxing? Why, because I, as slave, rely upon my idea of my private life, my thoughts, my worries, as being free in order to generate a version of mastery as freedom. I think that thinking is easy, and this is why I want to think that I want what I think I want, this is why I cannot answer if I am asked to discipline myself by deciding what I want. I transform this into a question that asks me whether I know what I want.

Response:

Whilst worry produces a version of itself as the proud silent type that needs to wake up etc., by so doing it reveals to us how it continues to sleep, for we produce it as being submissive, self satisfied, anti social subordination to appearances, to what it perceives the situation to be. Whilst worry imagines that it recognises what it needs it doesn't even work to achieve it. It is not that the master remains silent about the fact that decisions don't come easily to him, it is that worry cannot hear other's speech because it is so proud of itself. It doesn't know that it needs to listen, that it isn't complete. Worry notices that mastery and ease do not go hand in hand but shows its lack of depth by wondering whether the master might not be relaxing; when it should have worked to produce a version of thoughtful, social man as a character who relaxes in difficulty, who makes himself at home in intermediacy, through deciding and doing what he thinks is for the good.

Worry imagines in its lazy way that thinking is easy, impulsive rather than something that takes effort. We produce thought as argument, development, progress through effort, which may or may not be easy but which is necessary for us. Worry remains undisciplined by clinging to its version of thinking as impulsive and does not realise how we, by producing thought as a process, discipline ourselves in the strong, good sense of freeing ourselves from randomness, from unthoughtful impulse.

Analysis of Paragraph 42, 43

When I worry then I treat my thinking as a form of relaxation for I do not commit myself to any course of action, I treat my thinking as free for it seems to be the only thing that cannot be taken from me, that is my thoughts are free of other's demands. As a worrier, I think of my thinking as just looking on and as not participating, and I go on to transpose this idea of freedom onto the master, for I see the master as making demands but as having none made on him.

So now we can see how I, as a slave, treat my own thoughts or worries as all I own and as the symbol of my freedom, but I need to keep constantly in mind how this is just a reaction for it fails to address the question of the social and in this case unnatural nature of this set of social relationships. For, far from symbolising my freedom, my worries merely point to my oppressor: they need to show me that it is my that is, the slave's version of my freedom as my worries which contributes to, and sustains the presence of my oppression.

Response:

How possessive worry is here, i.e. it wants its thoughts to be left free of others' questions, for it sees others' questions as demands, but we know that this is the way that worry subjugates its subjects, for by being persuaded to treat their thoughts as valuable personal possessions they become cagey about what they think, but do not notice how it is they that are encaged by worry. Wanting to be free of others' questions is wanting to remain impulsive, encaged, static etc. it is deciding not to grow any more. By reducing its subjects to looking on, worry reduces thinkers/speakers/producers to receivers who imagine they have nothing to contribute. But by responding thoughtfully to others' questions we can work at freeing our thoughts from unthoughtful, merely conventional formulations.

However, worry assumes that other, like itself, only asks shallow questions i.e. questions which it knows the answer to. But we know that a thoughtful other is one that is prepared to ask himself and/or other stretching questions, but they are not demands, for they are not backed by force. By conceiving of them as demands worry deforms them in such a way that it can no longer understand their liberating potential.

Worry conceives of not committing itself to any course of action as relaxing, for it imagines that in this way it will avoid questions. Worry has been passive until this last ditch stand because it isn't sure whether it wants any of the things its subject previously had, for it can see disadvantages to all of them including for example its subject's freedom. But worry's efforts to avoid questions go further, for by reducing its own thoughts to impulse it can hurriedly try to forget any seemingly awkward questions that occur to it rather than to inquire into them. But we do not want to protect thoughts from others' questions in this manner for we want to become more thoughtful.

Worry continues by saying how it treats its worries as all it owns, and then correlates what it owns with symbols of freedom, by so doing, it reveals its possessiveness, but we would rather treat the disowning of possessions as a symbol of freedom for it is thoughtless possessions whether of, or by, objects or ideas, that create unnecessary limitations upon social progress by turning some away from what we have in common, what we share.

However, even although worry's speech seems to be beginning to recognise this, its subject still persists in not grasping that an active role must be taken, for she calls upon her worries to show her that it is worry's version of self etc. i.e. she even leaves it to her worries to do the work of showing. Our skilful speaker reveals very cunningly how those who worry would have a long while to wait for their worries could never do their own work for them.

Analysis of Paragraph 44, 45, 46

But again I must slow down for whilst I may be making some progress here I would certainly not have made enough if I thought that this supposedly new knowledge would be enough, or ought to make me a master. But even whilst I write I know that my excitement must show, and that the danger that this could occur is ever present. So now I need to clear the air for myself and perhaps one way of doing this will be to return to the question of substitutions mentioned in paragraph 7, i.e. firstly the philanthropist by the teacher and the poor by the student and latterly the philanthropist by the student and the poor by the teacher. What can this mean?

The first substitution need not delay us very long for we should see by now that the sort of gifts offered by the philanthropist do little if anything to teach the poor, in fact they hinder the learning of the poor, and leave the philanthropist in a blissful state of ignorance to boot. I am not commending that the philanthropist gives less here, far from it, I am demanding that the worrier, in this instance the philanthropist, begins to give i.e. that the philanthropist gives much more.

On to the second, what have the poor to teach the philanthropist? They need to teach him that his gift, though it may appear generous, is only a bribe, and that whilst both he and they refuse to speak to each other it will remain so. It is the refusal of both the philanthropist and the poor to address the social nature of their relationship which makes room for bribery and hence corruption.

Response:

Now worry wants to slow down, but not because it might be endangering other, there is no thought of other here, only of itself, and what of the 'reason' it offers for slowing down. We can read between the lines and notice that it was excited because it did think that this new knowledge would be enough, and ought to make it master, but it didn't want to say that for it feared that other might reveal that it was mistaken. By orienting to its fears in this way it shows us how knowledge, as something received, can never remove worry. Worry slows down here by treating its argument as knowledge that makes its subject aware. Again it separates its subjects from their productions by externalising those productions and starting to worry about them; rather than making the effort to display the good of those productions.

Clearing the air for itself is making it safe to stay where it is rather than moving, rather than doing something. Imagine restricting ourselves to clearing the air for each of ourselves in a gas chamber when we could be helping each other out through the door we are opening.

Whilst worry wants to correct previous work rather than to show how it is through what the previous work opens up that we can move on, our desire is not to correct and complete, but to open up and to thoughtfully stretch ourselves and others, and by so doing to seek to achieve more profound relationships. We are prepared to risk making mistakes rather than making the bigger mistake of waiting until we are sure we are not mistaken before we contribute anything.

What of these substitutions? Philanthropy as teaching: we know already that good work teaches/reminds self as well as other, and that the reduction of teaching to giving gifts shows us the weakness of worry's commendation. But, we are reminded here that in fact worry does foolishly conceive of ignorance as a 'blissful state' i.e. it conceived of others, i.e. the unworried as ignorant and envies them, seeks to be like them, hence its movement towards mindless activities e.g. drunkenness etc. But we are displaying how by becoming conscious of our ignorance we provide ourselves with reasons to continue inquiring/thinking and not to stay as we seem to be. To seek mindless activities is to reveal conceit of knowledge about what is good rather than to think about the good of thoughtful social actions.

When we turn to the second substitution we continue to hear something in what worry says, but what we hear is the poverty of worry's version of philanthropy as bribes, for worry needs not only to speak to other, but to listen in a productive way to its own speech.

67

Addressing the social nature of their relationship must be formulated not as looking from the outside but as getting inside and subverting what is going on. It is not a question of making room for ourselves beside corruption, i.e. of accommodating corruption, but, of making our society, our speech what we can live in and through. We have to get inside corrupt social practices in order to reconstruct them. We cannot settle for observation from the outside for we know we are already in, we cannot do the impossible. But, by not settling for observation we are beginning to construct more thoughtful practices.

Analysis of Paragraph 47

But now I must remember that it isn't simply a question of slowing down for I am not involved in a public debate i.e. my clarity of diction is not the issue. What I must remember is that I am these characters, I am involved in bribery and corruption for I, as worrier, help to produce it. By thinking of my thoughts as free and my actions/speech as unfree I make reference to the fact that I think I need to be induced to speak, and it is in this way that I come to produce everything I react to as an inducement, as an attempt to silence my thought. Every call to action becomes a threat or a bribe, and as a result when I do act or write, I begin by seeing my action or writing as at best irresponsible and at worst as the corrupt silence of the receiver of a bribe. I see then that worry begins and sticks with a conception of social relationships as corrupt, i.e. that worry produces corruption. (In fact worry is always a producer of bribes for they are seen to remove a danger, or risk, at least temporarily!)

Response:

Worry says clarity of diction is not the issue, when in fact, because of its refusal to take hold of its possibilities it can do no more than make clarity of diction the issue, for it acts as if it has no idea what the issue is. We are reminded by its speech that what we must remember is that we are not corrupt, and that by involving ourselves, committing ourselves to producing more thoughtful conventions rather than silently accepting conventions, usage, we become less complicated. By speaking/writing and questioning when we have doubts we free our speech and discipline our thoughts, that otherwise, i.e. if they remain private, do not have the advantage of others' collaboration. We produce our responses as inducing ourselves to do the work of saying what we think and being instructed by the conversations that develop from our questions. Every time we bring our thoughts into the conversation we produce speech that works to display the irrationality of a corrupt relation to convention. We do not produce our social relationships as corrupt, but draw upon our social relationships with ourselves and others and by doing so work against corruption. By calling ourselves to act thoughtfully we produce our writing, our speech as our response and not as irresponsible or corrupt.

Analysis of Paragraph 48

I begin to remember then, as a result of this speech how deeply my mode of thinking and of acting, and hence of thinking about the relationship between the two, is imbued by the grammar of worry, but this should remind me that I will not free myself of it in the way I might discard an empty ballpoint pen. Rather, I must remember that social relationships are not static, and that it is only by using and working with what I have got, i.e. what I am, that I can produce something better. My task then, as my struggle continues, must be to

68

make these words less empty.

Response:

We do not remember as a result of our work how deeply our mode of thinking and of acting is imbued by the grammar of worry, but how by thinking more deeply about ourselves, by producing less shallow selves, we display why we need not worry. Unlike worry we are not limited to an interest in me i.e. the 'I', but are concerned for ourselves, for our society as a thoughtful production, in effect as a going concern. By remembering how social relationships are not static we work with what we can be so as to improve what we at first sight might seem to be. Through our work, even with this portrait of worry, we are displaying how words are never empty for us. Worry, as it understands itself, produces words as empty to save itself the effort of thinking about what it says, but it cannot explain why it does this.

4 Manipulation

Our original speaker interrupts:

How eager you are to speak of worry as you also imagine it is!

But you would have done better if you had not been so ready to separate me from my speech, if you had thought more, and chosen not to do so. By trying to reduce worry to an 'it', i.e. to an unreflexive activity, as you were doing, you revealed your own shallowness. By reducing worry to an 'it' you imagined you could relieve yourselves of responsibility for 'it', and you did this whilst claiming to take on response-ability!

How can you, who have committed yourselves to producing selves as thinkers/speakers, at the same time commit yourselves to separating a speaker from her speech? How could you imagine you were respecting me by separating me from my speech? I thank you for your good intention, but ask you to be less hasty, less naive.

I did produce a version of worry as I imagined ordinary usage would have it, that is true, but my intention in doing so was to provide usage through which we could work together to show how worry could be a way of doing good, and I had expected that you would join with me in an inquiry into how to deepen the shallow version of worry I imagined ordinary usage would have produced. It was not worry that was shallow, as you suggest, but the version of worry that I produced, and that you were so ready to accept, only in order then to reject.

You imagined that by distancing yourselves from worry you could gain a clearer picture of 'it', and that then 'it' would be nothing for you to fear, nothing for you to worry about. You imagined you had distanced yourselves from 'it', and by so doing had yourselves become better than 'it'. That is, through your work you sought social distance; superiority and were tempted to think you had achieved it: that you were deeper than worry, and no longer had any real reason to listen to 'it'; you imagined you were no longer likely to be endangered by it.

So now it is you who need reminding of your shallowness: of the superficiality of your separation: of your manipulation, which was no more than sleight of hand. For how could you, who apparently imagined yourselves to be acting thoughtfully, believe that that separation could aid reparation?

But don't misunderstand me, I'm not suggesting that there was nothing of value in your responses. What I am suggesting is that I will not orient to your speech as something which I can extract certain elements from and then discard. I will not orient to your speech as you appeared to want to orient to the speech of worry.

I imagine that it is you who are now surprised, but we all have work to do so let's spend no more of our efforts speaking one against the other; when we can proceed by thinking about how worry could be a way to do good.

Response:

We were surprised by your interruption, and for a while it stopped us in our tracks, but given your stated commitment to thinking about how worry could be a way to do good we assume that you will not be so ready to accuse us of speaking against you, when we remind you, and ourselves, of what was said earlier. For in your haste to defend your person, i.e. what you imagine yourself to be, you do yourself an injustice.

We were not separating you from your speech, but trying to help you remind yourself how that speech was not you, i.e. was not yours; you were only speaking as if you were a worrier. We are committed, as you rightly point out, to producing selves as thinkers/speakers, but our commitment involves us in producing thoughtful, moral, social speakers, and not irresponsible careless talk. Would we be respecting you if we allowed ourselves to hear you as proceeding talking in a careless fashion?

However, your reminder about the shallowness of the version of worry we have so far considered is well taken, and we will try, as you suggest, to achieve a deeper version, but perhaps we will be stretching usage too far: if we think this is so we will do better to refer to this more moral, more thoughtful, more social activity by some term other than worry.

As to social distance, we do think our commitment is more thoughtful than worry's commitment (at least the shallow version), for if we did not, we would have no reason to work at preventing ourselves and others sliding into it. But we do not, and cannot transcend it, i.e. we don't get beyond it for we continue to have to deal with worries, we continue to be endangered if we fail to respond thoughtfully to others.

However, your interruption has helped us to remember an issue of more general significance, for by speaking of the shallow version of worry as how you/we imagined ordinary usage would have it, you/we have revealed how we were reifying, reducing ordinary usage. Response-ability for the weak version of worry appeared to be shared between ourselves and ordinary usage, and by being shared in this way we might have forgotten that it is we, as speakers and listeners, that both produce and consume ordinary usage. But we do remember how, by trying to be thoughtful interlocutors, the formulations we produce will be attempts to display the extra-ordinary depths of speech in its relation to Being, i.e. of the speaker's place.

Much earlier (P.12) we spoke of convention/ordinary usage as contrived, but as we proceed we are displaying how it is we who do take an active part in the contriving; and it was we who spoke as if we had to imagine what 'it' was, what 'it'/ordinary usage would produce. By making our relationship to our speech an issue of knowledge, as if of a separate object, we were erroneously separating ourselves from our speech, and could then, at best, only imagine what 'it' was.

As our speech continues we are keeping a grip, or regaining a grip, upon the productions of our dialectical engagements as speakers/thinkers, and only by so doing, do we continue to free our potential. Society, speech could only have constrained us if we had lost our desire to grip, if we had forgotten that society is our continuing production, and that through our production of society we are continuing to produce ourselves. By remembering this we do enable ourselves, and are enabling ourselves, to proceed thoughtfully.

We are committing ourselves not to proceed by reducing ordinary usage, and then showing ourselves to be superior to it by exemplifying difference through our reading: rather we are working and displaying our efforts to engage with ordinary usage in a friendly manner i.e. to think or theorise with, and for it in such a way as to collaborate socially, as would those seeking thoughtful social relations.

Perhaps you grasp now why we acknowledge that we do need to remember the shallowness of our beginnings but we do not hear this as an accusation, though perhaps you imagined you wanted it to be one; we hear it as calling us to continue working upon how to act more thoughtfully. Perhaps also our manipulation now seems less like sleight of hand.

Oh! you, as worrier, are surprised we say we are engaged in manipulating. We anticipated that this would be the case for we have come to expect that you, as worrier, begin with a version of other as manipulator, and manipulation as bad. So this is an issue we should now confront. (N.B. Unless we state otherwise, as this work proceeds we will refer to the worrier as you, but we remember we do not intend by this any specific self, or indeed any self at all.)

What do we mean then by our suggestion that you begin with a version of other (e.g. us) as manipulator? We expect that initially you see yourself as not acting, and want to see inaction as good, whilst seeing all actions as bad, i.e. as manipulation. For this 'reason' you might have asked us why we chose to raise the issue of worry, as if you would have accepted no action on our part as immediately just. You were puzzled as to why we should have raised this issue, as you did not conceive of it as our fault. Here your idea of forced confession comes to mind again, for your usage of responsibility is a way of producing speech as the acceptance of blame for a prior action, it must always be blame for as we have said you do see all action as bad. Consequently you would view us as acting irresponsibly by raising this topic: you imagine it would be better left alone. Perhaps you would prefer to forget about it, put it out of your mind? In this manner, you produce speech as a response that is limited to reaction, rather than being possibly active, and by so doing you commend inaction. But it has become clear to us that by ostensibly avoiding manipulative behaviour, ironically you also are engaged in manipulative behaviour, that worry is a form of manipulation. For your inaction is not without consequence, and it is chosen, hence in these regards it is analytically the same as action. We had instances often enough in Section 3 of the consequences of the worrier's inaction.

Very likely you will be angry at our suggestion that you are manipulating, but unlike those you view as manipulative you will not express your anger. You imagine it is unwise to express anger, for, given that you already hold a view of environment/other/manipulator as hostile, you imagine that expressing your anger would only be adding fuel to the fire. So whereas you view manipulative types as those who manipulate/channel their feelings, you choose to refuse to see how, by holding yourself back, you also manipulate. You imagine that the manipulative types become angry when the tide runs against them because when this occurs this threatens not only the manipulator's person, but also the activity to which he has committed himself. You imagine that the manipulative type wants other to be within his control, that the manipulative type seeks the comfort of a position of power from which he cannot be attacked or surprised. So you see the manipulative type as seeking ease, laziness.

The picture of the manipulative type you rely upon is as of one who seeks the calm that follows or precedes a storm. You imagine the manipulator sees the calm as his haven, for here chance is eliminated or controlled, for whilst anger or the storm is undesirable it will blow over and anyway is out of his hands. The manipulative type needs to control chance to keep his temper in check. Whilst you, on the other hand, imagine that it is when you feel happy-go-lucky that you need not worry, i.e. you see luck to be your companion, and imagine that it can be good or bad, but you place yourself in your companion's hands, you do not think of yourself as response-able for your own happiness, your own future. So, whilst you treat chance as your only possible friend, you also imagine that the manipulator treats chance as his sole enemy. You imagine that the manipulative type shares your view of all actions as bad, but that whilst you see this as a reason not to act, you imagine he proceeds to act anyway. By producing your lack of action as displaying your lack of corruptibility, i.e. by trying not to act in order to prevent your action being acted upon: by trying to constrain constraints by being constrained, you are showing a commitment not to act badly, and that could be praiseworthy, but in the process you have lost sight of the fact that it is bad not to act, or rather you forget that you are already acting. Whilst you imagine you are staying face to face with the problem, and that you suffer in silence, you also imagine that the manipulator tries to silence other i.e. to make other suffer before it by chance makes him suffer. So, whilst worry calls upon chance for assistance (i.e. whilst worry waits for miracles) it imagines that manipulation calls chance out in order to annihilate it, or control it, (i.e. worry imagines manipulation tries to produce miracles not to wait for them).

But we must proceed thoughtfully here for we know that we can neither produce miracles nor settle for waiting for miracles, and, that at the same time, we have need of efforts of miraculous proportions, for whilst we thought racism and sexism were bad this form of differentiation between self and other could have been much much worse for it goes deeper, and it could have isolated each individual from all others. And yet, even this most pervasive and vicious form of speech/life is, as we have said, a product of good intention, and by being so helps us to grasp why we need to converse more with each other rather than less.

Whilst you imagine you have good 'reason' to maintain social distance, and not to collaborate with other because of other's manipulative character; for you formulate manipulation as sleight of hand; we would rather display our formulation of how man-ipulation is what man, men and women do do. Man-ipulation, for us, means the activity of thoughtful, moral, social actors and not merely sleight of hand, deception, appearance. So now when we say that worry is a form of man-ipulation you need have no reason to be angry for we are speaking of its humanness, i.e. of what it shares with us. We choose to collaborate with you (worry),, to converse with you, for through this conversation our understanding of our 'place' is deepened. What can we learn from your current orientation towards other?

Perhaps we can begin to learn by formulating other as 'other than human' as 'other than intentional'. So now you collect all human actions and counterpose them to mere sleight of hand, to manipulation in the weak sense. When you say you are not acting you must mean that you are intending not pretending. Inaction must be read not as doing nothing but as being in action, i.e. involved in action and not as being an uninvolved actor. All actions, if and when viewed (i.e. from the outside) are mere manipulation i.e. sleight of hand, so you were right to ask why raise the issue of worry, but perhaps you were wrong to ask us and not yourself, for it is an issue for you as well as us, and this is why our actions could not and indeed cannot do your work for you, but at most can stimulate you to help yourself.

By placing man within an environment which is other than man i.e. nature; which is unintentional; mere sleight of hand; unthoughtful; you show us why forced confession i.e. the acceptance of blame for prior action is our effort to be becoming response-able, to begin to take on responsibility for that which we did not do, and by doing so to begin to interact more response-ably. If we merely raised the topic of worry and did no more, it would have been better left alone for it would have been vulgarised, and you would be right to put it out of your mind. Raising the topic of worry and doing no more could provide a very picturesque instance of sleight of hand. However, we know that your speech is, like all speeches, an intentional action, i.e. an instance of man-ipulation, and that by ironising manipulation, by speaking of it as something to avoid, hide from, (perhaps with your hands as in sleight of hand) you are asking us to engage thoughtfully with it. The conjuror also has intentions which we must not forget, if we are to preserve a human relationship with him, if we are not to treat him as a thing.

So now we appreciate that your anger would have been justifiable if by saying you were being manipulative we had meant in the weak sense. However our efforts to achieve a stronger, a more profound version of manipulation should allay your suspicions. As to your decision not to express your anger, we notice that your formulation of other as hostile leads you to begin with a version of both fire and tide as dangerous, but couldn't both fire and tide be resources if they are thought about. But, perhaps again it is we, not you, who are too hasty to imagine we understand what you intend, for perhaps we could formulate hostile as host-ile, i.e. as hospitable, host like, as welcoming, rather than as an enemy. So now not expressing your anger is read as not rushing, i.e. as not burning all your fuel at once, but as conserving energy. Holding yourself back is being reserved; thinking about how to act rather than being merely impulsive. Our formulation of man-ipulation is as a committed thoughtful activity, not as an activity to which we commit ourselves. How could we find a position in which we could not be attacked or surprised comfortable? To speak of surprises and attacks as similar in this regard is to betray defensiveness and a lack of adventure. It is to appear content with staying in the fort and surviving apparently safely behind its walls, rather than risking engaging with what lies outside its confines. Questions, like surprises, are deformed if they are reformulated as attacks. We choose to hear questions, and to ask questions, and by so doing to surprise ourselves. We choose to resist any inclination to treat questions/doubts as undesirable.

Your version of nature as manipulation in the weak sense is clearly presented by your usage of the storm analogy, and conventional usage does speak of the angry person as stormy. But, as we have said, our desire is to extend ourselves, our usage, to think about what we want to be becoming, and how we can continue working at becoming rather than to imagine we are such and such, and then finding ourselves with selves which we pretend we need to, but cannot control.

Whilst we do not fantasise that we can control chance, we do not rely upon versions of ourselves as resting completely in the hands of chance for we display our characters by responding thoughtfully, socially to what happens to us, and by doing so we extend the range of our intentions, of what we can think about and do something about. We treat chance as neither friend nor enemy for it is unintentional, and we do better by resisting such anthropomorphisms, for by doing so we rediscover our potential to work with our environment. We are responsible for what we do, for what we do displays our ability to respond, but we can also console ourselves by limiting the effort we expend upon what we decide we are not, and cannot be, responsible for. By concentrating upon our intentions we detect that the distinction between action and inaction could have misled, for both action and inaction can be intentional or unintentional, and our intentional effort is to be moving from the unintentional to the intentional for as thinkers/speakers we could not desire to eliminate or reduce thought/conversation.

Whilst as we said you imagine you are staying face to face with the problem, and that you suffer in silence, we would say that this action reduces suffering to putting up with, enduring, and that true suffering is a part of risking conversation, risking not remaining silent, for staying face to face with each other is what we are achieving by refusing to settle for modes of speech that rely upon imagined differences, barriers between self and other selves. We are involved in man-ipulation/conversation, but our intention is to work to hear what you have to say, and to instruct ourselves through it, not to reduce you to silence. Worry would need to wait for miracles for as long as it resists acknowledging that it has placed itself in the hands of chance. By raising chance to the status of only possible friend it shows its anti social nature, for it concomitantly reduces others, i.e. other speakers, to never achieving sufficient distinction from the rest of the environment to be specially treasured.

You imagine that actors have to know that their actions are good before and whilst they act, and that given your awareness that you do not have this knowledge, and your suspicion that others also do not have it, you formulate their actions as weak dishonest moves to avoid facing up to their ignorance. But by remembering that we cannot know that our actions are good, but that we can do what we have decided, what we have thought through as being for the good, and more deeply that this is what we all always do, we respect others actions as displays of their commitment. And we do distinguish them, as achievements, from the unthoughtful, unintentional environments out of which they have been drawn.

The man-ipulator offers formulations of others as having plans which are informed by good intention, but which are not complete, where that which is unplanned i.e. exigency, is not surprising, but where surprises are products of good intentions not of nature. Nature is pre-dictable in the sense of coming before speech. The man-ipulator's mode of interacting, with others, whom he formulates as acting with good intentions, is to question, to try to understand others' intentions. Ironically if others choose to remain silent when questioned, if others produce questions as unplanned for attacks, the man-ipulators effort to engage in instructive social interaction, i.e. to act in a friendly manner, will have been deformed by others into acts of aggression, of manipulation in the bad sense.

However the man-ipulator, the thoughtful interlocutor, encourages others to speak, i.e. the thoughtful interlocutor's speech intends to remind self and others of our ability to respond in such a way that we deepen our understanding of our intentions. We are pleased when we formulate other's speech as encouraging and requesting us to continue responding thoughtfully, socially, and whilst speech could have been used as a weapon to silence other, to force other to submit, we choose to speak in such a way as to draw ourselves, and others, out of submissiveness; we do not relate to other's speeches as commands for we are committed to deepening, strengthening our social relationships by no longer trying not to learn/remember what we can be, or better are.

The man-ipulator's usage of surprise encourages us to inquire into what we are; it stimulates us to stop hiding from ourselves by showing how revealing self's potential for inquiry enables self and other to work together to remember what they share. Whilst the manipulator wants to be able to predict but not to be predictable; wants to expose other and to continue posing himself, the man-ipulator has no need to pose for he remembers that he can only improve through exposure/conversation. The man-ipulator's actions may surprise, for by maintaining conversation they effectively risk keeping social interaction open indefinitely. The man-ipulator/thoughtful interlocutor does not settle for silence, but works to maintain thoughtful social relations. He uses his speech to display and maintain the social proximity which both he and others need if they are to continue engaging in man-ipulation, thoughtful conversation. The man-ipulator is not interested in what he or other is, i.e. in a conventional notion of social status, but is interested in conversing in such a way as to raise in stature. By recognising how stature is possibility not actuality, choice not nature, he keeps open social interactions that respect both self and other. Only in this way can the temptation to treat other or self with contempt be resisted.

By generating self as the possibility that we are response-able for, man-ipulators, speakers, thoughtful interlocutors refuse to succumb to a conception of self as limited in such a way as to be completely beyond our control and as such as diminishing our responsibility. As speakers we are able to choose how we respond, and we do continue stretching and extending our limits by engaging in thoughtful conversations.

And yet you (worrier not thoughtful reader) could have felt constrained to argue that the version we previously proposed you would have offered of other's actions as manipulation, i.e. sleight of hand, had not conveyed sufficiently well how threatening others' speeches (including ours) seem to you. Perhaps you would have spoken to yourself about the manipulator's speech in the following manner:

The manipulator sees other's plans as a threat but he knows that plans have limits i.e. are not complete, and that which is unplanned is exigency, chance, or perhaps surprise. His method of dealing with another who he suspects has plans (and he suspects all others of this) is to deal out surprises which prevent other from carrying out his plan. Ironically then the manipulator silences other by acting in a way that other could not have planned for. The manipulator's speech leaves other speechless i.e. his speech is designed to destroy other's ability to respond, the result being that the manipulator can now proceed to disregard other's plans. His fear is that other's speech will silence him, hence his need to speak first.

The manipulator's version of speech is as a weapon which can be used to silence other. He must control other's speech if he is to continue issuing commands. His version of listening is as submission, and the result is his desire not to listen, if he does have to listen he will be disappointed with his own actions; he will consider himself to have made a mistake which has allowed other not to conform to his plan; which has allowed other to take command of him.

The manipulator's usage of surprise gives us insight into why we are often forced to ask ourselves what the manipulator feels. The insight is that he, the manipulator hides in order that he can surprise, i.e. he doesn't want other to know his next move. He wants to be able to predict but not to be predictable. He doesn't want to be exposed and for this reason he appears stealthy but at times bold.

However, his surprising (bold) actions which initially could appear adventurous now appear more defensive for by stopping conversation they effectively close the door on risk. Having closed the door the manipulator feels contempt for other whom he sees as having failed to secure his objective, i.e. his actions are necessarily a slight on other's character. He uses his speech to maintain social distance which he needs to do his manipulating. Now he sees and treats other as lacking in stature, i.e. with contempt.

However, it was through our relationship with your version of the manipulator's speech that we were able to achieve the deeper version of man-ipulative speech that immediately preceded it. And through this effort to be reminded by your speech we have displayed how to listen in a manner which is not submissive. Thoughtful listening is neither mere consumption, i.e. acceptance, agreement, nor is it rejection, disagreement, i.e. refusal to consume; it is productive consumption; working thoughtfully with other's speech.

The man-ipulator, the thoughtful interlocutor, chooses a sense of adventure/of inquiry rather than choosing to give primacy to survival activities, for to opt for the latter is to restrict oneself to living on the surface, it is to restrict oneself to the shallows and to choose to have nothing to say. To give primacy to survival activities is to choose to ignore the fact that for speakers/thinkers survival has to be chosen. An orientation which gives primacy to survival generates a life as something to be consumed in the service of that which dies. Whereas the manipulator's choice of inquiry creates a relationship between self and other selves which makes productive living possible, the irony of survival activities, i.e. of running from death, is that their

77

lack of a sense of direction towards invites tragedy.

For instance, you would tend to feel responsible for further speech in social situations, for you imagine silences are dangerous, however whilst feeling responsible you do not feel response-able. But, rather than inquiring into what would be a thoughtful response, you produce the difference between responsible and response-able as providing a reason to say anything; you treat other and the conversation contemptuously by failing to recognise other's response-ability, and by failing to see the good of conversation, inquiry. However we show here how even your response, which displays your version of yourself as lacking the ability to respond, could be used by the thoughtful interlocutor to stimulate inquiry.

The virtue of speech is that we can provide, through it, good thoughtful intentions for speakers, and we can in this manner risk speaking response-ably, rather than simply from a feeling of responsibility which was itself mere personal protectiveness, i.e. fears of fantasised consequences of being blamed for the silence. By succumbing to these fears you would stop possible starts. You would stop the inquiry, the questions which could have enlivened yourself and others. You view the manipulator as consuming other, and imagine that you appear to consume yourself. It is by producing yourself as a consumer (by concentrating on the bad) rather than choosing to remember how you have produced other (the manipulator) that you are subjugated by your version of other, i.e. by forgetting you also are productive. The man-ipulator, the thoughtful interlocutor relates with other as a collaborator and works with other. We are working with you for our desire is not to reject you, or to succumb to your speech, but to deepen ourselves, and to achieve a less shallow reading of your speech through this conversation.

We want to continue being what we are, i.e. characters that can choose to continue freeing ourselves by engaging in thoughtful conversations with others. Whereas you want to stop being what you imagine you are, i.e. a threat to yourself, a brake, and you imagine the manipulator wants to stop others being what they are in order that he can stay as he is. We man-ipulators refuse to be dominated by images of our selves as worse than we can be. Whereas you are dominated by an imaginary version of yourself as having some utopian image of the self you ought to be, which, you then imagine yourself as not surprisingly failing to match up to. You do not work for better conditions, you want (merely wish you had) a self that could deal with any conditions. Secretly you wish you were the manipulator. But man-ipulators by focusing upon the fact that we do respond thoughtfully/intentionally, produce a relationship to any conditions which enables those conditions to help stimulate the desire for knowledge, the desire to live thoughtfully.

We choose to orient to other speakers in such a way as to work to display our essential sameness with them as speakers. The shallow worrier, 'you' in this work is a heuristic construct which reflects the limits of our current efforts to speak more thoughtfully, it does not display us pointing from a superior position at others e.g. readers. By working to display our essential sameness with other speakers we are working to show how, if we concentrate upon intentions, we do not limit ourselves to a conflict view of social relations, e.g. manipulator versus manipulated. Perhaps the manipulator would see the conflict view of social relations as providing a 'reason' to escalate the violence, maintain the social distance, and the worrier would use it as a 'reason' for not acting, and similarly maintaining the social distance, but we think about these different responses by showing how each is related to intention and a conception of what is good. Both are thoughtful achievements, but both seem thoughtlessly to try to deny or forget their achieved character. To 'have' a conflict view of social relations is to have been engaged in a dialogue, a thoughtful conversation which theorised about social relations and chose to rest with a formulation of conflict as struggle against, but to rest with that is to give up on struggle. Perhaps we do better to formulate con-flict as striking with others, collaborating with others, to think through what we could have misconceived as our beginnings. We could not reach a conflict view of social relations without having entered into social relations, and this displays the socially achieved nature of our conceptions, i.e. our dialectical characters. And, by doing so, reminds us to think about, work with, our concepts rather than be ruled by them.

We could also have felt contempt for our own feelings if we began to 'view' them, i.e. to externalise them, as being like everything else i.e. as being a matter of chance. In this way we would not have needed to accept responsibility for them, for we would have been opting to forget that our feelings are our responses, or are part of them, and that they display our choices, our decisions, and that whilst we could leave ourselves with nothing to do but worry, we can also choose to think of our feelings as our thoughtful products i.e. as social achievements, and by doing so we can become engaged in them rather than subject to them. We can deliberate and respond thoughtfully, rather than hiding behind the pretence that we are necessarily impulsive.

But taking on responsibility for our own feelings is not the same as concentrating on protecting them; perhaps this is the manipulative type's notion of responsibilities as possessions which call for protection, defensiveness. We own up to our feelings, rather than protect them, for by so doing, by submitting them for thoughtful attention, conversation, we can develop and change with them. We need not be contemptuous of that which we produce and can develop.

We are working with other selves, and by doing so display a commitment to social inquiry which recreates a social relationship between self and other selves which could have been lost if priority had been given either to the protection of feelings, or to contempt for feelings. The notion of commitment to social inquiry involves placing feelings in the service of thoughtful conversation. We need not be surprised when we remember that we do not need to defend our persons, but to offer our persons in defence of what we decide is for the good. Self defence could be good if self had been thought about, but if not it is thoughtless and does self a disservice for it displays lack of character.

What we are saying is that going to a lot of trouble, i.e. making an effort for someone, whether self or other, or something, is what we are all always doing, and that given this is so we can all as easily direct our efforts to more thoughtful social enterprises. Indeed once this is grasped it becomes impossible to choose to place our own efforts in the service of seemingly thoughtless activities. But, perhaps you formulate a lot of trouble/making an effort as painful, and refuse to grasp that engaging in painful activities could be admirable provided the engagement was thoughtful; was freely chosen. We could only choose to go to a lot of trouble for others if we had decided that their actions were products of good intentions. We do not choose to take pains with others in order to relieve others of pain, but we take pains with others, and our selves to improve ourselves (where ourselves includes other selves), for we are not becoming more thoughtful without effort.

The thoughtful interlocutor, e.g. Socrates, is one who leads a full life, for by taking pains with himself and other selves, by thinking about how he can respond more thoughtfully, by producing self as intentional rather than as subject, as choosing to take pains i.e. to make an effort, rather than as effortlessly submitting to pain, he and we are attempting to display the profound depths and morality of thoughtful life, of social interaction.

But you need to show that you are taking pains with/from other, like showing you are still breathing to prevent yourself being buried alive - and the result of this could be that some others see you as wallowing and this causes you further distress. You imagine you take pains with others to prevent yourself being buried alive, but by formulating your own actions in this way you diminish their worth. For if you were fully committed to the view that life was painful, where pain is something to be relieved of, you would do better to relieve others and yourself of life.

Perhaps you would 'view' actions of this sort as beyond you; as requiring a level of commitment you do not possess. But you only succeed in doing this by a committed and constant refusal to face up to and think about your own commitment, your own speech. That is, whether or not it does any good, or how it could be doing good. You treat your person, the way you imagine you are, as your 'nature', and by doing so refuse to think about and deepen your own actions by acknowledging that you choose them. You reveal your 'commitment' to a lack of commitment.

But still we must take care for our speech could persuade us that the work is for you to do, and not for us. We have contrasted the thoughtful interlocutor, whether writer or reader, over against the 'shallow worrier' in such a way that a reader, perhaps even ourselves, might have been led to believe that this work was doing us (the writer of the responses) no good. That we are merely engaged in lecturing you, and that if you went away the issue we are conversing about would do also. But, if this were so, and if we were being honest when we referred to our reader as a thoughtful interlocutor we would be offering him no reason to listen; for if it is doing us (the writer of the responses) no good, similarly it will do him (the thoughtful reader) no good. But we know ourselves better than this, for we have only been able to construct you (the shallow worrier) as one way of continuing to work at improving our version of self by thinking about what we could have been if we had allowed our inquiry to end at that point, and we write in the knowledge that our readers will be engaging in similar enterprises, and will not be put off by any clumsiness of style, but will perceive that the project though difficult, is necessary, and that even clumsy efforts may provide some assistance; that clumsy efforts are better than no effort. The shallow worrier is someone we could each of us pretend we are if we cut off our inquiry. However we are continuing to provide reasons for ourselves and other selves to do more than worry in the shallow sense, that is we are providing reasons to engage in thoughtful conversations through our continuing inquiry.

By suggesting that you, 'the shallow worrier' revealed your commitment to a lack of commitment, we meant to display our commitment to encouraging our selves, and other selves, to think about what we do. For your commitment to lack of commitment was not obvious in the manner of a revelation that is there for all to see without thinking. We choose to work at continuing to ensure that the obvious, the apparent, is not that which is taken to obviate the need for thought. Rather, by expressing to others what we find obvious, we continue displaying how thoughtfully or thoughtlessly we look at and hear what we respond to. We engage in conversations through which we can be changing ourselves for the better, rather than merely confirming over and over again what we could otherwise have come to conceive of ourselves as, and portray ourselves to be.

Original Speaker:

Earlier you spoke of how you were unaccustomed to hearing and giving lengthy speeches, and by trying to listen thoughtfully to what you have said after my earlier interruption I imagine that now I understand better your dislike for lengthy speeches. Yet, at the same time, I am tempted to apologise for my previous interruption, and in this way to put our conversation at ease. But, I'm not very good at apologising, so what I will do is say what comes into my head in the hope that you can make something of it, for I'm certainly impressed by what you have had to say so far, although the difference between you and me makes me feel very inadequate.

I think it is tempting both to offer and to accept apologies for they do provide a way for finishing conversations in order that other things can be done. An apology seems to me to be one way of relieving oneself of responsibility, it is designed to produce calm and provided the apology is not rejected its user can breathe a sigh of relief, for by silencing other he no longer needs to respond to other's questions.

But I have to admit that I don't like accepting apologies, (though I do accept them rather than say that!). My problem with apologies is that I hear them as couched in terms which lessen their giver's responsibility e.g. I didn't realise my actions might affect others: I didn't mean it, I was angry etc. You see I don't understand how anyone can apologise for something which is claimed not to be his/her fault. I can only see apology as being used to manipulate other. So perhaps my wish not to manipulate accounts for my reticence about apologising.

But, perhaps this goes deeper, for I see actions which have to be apologised for, as products of temptation's power to overcome our efforts at resistance, so the fault, i.e. the temptation in this way isn't the responsibility of the one apologising. I see temptation as providing time for activities which will later possibly require apologies. I treat my own actions, or rather inaction, as analogous to walking into the wilderness where temptation is at its strongest, for I see courage to lie in the resistance to temptation but not in its removal, for its removal would also remove the place for courage.

I treat abstention from involvement with other, i.e. from speaking or writing as my form of resistance, perhaps like the tea totaller, for I see my own actions as being submissions to temptation i.e. like the nonsmoker who just has one.

But I sense that you all (i.e. writer and readers) already have much to say, so maybe we should come to some arrangement, for though we will be able to converse more thoughtfully as our conversation progresses I cannot do everything at once. But I have heard enough to know that it is better to try to do something now than to pretend to be doing nothing. What I propose is that you speak whenever you have something to say, and that if I fail to take account of all you say directly as I proceed, you do not walk away, but stay to continue this conversation, for I am depending upon you.

Response:

You are right to notice that we already have much to say, though that you noticed this suggests you also had more to say! We agree that we need to come to some arrangement and further accept your proposal i.e. that we speak whenever we have something to say, and yet we know this means there are shocks in store. We begin by reminding you, and ourselves, that it is only through our work with your speech that we can act more thoughtfully with regard to this issue, so we have no incentive to walk away, on the contrary, we want to encourage you to continue choosing to walk, talk with us, for we hear your speech as reminding us of our response-ability. We will proceed by offering some thoughts on what we heard you to be trying to say a moment ago. By doing so we will be keeping open lines of thought that your speech helps us to reopen, and we display how we choose, and how you can choose, not to depend upon others. We want to display how you were proceeding yourself by inquiring into the grounds of the speech you could have made, i.e. into apology as excuse. Perhaps we could continue by risking formulating excusing as talking ourselves away from irresponsible actions towards response-able actions, i.e. excuses could be good if they are intended as active efforts to move beyond weak versions of self.

By saying that you were not very good at apologising you must intend to remind us, and yourself, not that we are different from you, for how could you know that? Rather you remind us that the version of apology we initially relied upon asked both too much and too little of apologisers. We share your lack of understanding about apology for it rests restlessly in the relationship between unintentional and intentional acts: in the uneasiness that both is the speaker's place, and that displays the profundity, and the morality of social life. You remind us that we take on response-ability for our acts by inquiring into how we did not know what we were, who were doing, when we previously acted. For instance, if we excused ourselves by saying we were angry, we would be raising to the surface the question of how we relate to ourselves as being angry, i.e. as being something. Conventionally if we had been angry we would also very likely say we were not ourselves. And we were not, for we are such that we do not and cannot know what we are, but are becoming what we are choosing to become. The existentialist notion of bad faith, e.g. Sartre's waiter is relevant here[1] for the waiter represents for us, not only one who mistakes what he isn't for what he is, but more deeply it represents one instance of resting too soon with a conception of oneself i.e. imagining that we know what we are, when to have done this would be to be binding ourselves in a speech by forgetting our place as speakers. To act either in the 'knowledge' that one is worried or that one is not worried is similarly to pretend to know too much. For we are not already this or that, and this is why speeches which stipulate that their authors already know what they are always contradict themselves.

We would not have said that we were impressed by what another had said, for by doing so we would be differentiating between ourselves and others, and could lead ourselves to forget how we necessarily played a part in formulating the reading we were impressed with. By offering impressive readings of others' speeches we make demands upon ourselves, and display how we desire to be better than we imagined we were. That is, we make the difference between other's speech and ourselves, so that difference cannot make us feel inadequate, but it can help us to recognise the potential we have to liberate ourselves. If we chose to apologise, we would formulate ourselves as taking on response-ability for our prior lack of response-ability, and by doing so directing attention towards how more thoughtful, more social actors would have chosen to act. And we dare say that thoughtful interlocutors decide to display their commitment never to relieve themselves of response-ability by externalising the production of temptation. As if temptation could provide time for! As if things provide for thinkers! As if we played no part in the production of that formulation of temptation! By continuing our inquiry we choose not to accept the situation as we imagine one who worries might formulate it; for your speech has reminded us that we could only have submitted to temptation if we had previously chosen to externalise its production, and to forget the part we are playing in the conversations which produce the versions we use of good and evil.

We choose to formulate apology as defence, as a political act: as a defence of man as a thinker/speaker i.e. as one who need not be told what is right or wrong, but who converses about, and decides what thoughtful men and women would want to do. All men and women are the same in as much as they are thinkers/speakers, and by drawing out as best we can what it is to be a speaker we raise the possibility of a dialectical politics i.e. a politics of doubt not dogma, where dogma is the error of hiding from doubt; is the error of not facing ourselves as thinkers, i.e. as those who do not know what is good but who choose to decide. We are concerned to produce political thought, and not to restrict ourselves by limiting ourselves to consumption; to digesting ideologies, including that of the apathetic/the apolitical, without showing how we must chew them over, think about them, if we are to gain any real sustenance from them. But we still have much more to do in our conversation with worry for this itself is a political act. Through this conversation we are helping those (including ourselves) who might otherwise have emaciated themselves to choose to emancipate themselves. We choose to work at making ourselves, our society, and cannot choose to leave that to chance, so let us return to our work with worry's speech.

By remembering how we play a part in the conversations that produce the version of temptation we hold, we do not have to restrict ourselves to resisting temptation. If we had done so, we would have restricted ourselves in the deep sense (i.e. strangled ouselves) quite unnecessarily by settling for a version of self as merely subject to temptation. That would have been lazy for that would have been accepting the situation as we imagined it was, rather than trying to situate, ground our imaginings. That is we would have been forgetting that we would not choose to walk into the wilderness, but out. Indeed worry's idea of the wilderness and isolation is very revealing for it reminds us not to conceive of self's crucial relationship as being with other than selves, but to formulate selves as speakers whose crucial relationships are necessarily with other selves through conversation. We are reminded by your speech that the wilderness and unintentionality could have been much closer to home, and could have resided in any talk which obstinately refuses to allow its depths to surface by listening in such a way as not to hear its own desire to be more profound, more social, more thoughtful. We do not imagine that being alone would be the wilderness for thoughtful interlocutors for we do not rely upon a version of ourselves as lacking control, as wild. We take the risk involved in our own actions, e.g. possible errors, but by so doing no longer need to prefer to be tortured, i.e. controlled by other, for by doing what we want we can make a real contribution and collaborate with others. By reminding ourselves that we are not controlled by others we show what we are in what we do, whereas shallow worriers, we imagine, are more afraid of freedom from others control than they are of others control, for the latter allows them to carry on worrying/complaining to themselves. Furthermore you remind us not to abstain from involvement with other selves for we can only be achieving more thoughtful characters through conversations, but conversation is a deeper invclvement and involves a deeper commitment than dependency upon other, for it involves grasping what speakers share and not settling for differences. We should not prostrate ourselves in front of others; we should not idolise others, but converse with them honestly so as to try to raise ourselves, bring ourselves back up. We think that restricting ourselves to not making errors, and in this way ostensibly not harming by not getting involved, can and frequently does harm. We dare say that the vestiges of a form of religious thought where god as observer and judge is omnipresent is very clear on the surface of worry's speech. And by taking this risk, we show how we do not need to wait for miracles, for we deepen the version of the environment as always containing both temptation and judgement by showing how it was itself a product of a shallow version of speech as at best imperfect consumption.

We dare say that if you had carried on talking you would have rested content with an ostensible description of what you are rather than thinking about what you could be. By risking offering a formulation of you, the worrier, as shallow, as one who holds onto a version of yourself as unalterably and essentially bad, we demand more of ourselves, in effect we remind ourselves that worry isn't good enough, that it doesn't portray or display social action as achievement. By risking arguing that you restrict yourself by reifying yourself; that you stopped inquiring any further about yourself when you imagined that you were your own worst enemy; that it was you that prevents your relationships with others becoming anything other than pretence; we provide reasons why you choose not to think about yourself, for you treat enemies as something to avoid. You cannot be befriending yourself, and this is how your conversation with yourself comes to appear to you as an altercation that does not progress, that leaves you unable to produce, to improve-ise, that leaves you with weak 'perhaps' and 'yes buts'.

Your version of yourself as your own worst enemy can also help us to remember why you see your relationship with others to be problematic, for you see yourself as possibly their worst enemy too. No wonder you get embarrassed when pointed at, for you allow the pointing to confirm what you already imagined was the case, and then you can at the most only ignore the pointing or gloss it over, for you have forgotten that it is only you that can do something about yourself by displaying your potential, your response-ability. Your version of other as observer and accuser rather than as collaborator and friend, shows us why you treat listening to others as painful i.e. as something to be endured. No wonder you head away from conversation into the wilderness, and refuse to work with others, with whom you could have risked learning and remembering.

By refusing to think about yourself you refuse to think about how you think, and this is sheer obstinacy, for if we wanted to improve the performance of a car for instance, or even to maintain its current performance, we need to think about how it works. Why then, given that we live through our thoughts should some choose to orient to their thinking/speaking as the one 'thing' they do not want to think about? What conception of a good life could elicit that response? Could it be nature as good, and thinking as unnatural i.e. man as worse than nature owing to this liability he has of having to think, of not fitting easily? We choose to commit ourselves to making the effort to show the good of thought/speech to rest in the uneasiness, the freedom through which we raise ourselves above the unintentional. We are not condemned to be free, but are free to condemn ourselves or to choose to think about/decide what we want to be becoming. By allowing your speech to stimulate our thoughts, by collaborating with it, in a productive relationship, we are displaying our choice to continue speaking/thinking about how we speak/think.

But we anticipate that you as worrier would not be satisfied with what we are saying for we propose that you equate satisfying with satiating, that you treat selves as receptacle-like i.e. you concentrate on limitations and boundaries and imagine that your actions will fail to satiate other i.e. you need to see other completely bowled over by your actions before you feel satisfied, and you do not accept other's word but need to see it. In this manner you see satiation as leaving no room for doubt, you try to push temptation outside the limit, and in this way to excuse yourself. But we allow the possibility of doubt as always being present as leaving room for desire, for thought, as ruling out satiation as a human possibility, and in this way our efforts are directed towards pulling temptation back in, in order to think how we produced it/in order to deal with it. We are not trying to push worry out but to pull it in with our questions in such a way that we can learn from it and not be subject to it.

Whilst you imagine that the manipulative type gets satisfaction from submission, and that he forces himself/his worries into submission and stops his conversation with himself, and by so doing produces the calm he pretends he is easy with. Whilst you imagine that other isn't worried because he isn't thinking, and that this is why manipulation could never work for you; that manipulation is oriented to making things easier, but fails to see that easier and better are not necessarily the same. We want to say that your failing is that you tend to see more difficult and better as the same. If being in difficulty and virtue were equivalent worry would be admirable, however we need brain as well as brawn, pleasure as well as pain, i.e. wisdom as well as stamina; otherwise we would merely be persistent; like the fly trying to fly out of the closed part of a half opened window.

Original Speaker:

'Now I am in a complete whirl, I no longer know what I am doing or what I will do next, and ...'

Response:

Stop there! You will not object to me interrupting for you remember our agreement, and what you are saying may indicate that we are now moving. However, we would rather not say 'I no longer know' for this suggests that previously you did know when, as we imagine, you really mean that you no longer imagine you know what you now admit you did not know. If this version of what you are now saying does better represent your thoughts we are beginning, and will be better able to inquire more thoughtfully into what we are doing. But we have to admit that we interrupted for we feared you would go on to give a bad reading of your condition, i.e. that you would go on to say that not knowing what you are doing worries you. However, we remember that it is only when we choose to be conscious that we do not know what we are doing that we can continue to inquire thoughtfully about it. To have said that not knowing what you are doing worries you would have been to have missed the point, for it would have revealed that you did imagine you knew what you were doing i.e. that you imagined you were worrying. And yet not knowing what you were doing is not a reason to worry for it is how we provide our impulse to proceed with active inquiry.

Original Speaker:

'But you did not know what I was going to go on to say, for how could you have known that? Yet still you interrupted in a manner that could be read as suggesting that you apparently choose to think more about what other is doing or going to do, than about what you are doing yourself. And this seems to be your way of not thinking about what you really want to go on to do. You used your energy speculating about what I was going to do in such a way that you could prepare for other's, in this instance my, speech by using other's, i.e. my, plan of action as something you could get a bearing from to make your present navigatable. But, by drifting away from a consideration of your own intentions you produce yourself as superfluous as at best merely orienting to, or from, other's needs. However, you and I know that as long as this is the case, as long as we rely upon a difference between worry, and we will now risk saying it, philosophy, which we do not continue inquiring about, we cannot be doing philosophy for we remain worried.

By orienting to other's plans, as you were doing, and producing yourself as superfluous you treat yourself as like driftwood, where you would formulate driftwood as causing no harm except when, if ever, it gets involved in, or collides with other's plans. In this manner your inclination towards separation is revealed. Still, our conversation ranges between collisions and collusion/collaboration, or better displays how collisions need not be catastrophies in the context of friendly relations, but play a part in the continuing production of the stimulation necessary for collaboration.

You, thoughtful interlocutors (i.e. writer and readers) will remember that I, the shallow worrier, was spoken about earlier as a heuristic tool. That you are making use of me, but perhaps now it is time, and perhaps it always has been time, for you to think more diligently about why you want to talk about me rather than to inquire more deeply about yourselves, and in that way to be displaying your potential! Could it be that you want to talk about what you imagine you already know rather than to risk thinking about, deciding what you want?'

(Note to reader: This could seem comical for only a short while ago (i.e. on P.84) we were hearing how the worrier's conversation with herself appears like an altercation, and yet here we have the heuristic tool that we ourselves have constructed apparently attacking us, i.e. using its speech as a weapon every time it is introduced. However all is not as it could seem for this appearance of altercation leads us to become increasingly aware of the problem the mode of discourse we have chosen allows us to bring to the surface, for I/you talk, or we/you talk could be how an altercation is represented. Incidentally our talk there of appearance, i.e. of the apparent can be deepened if we formulate the apparent as a-parent for we can grasp better how we could have been misled about our relationship to products of our thought i.e. to the apparent/the obvious, for the apparent, i.e. the a-parent does not father or mother us, rather we play a large role in the production of what we consider apparent. So now we grasp that if we continued to formulate we/you talk as an altercation, as a fight or dispute, as talk between two different 'I's or collections of 'I's we would be displaying our failure to grasp how self and other selves are intertwined in a manner that is necessary for their continuing production of themselves.

I must own up to the fact that I have been delayed for a long while at this stage of my writing, though nothing like as long as before I risked beginning, but this current delay has been related to my continuing uneasiness about how this work is being written. I want to be showing how one form of speech/life is drawn out of, through another through a friendly relationship between the two, and yet to write in terms of now and then could fail to display how the choice between the two is always now. I have used we/you talk, but the limitations of this mode of talk rest in the continuing tendency for it to be heard as a dispute. However if we formulate a dispute as a continuing reckoning between characters who will not, and cannot, settle for silence, for thoughtless lives we can better understand and display how friends never restrict or hold back their discourse, but through their discourse provide for continuing honest endeavour: where endeavour is formulated as the devouring of ends; where endeavour is the refusal to allow shallow talk to subject us. We abuse concepts, i.e. the ways we could have conceived, in such a way as to bring forth improved selves, an improving society. We do not orient to our concepts as limitations that we cannot stretch, for if we did we would be involved in self abuse, alienation. So we will return to the dialogue we have been producing/hearing, and not restrict ourselves to dismissing it, but make the effort to continue engaging with it.)

Response:

Your reference to friendly relations reminds us that we, you and us, must be formulating our collisions as stimulating collaboration. By doing so we formulate your decision in your next sentence to ask us to talk about ourselves, as displaying your friendliness; though we could have read it as indicating your unwillingness to continue; as indicating your decision to try to give your person a rest. But you could not have intended the latter for you know full well that the truth of the matter is that we are all always already talking about ourselves, and what we share, about our manner of theorising, even when we choose to remain silent. We might have offered a reading of you as being too ready to come up with objections that stifle our conversation, but ironically if we had done so we would have been displaying the weakness of our own persons for how could your questions be objections? Your questions encourage us to think about our own speech and provide for it, they encourage us to seek true character. If we are not merely to worry about worry we must display how our work provides for worry as a providential act, as intentional, and to do so we cannot rest with surface evidence, we must formulate intentions, and this does involve mutilating shallow personas. We cannot rest with a version of worry as debilitating but must be reforming it as making space for deliberation. When you spoke of a difference between worry and philosophy you could not have meant that the difference was there, as if you knew what philosophy is, what worry is, as if they were things. Your speech reminds us that we do not rely upon that difference, and that by continuing our inquiry we do not remain worried, in any shallow sense. To ask ourselves whether we are doing philosophy or not could be a question worth asking, and perhaps it is what all speakers are always doing. If it is, we are no exception. Perhaps we could risk saying this: that by making the effort to hear others' speeches, and our own, as the speeches of philosophers we are less likely to treat selves with disrespect. We return now to our theorising upon the speech of worry, and perhaps we can make our return by saying that we are less interested in which mouth a particular speech comes from, i.e. whether it be yours or ours, and more interested in the virtue of the speech in question. You pointed out that we had settled for a version of ourselves as superfluous, we could have reminded you that that was your construction not ours, but instead we will think about how the notion of superfluousness might be used by a thoughtful interlocutor, i.e. a philosopher, and we reach for our conceptions through the speech of worry. We will continue to refer to the worrier as you, for we can see the good of this given our new formulation of altercation.

Your production of yourself as superfluous ties in with your version of yourself as not harming, but you have to go a step further for deeply you are aware that this could not be good enough for you. You take another step and produce not harming as being steadfast, not budging, as being incorruptible, and, in this way, you formulate yourself as caring for others.

You do not do anything because you are never sure whether you mean it (cf., weak altercation notion accounts for indecision. But also you treat 'means it' as 'knowing what you are doing' rather than as 'intending whilst not knowing'). You imagine you are sure that it is not good to do things you do not mean. For instance, you imagine it would be better not to write a work like this, because you would not be sure that you knew what you were doing. This work itself shows to our readers why that would have been a far worse mistake. You are the sort of writer who would never have left the street you were born in unless you were forced. You want to consume and use theories and ideologies to shield your person in the same manner that some imagine others want the strength of the insurance companies around them, for you have forgotten to choose to make the effort to display how your unsureness was your asset. How fortunate that you are not our reader.

Your version of not harming as caring for is only an adequate version when nothing is required, but unfortunately for you, and fortunately for us, the only time nothing is required is likely to be in death, if that can be called a time at all. We offer the following caricature of you as dressed in the garb of a doctor who doesn't diagnose or prescribe anything as that way you feel you can do no harm. That doctor does not grasp that he could and must do much more, and so must we.

Your version of yourself as superfluous also leads you to end up talking to yourself for you imagine that you contribute nothing, you undervalue your own actions. Indeed even if you have a 'success' you would very quickly reduce it to being a matter of chance. You see yourself as wasting other's time, for you imagine that other could have no need for you, for you have not yet grasped how you need other.

But we draw out many lessons or reminders for ourselves through your speech for we would choose to formulate our superfluousness as displaying not that we are not needed, but that we are needed if we are to do any better than treating nature as good enough, and we produce the worrier's version of her own superfluousness as related to her forgetful version of her relationship to nature. By engaging in caricature we do what nature cannot do, we try to encourage those who might have worried (to say it once more ourselves) that pretending to be natural is not good enough for us.

Those who choose to view themselves as natural produce a version of speech/thought as a waste of time, they imagine they were better off before they learned to talk, but they are forgetting that they learnt that. An education that tries to teach us to be natural forgets its own social nature, if Kafka was referring to an education of this sort in his diaries he was very right when he said his education never did him any good. (Kafka 1972, pp15-21)

Whilst we are speaking of education we remember that for us a strong version of educating is educing, i.e. bringing out potential, we are wanting to reform views of education that are modelled on notions of imposing duties, for if we engage in imposing duties we would be fostering posers, i.e. actors who would not take on response-ability for their actions. Indeed the actions they dutifully perform would not be theirs.

The formulation of superfluousness we have offered also reminds us why we would not relate to conventional usage as being that which provides us with an easy way, for that would be to lean towards treating our conventions as natural and subjecting ourselves to them. We must be providing ourselves with thoughtful conventions for we do provide our usage, our conventions and if they are thoughtless that is our fault. We imagine that the worrier, that you, will try to hold on to a version of providing for that does not take response-ability to heart, for whereas your version of temptation revealed how you had forgotten that you were involved in its production, your version of responsibilities is as of duties in the weak sense mentioned above. You try to provide for things e.g. temptations, duties as if you have not had a part in providing them, and you fail to provide for them and for yourself as a result.

You imagine that providing for things is preparing for things, thinking about what might happen, and given that you concentrate upon seeing what you imagine is bad about things you tend to reduce preparing to various methods of avoiding. We are not concerned to provide for things, but to provide for ways of thinking in order that we do act more response-ably, and not allow our lives to be reduced to avoidance, perhaps dancing in the void. As we said much much earlier in this work preparing for us involves paring away that which detracts from our character i.e. shallowness, superficiality, and these efforts to work with the speech of worry are providing one instance of the level of our involvement/commitment.

NOTES

[1] How ironic that he chooses a waiter, i.e. one who waits!

5 Invention and art

In one breath you were speaking of caricature and yet in another you were speaking of paring away that which detracts from our characters, i.e. shallowness! As you yourself said, you are mutilating personas, for shallowness would test the best caricaturist, for it requires him to draw the featureless aspects out, in such a way that they dominate. And yet I see now how this does need to be done if they are to be pared away!

However, the issue of caricature helps me to raise much broader questions for whilst I do not deny that your speech displays inventiveness and the consummate ease of the accomplished artist, I reckon myself amongst those who are short in these qualities. And yet, more deeply, I have doubts about whether these are qualities at all.

I would like to go on to explain myself more clearly here, but each of the above issues suggests to me that it would be better if I did not, for (a) my uninventiveness suggests that I will not say anything you do not know already, (b) my lack of consummate ease suggests that you will say whatever I was going to say more skilfully anyway, and (c) my doubts about whether these characteristics of the artist are qualities or not suggest that to engage in artistic work i.e. in trying to produce an account could in any case be self contradictory.

Response:

Come on! Time and time again we have been saying it is time for you to contradict what you imagine is your self! After all we have been saying can you still want to remain silent; to let shallowness be the feature we must remember you by? Why not take this opportunity to converse about these issues in such a way that we can be deepening ourselves through our speech? Perhaps you are afraid that if your shallowness were removed nothing would remain! And perhaps you are right, but it could be that by making the effort to work at removing our shallowness we will be rebuilding the character you have irrationally come to fear you lack. And, by doing so, we will be remembering that we have never needed to fear other selves as being those who would merely reveal our shallowness only then to revel in it.

A few moments ago you said that you saw how, if we are to pare away that which detracts from our character it must be brought to the surface i.e. that you saw how it must feature in our conversation. Could not this help us to characterise a friendly conversation as that through which each interlocutor tries to draw the best out of other? Could anything less than this be friendship? We are at ease with our friends not because they ask nothing of us, or themselves, on the contrary, we are at ease in our friendly relationships for through them we continue to ask ourselves and other selves to improve.

Original Speaker:

> Excuse my surprise, but of late I have considered my friends to be those with whom I have felt at ease where ease involved no questions being asked. And yet now I can understand how that involved something more akin to unconditional acceptance of my person with all my faults, i.e. that version of friendship does not draw the best out of its members but allows them to degenerate, for it persuades them that no effort is needed to maintain the friendship. Friends of that sort would be our worst enemies. Furthermore this can remind us of one of the issues that we set out with i.e. that of the worrier's inability to befriend herself. Here we are showing that we were then relying upon an unexplicated notion of friendship as an easy silence. And yet by not settling for that silence we are showing that the worrier could have been beginning to befriend herself, and, more importantly, other selves all along by her questioning. Through our inquiry we are displaying how befriending ourselves could not mean merely resting content with ourselves, rather it means working together to draw the best out of each other. So now we grasp that we cannot expect to maintain friendships unless we are working at paring away our faulty personas, and by doing so are helping others to do the same.

Response:

Whilst much that you say here is praiseworthy we are concerned lest your manner of speaking could deter rather than encourage others and yourself, for at this stage, i.e. whilst you choose to dwell upon the dangers that could arise for those who choose to remain content with themselves as they seem to be, you do not yet display how enjoyable working to raise ourselves above thoughtless limitations can be. We will work in what follows of this section in such a way as to help ourselves to display how acting more thoughtfully, i.e. improving our-selves, our relations with others, is no hardship, and that the hardship lies in not doing this. But, perhaps we should say before we go any further, that we do not consider our work to be inventive, on the contrary, as we will be showing, it is you who invent, and are then trapped in the 'inventions' you forget you have produced. Neither do we consider ourselves to be accomplished artists, but this returns us to where this section began and provides an opportunity for you to offer more material which we can work together upon in such a way that we continue to deepen our speech, to make our speech more thoughtful, more social, more moral.

Original Speaker:

> 'Alright, let us get on for time and space are limited, and perhaps with your help we can provide material which we can use in our efforts to continue coming to grips with ourselves ...'

(N.B. However original speaker lapses into silence here.)

Response:

Now we could have appeared to assist you here by intervening, and speaking on your behalf, for we imagine that you have lapsed into silence as a result of your notion of yourself as uninventive. And yet we choose to ask you to speak, for by doing so you may help reveal to yourself and us how your decision to lapse into silence was a product of your inventiveness not your uninventiveness.

Perhaps you will be more prepared to proceed if we mention that through this inquiry we are leading ourselves to recall that through our formulations of educating as educating, and of friendship as drawing the best out of self and other selves, we are displaying how the worrier could, by choosing not to rest with, or be redirected by, lazy conventional usage, prove to be a good friend after all. But once again we ask you to proceed, for if you remain silent this could suggest that you are thoroughly persuaded by your own view of the situation, by your invention. That is, your silence could illustrate how it is you that are the accomplished artist, and how your persuasive art acts as your accomplice in the contemptuous deception of yourself and other selves in which you are unwittingly engaged.

Original Speaker:

> 'But this is a monstrous situation! No, I will not say 'is' for that would be to fail to consider how it is I that envisage the situation to be such; that would be to refuse to think about what I am doing. Indeed, perhaps if I always formulate seeing or viewing as envisaging I will be reminded of how I am actively engaged in the production of what I begin by imagining I merely see.

> So, by formulating seeing as envisaging we display how the appearances that perhaps we imagined we began with, are connected with what has previously occurred to us, but by working harder upon this mode of connection we display how it can shock us, and fragment any easy, persuasive, togetherness of what we had previously imagined to be the initial occurrence. A thoughtful response is not like a miracle then i.e. it does not wish to be good whilst denying its connectedness. Rather, by being a spontaneous reply (response), it displays that a thoughtfully connected act is an instance of productive consumption, it progresses, makes more out of initial images, by displaying what the initials stand for.

> When I began to speak a moment ago my speech displayed many of the features of anger i.e. it was impatient, rushed, unthought about, and full of excuses, I imagine it has always been this way for I conceive of myself as only producing, speaking, under duress, i.e. when I am forced. I only begin when the alternative is to end, i.e. when what I

imagine is a worse evil confronts me; hence my silence earlier. I connect with the past, or what I am in, in such a way as to conceive of myself as squeezed by it. I always want to pull my speech back, hence my 'yes - buts', because my version of beginning prevents me from having any resources for renewed beginnings.

Perhaps I rely upon a version of production as invention, where invention is analogous to creation ex nihilo i.e. the immaculate conception. How strange! For any impetus to rest within the confines of a language game, or form of life, is analogous to treating concepts as perfectly pure, i.e. as unable to be improved upon. But, this version of production is contingent upon the version of beginnings as the limit, i.e. of beginning as that before which there was nothing. So whilst I imagine that the manipulative type wants things easy, i.e. wants rewards without effort, i.e. wants something for nothing, I have relied upon a version of myself as wanting something from nothing.

Given this version of production as miracle, I am not surprisingly suspicious of all that purports to be production, and see my work to lie in showing that those creations were not from nothing, i.e. in showing the producers to be fakes. Perhaps it has been for this very reason that I have not wanted to be a producer, i.e. the fear of being shown to be a fake has prevented me from grasping that that fear was itself fake if it was mistakenly treated as original. So, if I had been reading this work prior to our conversation I would very likely have tried to show that it was not original, that it was like the work of so and so. I imagined that the only relationship of self to tradition was that of sheep to their leader. I would have tried to drag this work, and any work, down to what I imagined was my level, rather than risking allowing it to help me grow.

Response:

So now be kind enough to tell us how you might have spoken about inventiveness etc. in order that we can continue actively contemplating, thinking about, drawing the best out of, rather than merely recounting or reflecting, or for that matter ignoring or rejecting, the modes of thought/speech in which you were engaged when you began by referring to this situation as monstrous. By doing so we will be stretching ourselves out of a mode of speech that requires us to be squeezed, strangled, before we will speak. And, we will be reminding ourselves that we do not, and cannot, create out of nothing; we do have to relate through our material, we are intermediaries, and we choose to squeeze and work upon our material i.e. the forms of speech we could have used, that would otherwise use us.

Original Speaker:

'I will proceed by telling you the worries I have about inventiveness, for I may as well admit that had you agreed with my suggestion that your work was inventive this was what I was going to do anyway.'

(Note to reader: we include a further appendix at this stage in order that you can if you wish work through this speech without our responses, but we will then, as before offer readings of each paragraph to try to draw the best out of, i.e. to offer formulations of, this speech about worry and inventiveness, i.e. to say what it reminds us of.)

Para. 1   So, worries about invention: firstly, it is this version of invention as miracle, i.e. as something to be waited for which reduces the worrier to wasting, consuming time, she sees there to be nothing she can do. Worries about this though are that it is only a worry if consuming time is bad.

Para. 2   Secondly, and a much more dramatic worry, is that as yet we have failed to bring to the fore the inventors potential to produce monsters as well as, or in the place of miracles. Some sort of Frankenstein analogy might be appropriate here, i.e. whereas manipulation merely leaves dead bodies behind, invention is more like bringing to life. It is in this sense that the manipulator can become the tool of manipulation, i.e. manipulation can get out of hand. The monster is created and then consumes its creator, examples might be capitalism, bureaucracy, speeches or hearings that have forgotten to continue inquiring into their speaker's or hearer's place.

Para. 3   One point that could provide interesting work is why the worrier invents a monster in the sense of producing the environment as something which cannot be trusted, i.e. as something to be afraid of. The worrier produces the environment as a monster and then chooses not to accept responsibility for her production. Because she conceives of the monster as having got out of hand she can wash her hands of her responsibility, i.e. her part in its production. She can sit back and hope it does not devour her. A monster is precisely that to which you cannot be expected to be responsive. With both monsters and miracles all you can do is sit back and hope.

Para.4   Perhaps we can make more sense now of the worrier's distrust of others, for she views them as acting as though they were or are not productions, i.e. as if they have a life of their own (in the same sense as Frankenstein's monster), and as if their life is dependent solely upon consumption. The worrier is like the child who relates only to parents who she imagines have forgotten their childhood. That is, who she imagines see themselves as complete, and hence as no longer needing to produce themselves, but only to consume. Monsters do not grow, in the strong sense of grow better, and in this sense they are complete, i.e. all they will ever be. (Convention as mere persistence now starts to sound like the monster!)

Para. 5   Furthermore, this reminder of the inventor's potential to create monsters as well as miracles reminds us that the worrier's version of production as invention is yet a further indication of the worrier's wish to remove herself from responsibility. For, what the worrier likes about invention is its lack of responsibility for the invention's uses, i.e. she merely invents things, she does not use them. She could work for anyone. More than this though the inventor is, in a deep sense as inactive as the worrier for she requires an entrepreneurial alter to do things with her inventions i.e. she provides things for others to act with. She evades the decision (or pretends she does) about what ought to be done. So now we can see why invention is not a strong formulation of action.

Para. 6   Thus even the worrier's utopian image of herself is as a creator without responsibility. The inventor produces inventions that will not ask anything of her i.e. the inventor wants admirers (gasps) not friends, she wants to remain a mystery. The inventor then is one who tries to stop conversations by producing i.e. the inventor has no time for speech as she sees others as uninventive (as dummies). Her inventiveness separates her from others, and her tendency to mumble, and speak incomprehensibly suggests a lack of need of other. The inventor relies upon the separation of her product from her resources to retain her respect from others.

Para. 7   Inventors often seem to be uncommitted except to invention, and perhaps this accounts for why they can produce monsters or miracles. But, it might be that their mumbling, their lack of ability to converse with others accounts for their apparent lack of commitment to anything other than invention. Their lack of commitment is a product of loneliness, the same loneliness that the worrier experiences as a result of her urge for separation, which is in turn a result of seeing connection as pollution.

Para. 8   The worrier by producing her version of production as miracle also produces her version of dialogue as the process of yes-but, i.e. invention followed by worry/interrogation, where worry is equivalent to seeing what is wrong with the invention, or what could go wrong with the invention. The worrier relies upon a notion of perfection as being without limits, so she sees imperfection as extending limitlessly i.e. as far as limits go, and furthermore she sees imperfection as bad. So her version of providing for is showing the limited nature of, and this becomes equivalent to showing the bad. In this way she creates monsters out of the same material from which 'miracles' could be created. Furthermore, this version of bad as extending to limitlessness also suggests why the worrier produces seeing the good as irresponsibly taking a holiday. She produces rewards as that which should follow work, and as she sees her work as limitless, she never gets to see the good of anything, she never gets a holiday. She sees imperfection as bad, but fails to see that imperfection also involves good, i.e. that that which is imperfect is not all bad. This is how she creates monsters.

Para. 9   This version of the worrier's speech as seeing the bad also helps us see why she sees other's speech as accusation i.e. whilst her wish to see problems or what is bad does provide room for more talk, which is good, it limits talk to court talk, which is bad. It reduces dialogue to prosecution and/or defence. The worrier either submits and accepts that the invention is original, i.e. that she has witnessed a miracle; the only way presumably she would ever do this is because of lack of evidence to the contrary, or the worrier/prosecutor forces the inventor to submit and the miracle is shown to be fake. There is little or no time or space, given the limits of the court, and its version of dialogue to see the good of anything. Also, the worrier (as prosecutor) successfully produces herself as having no part in the crime. The prosecutor/worrier plays the opposite trick regarding responsibility to that of the inventor, i.e. whilst the latter invents but does not use, the former uses things (e.g. the law) but disclaims responsibility for the production of those things.

Para.10   The worrier needs new things/inventions to criticise in the same way that the courts need crimes. This is another way of saying why it can never get to seeing the good, or having a holiday, for it can always find plenty of its work to do.'

ANALYSIS OF APPENDIX B

Response:

Our relationship to this speech has requested a great deal of work and effort from us, for whilst we might have begun by dismissing it as a lazy regress, perhaps in part induced by a misreading of our earlier intimation of friendship, we are finding that by working upon, and with it, we are better getting to grips with how our relationship to what we read or hear can be a relationship of productive consumption. What we make out of this speech, and our relationship to it, may well be such as to make unrecognisable material almost recognisable. We will work through the speech paragraph by paragraph for from, and through, each paragraph we draw out elements of that which we are producing in this section, but this methodological or meticulous routine will not hide from us that our form of examination of text does not simply require a microscope and a cataloguing process. Our relationship to this speech and to all speeches including our own has more in common with the artist's relationship to his materials, but as we will very likely be speaking about art in the near future we will say no more on that issue at present. So we proceed to work with each paragraph in turn.

Analysis of Paragraph 1

So, worries about invention: firstly, it is this version of invention as miracle, i.e. as something to be waited for which reduces the worrier to wasting, consuming time, she sees there to be nothing she can do. Worries about this though are that it is only a worry if consuming time is bad.

Response:

This paragraph reminds us to choose to hear your speech as choosing not to be reduced to worrying about invention as miracle, for we hear you as saying that that is how the version of invention as miracle would have reduced those who used and relied upon it to worry. That is, we hear your speech as actively seeking, working to achieve, a better version of good speech than invention as miracle. You start to display this for us by saying that wasting time is only a worry if consuming time is bad and this prompts us to ask ourselves why, or whether, we might have relied upon a version of time as some thing we can waste. But we can only waste, in the sense of use up, that which we see to be limited, so it could be that what we are uncovering here, with the help of your speech, is how even time can be reduced to a personal possession, a commodity, by those who imagine they already know what it is good to do or be. Perhaps this notion of wasting time is related to versions of man's mortality as something to fear, and yet there is something irrational about wanting to save, in the sense of stock up, time. By deciding not to orient to time as a personal possession that needs to be preserved, in the sense of not wasted, for how could we save it? and what for? we better grasp that we are always acting intentionally, thoughtfully now. That is we grasp how our selves are in time but do themselves no good by worrying about the movement of time. If we are to act more thoughtfully we must at least be prepared to ask ourselves whether what we are doing is what we would decide is worth doing, and not to pretend we already know, i.e. that we do not need to think about that.

Analysis of Paragraph 2

Secondly, and a much more dramatic worry, is that as yet we have failed to bring to the fore the inventor's potential to produce monsters as well as, or in the place of miracles. Some sort of Frankenstein analogy might be appropriate here, i.e. whereas manipulation merely leaves dead bodies behind, invention is more like bringing to life. It is in this sense that the manipulator can become the tool of manipulation, i.e. manipulation can get out of hand. The monster is created and then consumes its creator, examples might be capitalism, bureaucracy, speeches or hearings that have forgotten to continue inquiring into their speaker's or hearer's place.

Response:

So frequently your speech could have frustrated us, as it seems to frustrate, yourself, for couldn't you have said not 'we have failed', but we now succeed, or alternatively couldn't you have said, we have previously succeeded in not bringing the inventor's weakness to produce monsters to the fore? Of all the 'things' an inventor could produce, your speech chooses to concentrate on the monster!

We become impatient for we want manipulation to get out of hand, we want man-ipulation to be thoughtful, ruled by heads if you like, and we want to bring back to life the forms of speech, i.e. like yours is at present, that could deaden the lives of their speakers and hearers. The analogies you use reveal the points at which you decide to discontinue your inquiry, but we are showing how you could have got the best out of your own speech by displaying how it helps you to proceed with inquiry, rather than by imagining it brings it to a close. We do not choose to move from miracles to monsters, but from miracles and/or monsters to continuing human achievements. We are reminded that we do not orient to your speech as either a miracle or a monster i.e. our concern is not with easy, thoughtless acceptance or rejection, rather, by orienting to your reading of your circumstances as a continuing human achievement we can work towards a more thoughtful understanding of what we share. But, the more profound and deeper issue we are raising here is that we should not differentiate our speech/thought in such a way as to treat it differently to the speech of others, and by relating to our own thoughts in this same manner we should work with and on our thoughts and not orient to our thinking as a work process which if successful can be terminated in easy thoughtlessness. Thinking which does enjoy itself, i.e. thinking which is social has no need to terminate itself, and we take this opportunity to remind ourselves that we do not separate thought from action in any vulgar manner. By commending that thinking does not terminate itself we are not commending inaction, but we are commending an end to any urges towards thoughtless actions.

Analysis of Paragraph 3

One point that could. provide interesting work is why the worrier invents a monster in the sense of producing the environment as something which cannot be trusted, i.e. as something to be afraid of. The worrier produces the environment as a monster and then chooses not to accept responsibility for her production. Because she conceives of the monster as having got out of hand she can wash her hands of her responsibility, i.e. her part in its production. She can sit back and hope it does not devour her. A monster is precisely that to which you cannot be expected to be responsive. With both monsters and miracles all you can do is sit back and hope.

Response:

(a) Regarding interesting work, we are reminded by this that we will always ask ourselves what it is or why it is that some thing or topic interests us, for by doing so we will encourage ourselves to think about what we are doing, what we are, and by doing so will choose to act in a more thoughtful manner. Perhaps what interests the worrier are ways to avoid facing up to that which she imagines she fears. So, when she says 'one point that could provide interesting work ...', we could hear her as revealing her temptation to conceal from herself the fact that deeply she imagines that she is afraid to ask herself about why she is interested in what she says she is interested in. She might try to laugh this off, but she would do better if she honestly admitted that she did not know what she was interested in for then she could work with us to produce thoughtful interests. We do not skate over the issue of interests, for if we did we would be restricting ourselves to the shallows, and restrictions of that sort are uninteresting to thoughtful social, characters.

(b) She speaks of that which cannot be trusted as something to be afraid of, but fear is not the only response possible, for isn't it the stranger i.e. the one we do not know that we cannot yet trust. So isn't a possible response to that which we cannot trust inquiry, i.e. the effort to seek to get to know, to create a relationship of trust with? Furthermore the worrier claims to know too much for she says that the environment cannot be trusted, we would rather say that we do not yet know whether it can be trusted or not, i.e. we would not prejudge the issue. Also, by redirecting her attention to other, the environment, the worrier reveals her trust in her self as she appears to herself to be. We are showing that she would do better to orient to that which she imagines herself to be as something to distrust, if that distrust could stimulate her into thoughtful active inquiry and not fearful avoidance.

(c) Whilst she conceives of the environment as having got out of hand, we conceive of our environment as that which has always been out of hand, but that which we have to work to take into our thoughtful hands. We are washing our hands, thinking about our methods, in order to work well with our materials, our environment. That is, we are doing this work, i.e. writing this piece, before we offer readings of other authors etc. in order that our hands/methods do not unnecessarily dirty our material. We want to be becoming better able to respect our materials.

(d) We would rather say that a monster is that to which you cannot choose not to respond, and in that sense we would not be unduly concerned if this work strikes you as monstrous, for if it does it will at least encourage you to think about how you are responding, and not to imagine yourself to be inactive, i.e. merely sitting and hoping, or perhaps judging as if from the outside!

(e) By producing a version of the relationship between self and other selves as that between self and monster we hear you as revealing an urge to live without speech, i.e. an urge for you to live your personal life even at the cost of thought/society, for there is no place for conversation with a monster. Questions are avoided like the plague. But that would be no life at all for a thinker/speaker it is not a human possibility. It is to reduce thoughtful questioning, interrogation to in - terror - gation.

Analysis of Paragraph 4

Perhaps we can make more sense now of the worrier's distrust of others, for she views them as acting as though they were or are not productions, i.e. as if they have a life of their own (in the same sense as Frankenstein's monster), and as if their life is dependent solely upon consumption. The worrier is like the child who relates only to parents who she imagines have forgotten their childhood. That is, who she imagines see themselves as complete, and hence as no longer needing to produce themselves, but only to consume. Monsters do not grow, in the strong sense of grow better, and in this sense they are complete, i.e. all they will ever be. (Convention as mere persistence now starts to sound like the monster!)

Response:

But what good does it do you, or any other for you to rest in distrust of other? We choose not to rest there, i.e. not to distrust others e.g. perhaps the worrier, but through our conversations to relate in such a way as to display how by acting thoughtfully, asking questions we can enliven ourselves and other selves. We choose not to relate to the worrier as parent to child, or as child to parent, but as we would with collaborators, friends who do not consider themselves complete, and who are seeking to grasp the monstrous nature of any selves that choose to imagine they are complete. We could not have a life on our own for we are not one, and, if parents were to have been those who imagined they were complete, we would not choose to grow up. Furthermore parents' very desire to have children could be an expression of their deep awareness of their lives lack of completion. But, by committing ourselves to lasting childhood we display the child's response-ability, and are not treating childhood as a way to avoid responsibilities. The child has potential to improve and we are making the effort to continue to share in that.

Analysis of Paragraph 5

Furthermore, this reminder of the inventor's potential to create monsters as well as miracles reminds us that the worrier's version of production as invention is yet a further indication of the worrier's wish to remove herself from responsibility. For, what the worrier likes about invention is its lack of responsibility for the invention's uses, i.e. she merely invents things, she does not use them. She could work for anyone. More than this though the inventor is, in a deep sense as inactive as the worrier for she requires an entrepreneurial alter to do things with her inventions i.e. she provides things for others to act with. She evades the decision (or pretends she does) about what ought to be done. So now we can see why invention is not a strong formulation of action.

Response:

You remind us that we would rather have said that our potential to act with thoughtful good intentions reminds us that our version of production, as thoughtful response, is deeper than inventiveness for it indicates our desire to become ourselves by taking on response-abilities. For what we like about thoughtful responses is that they claim response-ability. We do not differentiate between self, and other selves, in such a manner that our thoughtful response is good for one and not the other, our responses display our community with others. We work for ourselves, and with ourselves, and do not shift responsibility for our products on to others e.g. employers. We are active, and do not require others to act in a different capacity to ourselves, for we want others to think about, and collaborate in the improvement of our ways of speaking/thinking/living, as we are doing. We are making the effort to provide for ways of thinking/acting such that we decide what we ought to do, for there is no way we can leave that decision to others. So, we are working with the worrier's speech to formulate more thoughtful/social modes of thought/action and by doing so deepen ourselves.

Analysis of Paragraph 6

> Thus even the worrier's utopian image of herself is as a creator without responsibility. The inventor produces inventions that will not ask anything of her i.e. the inventor wants admirers (gasps) not friends, she wants to remain a mystery. The inventor then is one who tries to stop conversations by producing i.e. the inventor has no time for speech as she sees others as uninventive (as dummies). Her inventiveness separates her from others, and her tendency to mumble, and speak incomprehensibly suggests a lack of need of other. The inventor relies upon the separation of her product from her resources to retain her respect from others.

Response:

We are reminded by this paragraph that our version of ourselves is as response-able, thoughtful, social actors. We produce our actions as asking the same of ourselves as from other selves, for we choose to display our selves in order that through, and with, others' collaboration we can demystify our actions, and get a better grip upon what we do. We try to start and maintain conversations with, and through our formulations, for we have no time outside our conversations/thoughts, outside our friendly relationships. Indeed we would become dummies if we could have chosen not to hear what others had to say. Our response-able actions collect us with others, i.e. display what we share, and if we have a tendency to mumble or speak incomprehensibly we are reminded by this of our need of other, rather than our lack of need. We are working to recollect how we are using our resources in our conversations in such a way as to respect other selves and our own selves. And we know that by differentiating in shallow ways we cannot create conditions in which we truly respect other selves and our own selves.

Analysis of Paragraph 7

> Inventors often seem to be uncommitted except to invention, and perhaps this accounts for why they can produce monsters or miracles. But, it might be that their mumbling, their lack of ability to converse with others accounts for their apparent lack of commitment to anything other than invention. Their lack of commitment is a product of loneliness, the same loneliness that the worrier experiences as a result of her urge for separation, which is in turn a result of seeing connection as pollution.

Response:

We want to ask what the worrier would do with inventors, or more strongly what the worrier would do with all of us, for she seems capable of producing bad versions of each and every one of us, including herself. What could the good of this be? Perhaps it could direct our attention to what we all share, i.e. our incompleteness, and by doing so she could be calling upon us, and herself, to raise ourselves above the pretence of either phoney commitments or phoney uncommittedness. Our commitment can only be our continuing engagement in the effort to be freeing ourselves from activities which are degrading. Freeing ourselves from activities which require us to deny, and/or forget, that we do not know what is good, and cannot know, but do decide through conversation. We are committed to listening to others and ourselves in such a way that we hear speeches as calling for thoughtful responses. You have spoken to us of the worrier's urge for separation, but the fact that you continue to converse with us displays either that you are not the worrier in which case how do you know that she wants separation? Or that worry's, your, urge is not for separation from all others, but from polluted speeches that would degrade their speakers. So your desire is for yourself, and other selves to stretch speeches in such a way that those speeches are worth listening to, connecting with.

Analysis of Paragraph 8

> The worrier by producing her version of production as miracle also produces her version of dialogue as the process of yes-but, i.e. invention followed by worry/interrogation, where worry is equivalent to seeing what is wrong with the invention, or what could go wrong with the invention. The worrier relies upon a notion of perfection as being without limits, so she sees imperfection as extending limitlessly i.e. as far as limits go, and furthermore she sees imperfection as bad. So her version of providing for is showing the limited nature of, and this becomes equivalent to showing the bad. In this way she creates monsters out of the same material from which 'miracles' could be created. Furthermore, this version of bad as extending to limitlessness also suggests why the worrier produces seeing the good as irresponsibly taking a holiday. She produces rewards as that which should follow work, and as she sees her work as limitless, she never gets to see the good of anything, she never gets a holiday. She sees imperfection as bad, but fails to see that imperfection also involves good, i.e. that that which is imperfect is not all bad. This is how she creates monsters.

Response:

The thinker, by producing a version of production as thoughtful response also produces a version of dialogue as a process of questioning, i.e. statements followed by questions where the questions are equivalent to asking what the good of the state of affairs suggested by the statement would be, or could be. We produce our notion of dialogue, i.e. thoughtful life as being without limit, for it does not rely upon specific embodied persons, so we produce dialogue as extending limitlessly, and furthermore we produce dialogue i.e. that which does not end, as being worthy of our commitment i.e. as being our expression of our thoughtful good intentions. So our version of providing for is showing the unlimited nature of dialogue, and this is equivalent to showing the good of thought as opposed to thoughtlessness. In this way we can continue speaking thoughtfully rather than settle for monstrous versions of ourselves as seeking thoughtlessness: i.e. an end to dialogue. Our version of the unlimited nature of dialogue and the good of thoughtful intentions reminds us why displaying the good of dialogue is not taking an irresponsible holiday, but is working in a fashion that does us good. By seeking to deepen our understanding of our place as speakers we are showing how we must be thoughtful, i.e. willing and able to reflect upon our own speech/action, if we are truly to enjoy doing what we do; if we are to be becoming engaged in what we are doing; if we are to be displaying our social characters. We have no way of conceptualising how we could separate our work, i.e. thinking, from rewards, for we only engage in work/thought that is good for us, and as we also can conceive of no end to our work we are in a sense always on holiday. We show the good of imperfection to rest in the choice, the freedom, we offer each other through our place as intermediaries. By remembering that that which is imperfect is not all bad we make space for our thoughtful good intentions, and can continue to work in such a way as to be improving upon otherwise monstrous versions of self.

Analysis of Paragraph 9

> This version of the worrier's speech as seeing the bad also helps us see why she sees other's speech as accusation i.e. whilst her wish to see problems or what is bad does provide room for more talk, which is good, it limits talk to court talk, which is bad. It reduces dialogue to prosecution and/or defence. The worrier either submits and accepts that the invention is original, i.e. that she has witnessed a miracle; the only way presumably she would ever do this is because of lack of evidence to the contrary, or the worrier/prosecutor forces the inventor to submit and the miracle is shown to be fake. There is little or no time or space, given the limits of the court, and its version of dialogue to see the good of anything. Also, the worrier (as prosecutor) successfully produces herself as having no part in the crime. The prosecutor/worrier plays the opposite trick regarding responsibility to that of the inventor, i.e. whilst the latter invents but does not use, the former uses things (e.g. the law) but disclaims responsibility for the production of those things.

Response:

Our version of the thinker's speech as seeking to continue engaging in dialogue also helps us display why we do not choose to hear other's speech as accusation, but as friendly questioning which encourages us to think more about why we are doing what we are doing. Our desire to achieve greater understanding of what others understand as good about their actions does provide us with room for more conversation, and by refusing to limit our speech to court talk, we refuse to reduce the friendly relationship that is dialogue to a matter of prosecution and/or defence. For we speakers are working to produce thoughtful decisions about good and bad, not to produce evidence in order to support or reject a specific instance in respect of previously unquestioned but adhered to rules.

The thinker neither submits and accepts that the invention is original, nor does she reject it because it is not original, rather, through conversations with the 'inventor' she is reminded that the inventor is like herself, i.e. is also engaged in the effort of getting to think about the place of self. Our version of dialogue enables us to need no time and space for any activities other than those of conversing in such a way as to display our thoughtful social relationships, for why would we want to use our selves doing what we did not think it was good to do?

Furthermore, this paragraph reminds us that we are choosing not to produce versions of all others as worriers (cf., prosecutor as worrier, inventor as worrier etc. etc.), for our work is engaged in showing how all speakers are engaged in the activity of displaying the place of thinkers/speakers/social actors. The worrier speaks in that paragraph of the prosecutor as playing the trick of using things, e.g. the law, but not being responsible for the things, and of the inventor as producing things, but not being responsible for their uses. We, however, choose to claim responsibility both for our productions and for the uses of our productions. We are responsible for both the worrier's speech in this work and our own, and this can remind us how, whenever we read or converse, i.e. all of our thoughtful lives, we are responsible not only for the versions of ourselves that we display, but also for the versions of other that we choose to respond to. Of course this does not lead us to be overwhelmed with the effort we must make, for we remember that we are already making that effort, and always have been. Now, by thinking about how we are making it, we can choose to waste ourselves less in shallow misunderstandings.

Analysis of Paragraph 10

> The worrier needs new things/inventions to criticise in the same way that the courts need crimes. This is another way of saying why it can never get to seeing the good, or having a holiday, for it can always find plenty of its work to do.

Response:

By formulating our relationship to ourselves and other selves as one of friendship, of membership in the same community, we always have dialogue to engage in, questions to ask. But this is not criticism, for criticism, as conventionally understood, involves the invocation of criteria that we do not claim to have access to, knowledge of. Our questions display our commitment to continuing dialogue; not the unthoughtful decision to reduce ourselves to offering answers we cannot support. We are not on the look-out for crimes, and/or inventions in the manner it is suggested in that paragraph that the courts and the worrier are, but, even so we are, fortunately, never short of work to do.

Original Speaker:

> I wish I could feel optimistic about the future, i.e. about my achieving your understanding, but I lean toward pessimism for I have grave doubts about my ability to do so!

Response:

You speak as if both the optimist and the pessimist are in better situations than yourself, for you too hastily seek the security that you imagine their views of the future offer them i.e. even the pessimist need not worry for there is nothing he can do. You imagine yourself as being in a situation of greater suffering, and yet we would say that you are right neither to be an optimist, nor a pessimist, for each claims to know too much about what factually will happen, and, more importantly, about whether what will happen is good or bad. You remind us that we do not know the future, but we do know that it is not what happens that is good or bad, but how we respond, and that is why we can choose to act with thoughtful good intentions now. That is why we can affect what happens. Our security rests in the fact that we know that what happens cannot detract from our thoughtful good intentions; which is not to say we cannot make mistakes. We produce your doubts about your ability as doing you credit, and enabling you to proceed, i.e. ironically they display your ability. They enable you to raise, rather than lower, yourself, they are important, but not grave. However, we imagine that in your eyes important matters are grave, serious, and by remembering this we can move on to speak about art as we earlier intimated we would.

We imagine that you conceive of art as a reward, that is as analogous to a sweet that follows the main course, or as something to be consumed after the work of sustaining has been done, and that this leads you to view art as being dispensible i.e. able to be done without. Yet we would say that in this as in so many other matters you have the true order of man's place backwards, for does not that which needs to be sustained first have to be produced? We all engage in thoughtful art work when we are producing the versions of ourselves that then need to be sustained.

You who imagine you can sustain yourself without art, or before bothering with art have come to paint a picture of yourself as natural, and are so taken in with what you see that you forget you painted it. And then you go on to forget that you are always painting for you have come to imagine that you cannot paint at all.

You make art sound like something you can leave behind, for you tend to want to travel light, but you forget that where you decide to travel is part of your self portrait. By treating art as inessential you would reduce your travel to mindless wandering for you want to let nature make up your mind for you; you want to be blown by the wind. So here we show how if we rested with a view of the social as a topic for science we would be engaged in the reduction of ourselves to nonselves. You might have offered a version of what we are saying as nonsense without noticing that non-sense could be good if we can show how it makes room for us as truly response-able, social, thoughtful, moral actors rather than as sensible little things.

This writing is exciting and enjoyable and that is good, but we do not rest back, for we are engaged in instructing ourselves in how to paint, i.e. we take pains with ourselves to be becoming more skilful painters, for here is where we part company with the conventional notion of art. Our work is not a matter of inspiration, or natural genius, but of human effort, of human achievement. Our lack of ability to produce a perfect speech does not rest in our difference from others, but in our sameness, and this is why we are engaged in a relationship of friendship which is denied to speakers who hide behind social distance, who imagine they are, or are in the company of, accomplished artists. This is how we could earlier speak of ourselves as the same as Socrates, and can say here that you are the same as us. But of course, excitement and enjoyment must also be thought about. The former is conventionally taken as getting out of oneself e.g. being overcome with emotion or whatever, however, we produce excitement as thoughtful involvement. It is only those who rely upon a disintegrated version of the relationship between self and other selves that imagine they are drawn out of themselves when they get involved with others. As to enjoyment, we will be addressing this topic throughout the remainder of this section, but we can say that for us enjoying is not mere consumption, but taking things further, adding joy to things by deepening, by making more thoughtful.

The manner in which we imagine you separate consumption and production leaves you unable to remember how you are producing yourself, and if this view were generally adhered to it would reduce men's capacity to produce in a manner that could please only a misanthrope. But we think of selves as lovers of mankind. However, we imagine that you who hide from your response-ability, i.e. from the fact that you are a thinker, would see speech about love as very out of place here, for you cannot distinguish between pleasure and seduction. You see knowledge, for example sociology, as a means to enclose and define, i.e. as a way to fill in the gaps, rather than as a way to actively seek friendly relations, i.e. as an inquiry which opens and liberates those engaged in it. Stripped of its rhetoric we find that social science could be the seducer that would unclothe men of their finest garments, i.e. of their ability to move and improve. And yet you are perplexed, though you seek to hide this, for whilst you commend seriousness you only enjoy yourself when you are unserious.

You see art as equivalent to alcohol and accuse both of being seductive i.e. of reducing men's productive capacity, you would accuse us as well, but you are perhaps a little nervous at present. And yet there is something in your accusation if art is treated as for consumption, and for this reason we would ask you not to orient to this work in that way, for if you do you will be forgetting the unproductive, i.e. the seductive, nature of your own activity. We imagine you equate seduction with temptation, and art, because it is moving, with seduction, you want to remain unmarked by what you read, on top of it, for you imagine that seduction occurs outside work, where work is constrained, i.e. is an imposed duty. But we remember how we need not be seduced by this persuasive though enslaving notion of work. For we remember that seriousness fails to differentiate between good and bad, i.e. that a rapist could be very serious in the pursuit of his victim, but would that increase the worth of his action?

Our speech begins to irritate!! We expected as much for you can only tolerate art as long as it does not claim to have anything to say. As soon as the artist asks you to answer for yourself you imagine he is being pretentious, and we would agree with you if that artist was raising himself on a platform in such a way as to differentiate between his ability and that of his audience, but this need not be the case. Furthermore, and of greater importance, is your deep awareness that whilst you charge art with pretentiousness you refuse to recognise how your usage of alcohol to hide from ugliness is also pretentious i.e. that hiding from, or not facing up to, what you claim you know is bad is pretending.

You want to make or keep your routine, your life, tolerable and you use alcohol, acquaintances, or whatever else as a way to take the edge off your pain, you will try to slot our speech away somewhere in order to make it handleable, for your interest is in getting through unscathed. Your irritableness could surface in an attempt to listen no more, for you want to charge us with speaking dishonestly, for you imagine that we do not know what we are talking about, and this is why you distrust others, for you always feel they do not really know what they are talking about. But, you rest content with versions of others as either fools or liars, and neither instils in you any trust, or any desire to pursue a conversation. However, you could have seen those who talk about what they do not know as men, i.e. as philosophers, who take the risk of engaging in conversation, i.e. of allowing themselves to ask questions and to be asked questions. You imagine you want to have the courage to call others liars and fools, whereas we call ourselves to courageously join in the conversation in such a way that we can collaborate with other. You imagine that you need knowledge to speak e.g. you draw back from accusing other when you realise you do not yet know enough to go through with your accusation. Whereas we see those who speak, including yourself, as expressing the desire for knowledge rather than the possession of knowledge. You imagine you are either deeper than others, i.e. not as foolish, or not dishonest like others, i.e. not a liar, but it is you who are too foolish to notice how your silence is a lie. By conversing openly with others we risk having our foolishness remarked upon, but only in this way can we proceed to try to act more thoughtfully. We do not wish to allow ourselves to become settled in a foolish routine.

Original Speaker:

But you must remember that you are imagining all of this, that I am only an imaginary speaker, for it is this very tendency to reify, as you are reifying the worrier, i.e. to speak as if she is there, and is not a product of your theorising that exemplifies the worrier's error with the bad. That is, worry reifies the bad, and yet it is aware that it does not know what is good, for it imagines good is beyond it. However, it does imagine it knows, that it can see, what is bad, indeed it imagines that its lack of ability to see the good is bad! How much better if it can come to remember the good of not being able to see either the good or the bad, i.e. that this enables us to choose, to think about, talk about, what is good or bad for us. You do not know that I, the worrier, am bad, you do not even know that I am, but through your speech you are displaying how you are committing yourself to act in certain ways, and you need to remember as you continue speaking that it is your intentions that are always worthy of analysis rather than the accuracy or equivalence between your speech about an object and the object itself, for the latter is no more accessible to you than it is to me and we need not converse about it. Are you giving enough thought to your readers? Why should they be interested in your imaginings?

Response:

Thank you for the reminder, so now it is not a question of whether worry is or is not, or of whether worry is or is not bad, but of our thoughtful decisions. We can, and always do, speak about, converse about possibility, and in this manner orient our actions rather than merely submit to knowledge claims which we know claim too much. We are not engaged in pointing at, or accusing, those who worry, rather, by thinking about worry as a form of life, we are offering ourselves pointers. As to our readers, perhaps they had drifted from our thoughts, but given that we do not differentiate between ourselves and other selves in terms of access to knowledge etc., and given that we have been enjoying our engagement in this conversation we dare to say that they also will be enjoying it, for we know that they will not be consumption oriented. We know that they do not imagine that they should not enjoy what they enjoy. Worriers would worry because they did not enjoy art and they thought they should, but our readers are not worriers for they are thoughtful interlocutors who do not need to be drunk, and in this sense unserious, before they can enjoy anything. They do not need to be entertained to pass their time, for they also are engaged in our inquiry and they are well aware of the foolishness of the tragedies that always result from lack of involvement, i.e. from trying to stay out of things/conversations. There is a deep irony here for if the sociologist is one who formulates his own place as that of observer, i.e. as outside, we see that as such he can never get below the surface and his speech will necessarily remain shallow, and if listened to would play a part in the reduction of man to silence. But, of course no character in his right mind, i.e. no thoughtful interlocutor, would choose to engage in such a self destructive enterprise, and we produce our version of the sociologist as engaging in a productive dialogue with the forms of life in which, and through which, he seeks to produced more thoughtful, more social, conventions.

We want our work to encourage you to risk being moved, and to move ourselves, for we do not settle with a version of being moved as bad i.e. as being corrupted. We do not succumb to fears about expressing our feelings, for only by expressing them can we be instructed through conversations with others as to the possible society that could arise around them. And, as we have said, we do not rest with a version of other as untrustworthy. Whilst the worrier, as disintegrated man, has, through her undialectical version of thought, come to imagine that when others are involved in the movement of her feelings, her feelings are no longer hers, we are working to display how both self and other are always involved in social relationships. We do not seek separate survival but to live more thoughtfully by increasing our involvements with others.

6 Seriousness

Original Speaker:

But if one of the elements of what you were doing in the last section was alerting me to the fact that seriousness can be seductive i.e. that both good and bad can be seriously pursued isn't the very fact that you alert me to it like telling me to take it seriously? If you want me to be more than startled surely you need to produce a stronger version of serious such that the difference between serious and unserious activities can help me to choose what I do. You need to show me why 'more deeply' and 'a stronger version' are not simply other ways of saying 'more seriously' or 'a more serious version', when, as yet, you have not shown me the difference between serious and unserious.'

Response:

We think that we can be more than startled if we make the effort to think about what it is about seriousness that we could have imagined was good. Whilst you imagine you want us to become things that help you choose what to do, perhaps to reduce the choice you have i.e. to make you more like a thing, we want to be becoming able to help ourselves (including you) to choose well. And we do so by listening to our own speech in such a way as to display how we are all already always choosing. With regard to your request that we show you why 'more deeply' and 'a stronger version' are not simply other ways of saying 'more seriously' and 'a more serious version', if we replied that they could be, we would perhaps be accused of facetiousness, but that is what we do reply, for until we have conversed about how we could have used the notion of seriousness, about why you for instance chose to begin by treating 'more deeply' as 'more serious' our conversation will not progress.

To put this in another, perhaps more risky, fashion, in the last section we made reference to the fact that a rapist could pursue his victim seriously, as a way to illustrate how seriousness was not enough. And yet we used this example in the context of a section through which we came to reveal how we imagine the worried type reifies the bad, i.e. believes she can see what is bad. But we know that no thing is good or bad. That we, as social actors, think, converse about, and decide how we want to differentiate between activities, things, or whatever, in terms of good or bad. So, we could have chosen to formulate rape as good! That we do not choose to do so is not because of any goodness or badness which is inherent in rape, indeed it is not because of anything, rather it is in order to display our commitment to the sort of community we desire, the sort of characters we want to be. Forms of speech/life which rely upon reified versions of good or bad would have committed rape of a much deeper order if they could have oppressed us, as speakers, and deprived us of the profound enjoyment that speech which displays our awareness of our place as social actors provides. That is as those who do continue to collaborate in such a way as to choose how we want to live.

But, as yet, you do not appear to be sharing in this enjoyment, perhaps you will continue to collaborate with us by informing us as to how you imagine a worrier would speak about seriousness. After hearing you speak we will once again relate to, and through, your speech paragraph by paragraph.

(Note to reader: Again we choose to resort to usage of an appendix, but it occurs to us to say that the placing of these appendices in the body of the work displays how they have been, for us, an integral part of our work; how we have no desire to cut them out, or dismiss them, but seek to be deepening ourselves through our friendly relationship to them. You, being a thoughtful interlocutor no doubt choose not to orient to the speeches of others as appendices which give you pain and which are better removed. No doubt you will be orienting to others' speeches as helping you to provide for yourself the pains of conscience so necessary for thoughtful actions. We are all doing far better by not shoving those pains to the back of our minds.)

APPENDIX C

Original Speaker:

Para. 1   Perhaps a worrier conceives of a serious situation as one where worry is a reasonable response. Perhaps she perceives the situation to be serious when she has some responsibility to act in the situation which she imagines she may be perceived by herself and others to fail to fulfil. Also, the more the outcome is irreversible the more serious it appears. Thus the parents whose child dies in childbirth may for good or bad reasons tell themselves that they can try again later, or adopt, or whatever, and in this way make the outcome appear less final. Finality, then, can be treated as an important feature of seriousness. It is worth noting that the idea of finality seems to oscillate between the notion of limit as an idea of finiteness, and limitlessness, in the sense that absolutely nothing can be done, hence its irreversibility is complete rather than incomplete. This idea of finality also has a bearing upon that of responsibility, for being responsible for something serious, i.e. final, is producing something that cannot be responded to, (that is, if a response is seen to contribute to, or alter the original in some way) precisely because that which is final is that which cannot be changed. The worrier doesn't want to be serious because it would involve him in producing an outcome which he could not change. If a person is responsible for a serious situation (e.g. a motor accident) her problem is that she cannot do it again and correct her mistake, it is final, past.

Para. 2   Somehow worries have a sense of finality in that they are only replaced by other worries, in a very real sense then the worrier lives in the past, where the past is final, i.e. persists. Finishing off, or finalising now is like making something persist as it is. Finishing off is reifying, and yet the worrier treats that which is unfinished as something to worry about. The worrier treats thinking or worrying as a means to complete that which is incomplete, she sees worry as complementing and complimenting (in the sense of taking seriously) that which is dealing with i.e. worrying about. The worrier then sees treating something seriously as adding to it whereas she sees treating something unseriously as detracting from it. Her version of work then is such that she sees taking other seriously as meaning that other cannot give, for to accept from other would be to take away from other which is to treat other unseriously.

Para. 3   Now I'm thinking that this talk about finality is a way of passing the time, and nothing more, i.e. I am not too sure how it helps except that it is saying something. Now I am thinking that it is this paragraph that is a way of passing the time, and I am unsure what it would be not to be merely passing the time! This though is providing another way on for perhaps being serious is doing more than merely passing the time i.e. merely passing the time is being unserious e.g. chatter, jokes, greetings, all of these are ways of getting through i.e. rather like ways of avoiding awkwardness or embarrassment. Here then we can begin to see that the serious and the unserious are not opposites, rather, whilst the unserious doesn't do any more than merely pass the time, somehow the serious is seen as doing more. The unserious merely passes the time in the sense that it has no impact upon it, i.e. it leaves things as they were, whereas the serious has an impact i.e. the serious needs to be recognised. The serious then, like an impact is something you have to face up to i.e. it cannot, or should not be avoided. The worrier by taking everything seriously sees herself as being stoned, in the tough sense, and only acts in such a way as to avoid impacts. She takes the proverb that people who live in glass houses shouldn't throw stones too much to heart, and sees all others as being those at whom the proverb points. She sees herself as also living in a glass house but not as throwing stones. She treats others then as dopes who fail to see the foolishness of their ways, and she foolishly thinks she can differentiate herself from them by having no ways.

Para. 4   Ways here are analogous to methods or routes, and this raises another aspect of the serious, i.e. a serious person is methodical where method is following rules, this is necessary if all you require of yourself is that you do not make mistakes. By treating the serious as the methodical we can do a disservice to the former and too great a service to the latter. For one result of this is that the unserious comes to mean haphazard, chance or randomness, and this does resonate with comedy, and yet isn't this to reduce seriousness to monotony and comedy to slapstick? Whereas, by treating the methodical as serious, we fail to see the haphazard, chance or random nature of methods. The worrier wants to feel secure, i.e. to have a method, but in some way wants this method to be a miracle i.e. not to be haphazard, chance or random. Being unserious, unmethodical comes to mean to the worrier acting in contempt, i.e. randomness comes to be seen as movement, i.e. lack of method, and is seen to be the result of a failure to resist temptation. Being unserious could then lead to a charge of disorderly conduct.

Para. 5   The point about orderly conduct, or serious conduct, is then that you know what will happen, and this comes to be one step worse than the worrier, for whereas the worrier lives in the past i.e. treats the present like history, the serious dope wants rules to be followed so that the future is known in the same way as he thinks he knows the past. The serious dope thinks whatever will be will be, in this way he is totally fatalistic and this is why he doesn't worry. But the worrier somehow wants fate, chance to intervene on her behalf. It is not then simply that the serious dope trusts everybody, and the worrier doesn't trust anybody, rather it is that the serious dope doesn't need trust. Now the worrier doesn't trust anybody, and that is why she needs fate to intervene on her behalf, and the 'reason' she doesn't trust others is because she thinks you could only trust perfection. Somehow she needs to remember that we can trust ourselves to do our best, and that this trust need not be seen as misplaced if success is not achieved. Whereas the naive person has a misplaced trust in himself i.e. he thinks he knows he will succeed, the worrier has a naive version of trust as a complete guarantee, when she sees that guarantees cannot, or have not been given she sees this as providing room for worry. She treats trust as an end or reward for work and as a result cannot work, for trust is an ingredient of beginning to work. The worrier's version of trust as a guarantee of success is closely related to the manipulator's view that you can only trust that which you can control, the manipulator's version of trust is trussed up, tied up, only able to submit. Questioning is one tool the manipulator can use to force submission, answering becomes answering to. However, whilst the worrier questions her ability to answer she fails to question other's, i.e. the manipulator's, right to ask, in this way she is submissive. The worrier adopts the manipulator's version of questioning as forcing submission but applies it more rigorously i.e. she includes herself and her own ends as well, in this way we might wish to say that the worrier is more serious than the manipulator. Both the manipulator's and the worrier's versions of trust involve treating others as means i.e. as tools, and a trustworthy tool is one which does the job you use it for well, i.e. it does not break down, is not faulty. The difference between the manipulator and the worrier is that the latter applies this version of others also to herself and the result is that because she treats herself as a tool she needs to be submissive and told what to do. She treats her failure to do what she is told (i.e. to submit) as a further fault.

Para. 6   The idea of submission here brings out the forceful nature of the serious as that which has an impact, and reminds us that the serious is unlike the unserious in being something which can instil fear. The absent minded professor appears as an example of someone with no fears i.e. he doesn't care above survival, caring about survival can mean then being present rather than absent. For the absent minded professor time simply passes, nothing seems to have any impact upon him, at least nothing other than that which totally absorbs him, whatever that might be. Perhaps though the worrier is much closer to the absent minded professor than it originally appears, i.e. she is absorbed by her worries and recognises little else, or better, her worries involve her in trying to recognise absolutely everything. The difference between the absent minded professor, the worrier, and Socrates, could then be one of subject matter i.e. of what matters to them, or how things come to matter for them. Somehow the absent minded professor seems to me to be a pretender (I don't trust him) so I'll forget him; the worrier and Socrates seem to differ greatly on their versions of the serious, for the worrier what matters is that which is causing trouble i.e. the bad, evil, whereas the only concern to be treated seriously by Socrates is the pursuit, in an active, productive sense, of the good.

Para. 7   The worrier sees taking something seriously as trusting, yet she seems to equate trust with knowledge, or to see knowledge as a prerequisite for trust. She thinks that being truthful (i.e. trustworthy) involves knowing whilst at the same time she feels/knows that both others and herself do not know. The result of her confusion is that she sees taking other seriously as being a slip into laziness i.e. as being seduced. An example of this would be how she is unable to feel pleased or glad about another's acceptance of her work for more than a few moments, before she starts to worry again about whether she is right to allow her own opinion of her own work to be changed so easily.

Para. 8   For the worrier then, unserious becomes untruthful and she equates untruthful with dishonest, at the same time she sees the unserious as something you need not be afraid of, i.e. as something you can enjoy. We can see how in this way she comes to see enjoyment as bad.

Para. 9   Somehow now we must see whether worry could be serious, i.e. whether worry could have an impact, which would be like saying that it wasn't merely a failure to do, as it did do something. The point here is that if worry has no impact it is unserious given this version of serious as having an impact. This sounds odd now though, for, having an impact really does sound like a worrier's negativistic version of action i.e. it has no sense of direction or progress/purpose. This suggests then that the versions of serious i.e. re having an impact and being final are still too shallow, in the sense that talk of stopping and starting only really make sense in the context of a recognised direction. Indeed being too shallow is like coming to an end too quickly. Being serious still then means to the worrier something bad, also being unserious means something bad to the worrier, in this way the worrier shows us that her versions of serious and unserious activity still fail to provide any help in her choosing of what to do. The point here is that her version of herself as a tool requires her to deny her ability to choose, and given this denunciation she does need help about what to choose. She needs to be reminded that in seeing the bad she is in a way exercising her choice.

Para.10 Somehow on rereading what I have said it seems to me that the shallowness of this version of seriousness needs to be emphasised for it does seem as if whilst it does tell us more about the worrier, it still falls far short of telling us anything about a strong version of seriousness. Somehow this speech in spite of its remarks on finishing off as reifying still looks like fishing or searching for something complete, i.e. a good version of seriousness. Somehow the idea of fishing whether methodically or not seems lazy, whereas being serious seems to involve something much more like effort or work, even if because of the seductive nature of the serious it is bad work. It seems now that something which is serious is something which is unfinished i.e. something that required work more like the future than the past. The worrier would then be right to see the unfinished nature of things but wrong to see this as being a fault, at least as a fault of the things, for she must see her own responsibility for what she produces before she can see choosing as an activity she can take part in.

RESPONSE TO APPENDIX C

Your speech on this issue puts us in a whirl, and by doing so encourages us to deepen our understanding of the usage of the notion of seriousness, and enables us to proceed by raising questions about the grounds of our speech. One way we read our analysis here would be to orient to each response as a continuation of each of your paragraphs. The continuations or responses display how issues surface for us through your speech which would not have done so had we heard it as complete i.e. if it had been heard as complete that hearing would have covered over its grounds. The multiplicity and profundity of the issues you have helped raise for us in such a short space display the virtue of inquiry, but also display why we choose to continue working with increasing vigour to be continually remoulding our forms of speech/life.

Of course each paragraph we write will also require deepening, but that is why we continue to write, to speak to, and with, each other. Our intention is not to speak as if from a platform which would prevent us from hearing others' questions, but to speak in such a way that others choose to question, and,, by doing so, desire with us to be engaged in the deepening of our community through continuing questioning.

Analysis of Paragraph 1

 Perhaps a worrier conceives of a serious situation as one where worry is a reasonable response. Perhaps she perceives the situation to be serious when she has some responsibility to act in the situation which she imagines she may be perceived by herself and others to fail to fulfil. Also, the more the outcome is irreversible the more serious it appears. Thus the parents whose child dies in childbirth may for good or bad reasons tell themselves that they can try again later, or adopt, or whatever, and in this way make the outcome appear less final. Finality, then, can be treated as an important feature of seriousness. It is worth noting that the idea of finality seems to oscillate between the notion of limit as an idea of finiteness, and limitlessness, in the sense that absolutely nothing can be done, hence its irreversibility is complete rather than incomplete. This idea of finality also has a bearing upon that of responsibility, for being responsible for something serious, i.e. final, is producing something that cannot be responded to, (that is, if a response is seen to contribute to, or alter the original in some way) precisely because that which is final is that which cannot be changed. The worrier doesn't want to be serious because it would involve him in producing an outcome which he could not change. If a person is responsible for a serious situation (e.g. a motor accident) her problem is that she cannot do it again and correct her mistake, it is final, past.

Response:

You remind us that situations are conceived, and then responded to, and that we choose to conceive all situations in such a way that we continue responding thoughtfully. When we theorise we uncover the response-ability we have to act in a thoughtful manner, we direct our attention towards the difference between a thoughtless response and a more thoughtful response, rather than upon the difference between what we cannot even arrive at, i.e. think of, i.e. some perfect response beyond even our fantasies, and what we imagine we could most easily do. Also, by directing our attention towards our own intentions, our own responses, we remember that our responses are never irreversible, i.e. we can always change our mind for the better, we can always contradict our previous talk. Furthermore, the instance you provide of the parents' response to the child's death in childbirth reveals how you overcome a preoccupation with issues of life and death by bringing to the forefront the issue which is worth conversing about, i.e. how to respond to tragedy, or how to decide to lead a good life. By focusing upon what they could do they do not merely 'appear' to make that less final, they do make it less final.

But what of this issue of finality, which you quite rightly raise? Perhaps it reveals the extremism of a form of speech which tries to be all or nothing, for neither of these are human possibilities. Indeed the notion of 'perhaps' itself reveals speech which allows itself to be trapped between unacceptable extremes rather than finding a way to moderate its extremism. So if we had formulated the preoccupation with life and death as being pre-occupation, i.e. that which precedes work and had denounced pre-occupation as being in opposition to work we would have been engaged in the same type of extremism. But if we formulate a pre-occupation as that which calls for work we release ourselves.

If it could, worry would subject those it tries to subject by reducing them to oscillating between the fantasy of doing everything, perhaps preparing for anything that might happen, and the fantasy that nothing can be done i.e. that everything is beyond those it subjects. These twin fantasies would have restricted the worrier to a love/hate relationship to death, but by doing so would deny her everything other than a fantasy life. We are saying that we formulate the thinker's life, the human life, as intermediate, as always doing something, i.e. as the active thoughtful effort to seek through friendship to live our specifically social condition. Human actions are profound as they are the effort to achieve a just society, and are not centred upon the actors continuing personal survival at any cost.

It is said in this paragraph that the worrier does not wish to be responsible for something final because the final cannot be responded to, but we, by being thinkers, i.e. those that always respond can have no final products, nothing is final for us, we always have more to do. We want to be thoughtfully producing, i.e. to be involved, for if we were not we would be unchanging, we would have become outcomes rather than continuing to be continually coming out. We would rather have said that accidents are what selves were not responsible for, but that selves can learn from accidents. So we would hear you as saying that that motorist could do it again if she refused to think about what occurred, if she refused to learn through her formulation of her past, i.e. if she refused to allow her past to befriend her. Our problem is not that of making mistakes like Skinnerian rats, but of reaching decisions about how we choose to live, and that is a good problem to continue to have.

Analysis of Paragraph 2

Somehow worries have a sense of finality in that they are only replaced by other worries, in a very real sense then the worrier lives in the past, where the past is final, i.e. persists. Finishing off, or finalising now is like making something persist as it is. Finishing off is reifying, and yet the worrier treats that which is unfinished as something to worry about. The worrier treats thinking or worrying as a means to complete that which is incomplete, she sees worry as complementing and complimenting (in the sense of taking seriously) that which she is dealing with i.e. worrying about. The worrier then sees treating something seriously as adding to it whereas she sees treating something unseriously as detracting from it. Her version of work then is such that she sees taking other seriously as meaning that other cannot give, for to accept from other would be to take away from other which is to treat other unseriously.

Response

This paragraph reminds us how worry is not a human possibility, for as thinkers, humans live very much in the present, and by formulating the present as unfinished and as always unfinished we do not give ourselves something to worry about, but actions to do. Perhaps we would have something to worry about if we ever finished something off, but that is beyond the limits of thought, and is not worthy of, or accessible to our thought. We consider thoughtful actions as those which display the incompleteness of that which might erroneously have been taken as complete. So our work compliments that about which it speaks by displaying how the speech it topicalises is deeper than it would have appeared if it had been read as feigning completion. We are instructed by unfinishedness for it allows us to continue engaging in worthwhile conversations, and we display the possibility of improvement through them. We do not come to the worrier as Father Christmas comes to the child, nor are we simply waiting for a Father Christmas, e.g. a good theory, rather we engage in friendly conversations now.

Analysis of Paragraph 3

Now I'm thinking that this talk about finality is a way of passing the time, and nothing more, i.e. I am not too sure how it helps except that it is saying something. Now I am thinking that it is this paragraph that is a way of passing the time, and I am unsure what it would be not to be merely passing the time! This though is providing another way on for perhaps being serious is doing more than merely passing the time i.e. merely passing the time is being unserious e.g. chatter, jokes, greetings, all of these are ways of getting through i.e. rather like ways of avoiding awkwardness or embarrassment. Here then we can begin to see that the serious and the unserious are not opposites, rather, whilst the unserious doesn't do any more than merely pass the time, somehow the serious is seen as doing more. The unserious merely passes the time in the sense that it has no impact upon it, i.e. it leaves things as they were, whereas the serious has an impact i.e. the serious needs to be recognised. The serious then, like an impact is something you have to face up to i.e. it cannot, or should not be avoided. The worrier by taking everything seriously sees herself as being stoned, in the tough sense, and only acts in such a way as to avoid impacts. She takes the proverb that people who live in glass houses shouldn't throw stones too much to heart, and sees all others as being those at whom the proverb points. She sees herself as also living in a glass house but not as throwing stones. She treats others then as dopes who fail to see the foolishness of their ways, and she foolishly thinks she can differentiate herself from them by having no ways.

Response:

You say that speaking about finality is a way of passing the time, and we think you are on to something here, but that you could have taken your discussion further by saying what you think would be not merely passing the time. Whilst you try to still your unsureness by proposing that being serious is doing more than passing the time, we can now, through our reading of your speech, display how being serious is merely passing the time if it reveals an overwhelming interest in finality and/or survival, for we would say, and do say, that what you speak of as unserious, i.e. chatter, jokes and greetings all have a better conception of social relations than does seriousness as you formulate it. At least chatter, jokes and greetings have some relation to others, and furthermore all relate to others in a friendly manner, though we would want to deepen their notions of friendship. At least they have some conception of their need of a relationship with other. The serious type seems limited to a tragically isolated life i.e. a dead life. Your reference to chatter, jokes and greetings as ways of getting through could have been a beginning, but instead of showing the good of getting through and how it can be deepened you choose to speak of getting through as avoiding awkwardness and embarrassment. Yet we, writers and readers, know that it is only through awkwardness and embarrassment that we learn deep lessons. We do not seek to avoid embarrassment but to be embarrassed so as we can remember all the better how to truly embrace.

We say that you want to see the serious as doing more than passing the time because you want to compare yourself with those that chatter, joke and greet, in such a way that you imagine you are superior, but as we are showing your unthoughtful commitment to seriousness leaves you without friends for you imagine that nobody other than yourself is worth talking to. You say that the

116

serious needs to be recognised, but you never cease to be amazed at the fact that you are not recognised, that your speech though it may have a momentary impact leaves others unmoved.

We choose not to recognise the serious but to think about it. If the serious were formulated as an impact we would be forced to face up to it for we could not avoid it, but what we are showing is how the deeply serious issues for men and women are those they need to choose voluntarily, those they can turn their backs upon. More deeply, that whatever we do we do voluntarily. We take every speaker seriously, but we do not take things, for instance words, seriously. By taking speakers seriously we respect them and do not differentiate between what we require of others and of ourselves. By not differentiating between selves in the manner you imagine the worrier does, we can be becoming less foolish, i.e. the worrier in your speech does not see the dopiness of not speaking to others. She does not see that she invites the stoning by her refusal to converse, which she rationalises as passivity, i.e. by her refusal to engage in neighbourly, friendly relations. But we who are writing, and speaking about the human place, i.e. all of us, engage in conversations that reveal our own foolishness rather than pointing at the foolishness of others. But we are not revelling in this foolishness we are seeking, as our inquiry displays, to continue doing something about it.

Analysis of Paragraph 4

Ways here are analogous to methods or routes, and this raises another aspect of the serious, i.e. a serious person is methodical where method is following rules, this is necessary if all you require of yourself is that you do not make mistakes. By treating the serious as the methodical we can do a disservice to the former and too great a service to the latter. For one result of this is that the unserious comes to mean haphazard, chance or randomness, and this does resonate with comedy, and yet isn't this to reduce seriousness to monotony and comedy to slapstick? Whereas, by treating the methodical as serious, we fail to see the haphazard, chance or random nature of methods. The worrier wants to feel secure, i.e. to have a method, but in some way wants this method to be a miracle i.e. not to be haphazard, chance or random. Being unserious, unmethodical comes to mean to the worrier acting in contempt, i.e. randomness comes to be seen as movement, i.e. lack of method, and is seen to be the result of a failure to resist temptation. Being unserious could then lead to a charge of disorderly conduct.

Response:

Unlike your hypothetical worrier we do not seek to differentiate our selves from other selves, i.e. to be showing one way to be better than another, for we do not rest with shallow comparisons for we seek companions. It is not that we have no method and others have methods rather it is that our method is not the following of rules, but the ongoing production of our rules. To orient to rules as something to follow, rather than as something to think about, question, decide upon, would have been to deny our dialectical characters. But the thinker in seeking the truth i.e. in seeking to act more thoughtfully, is not limited by any terror of being found wanting, i.e. of being found to have made mistakes, for mistakes are inevitable in any genuine inquiry. To rely upon a method in order to avoid being seen to make a mistake is to display mere survival orientation, and it shows the slapstick nature of tragedy if tragedy is oriented to as merely recounting the body's mortal nature, rather than as displaying how we, as thinkers, raise ourselves above this morbidity and through continued consideration of the possibility of good lives, good society, are producing enjoyable thoughtful lives and are contributing to our ongoing dialogue.

Whilst your imaginary worrier seeks the security of a miraculous method we come out against that search for security as the good, for we remember how secure prisons can be. Our security is social, it is friendship and it is displayed through our search, our inquiry, for we know that thoughtful interlocutors are joined with us in opposing and deepening forms of speech that reduce choice to randomness/chance only then to outlaw and legislate against choice as unmethodical. We are, and continue to be disorderly if order is imposition i.e. if it reduces lives to taking exercise in a prison yard, for who would acquiesce to those orders!

Analysis of Paragraph 5

The point about orderly conduct, or serious conduct, is then that you know what will happen, and this comes to be one step worse than the worrier, for whereas the worrier lives in the past i.e. treats the present like history, the serious dope wants rules to be followed so that the future is known in the same way as he thinks he knows the past. The serious dope thinks whatever will be will be, in this way he is totally fatalistic and this is why he doesn't worry. But the worrier somehow wants fate, chance to intervene on her behalf. It is not then simply that the serious dope trusts everybody, and the worrier doesn't trust anybody, rather it is that the serious dope doesn't need trust. Now the worrier doesn't trust anybody, and that is why she needs fate to intervene on her behalf, and the 'reason' she doesn't trust others is because she thinks you could only trust perfection. Somehow she needs to remember that we can trust ourselves to do our best, and that this trust need not be seen as misplaced if success is not achieved. Whereas the naive person has a misplaced trust in himself i.e. he thinks he knows he will succeed, the worrier has a naive version of trust as a complete guarantee, when she sees that guarantees cannot, or have not been given she sees this as providing room for worry. She treats trust as an end or reward for work and as a result cannot work, for trust is an ingredient of beginning to work. The worrier's version of trust as a guarantee of success is closely related to the manipulator's view that you can only trust that which you can control, the manipulator's version of trust is trussed up, tied up, only able to submit. Questioning is one tool the manipulator can use to force submission, answering becomes answering to. However, whilst the worrier questions her ability to answer she fails to question other's, i.e. the manipulator's, right to ask, in this way she is submissive. The worrier adopts the manipulator's version of questioning as forcing submission but applies it more rigorously i.e. she includes herself and her own ends as well, in this way we might wish to say that the worrier is more serious than the manipulator. Both the manipulator's and the worrier's versions of trust involve treating others as means i.e. as tools, and a trustworthy tool is one which does the job you use it for well, i.e. it does not break down, is not faulty. The difference between the manipulator and the worrier is that the latter applies this version of others also to herself and the result is that because she treats herself as a tool she needs to be submissive and told what to do. She treats her failure to do what she is told (i.e. to submit) as a further fault.

Response:

As an aside we would say that speeches which refer to 'the point of', 'the point about' etc. are lazy for they conceive of themselves as having reached a conclusion, and one worth speaking of at that, i.e. they orient to finishes rather than to continuing. Your differentiation between the worrier and the serious dope is interesting, and it reveals the depths to which a continuing emphasis on comparison as a means to raise one's person can extend. Your discussion of the worrier's orientation to trust helps us a great deal, and helps us to console ourselves in our writing for it reminds us that we do not orient to success/finish and consequently cannot fail, for that orientation would have displayed the excesses of a survival orientation rather than the desire to continue working, collaborating together. We are able to differentiate ourselves from naivety which would have a misplaced trust in that it not only orients to success but also imagines it will succeed. Furthermore, we commend that the good of not being given the guarantees by others that you say the worrier seeks, and is distressed at not receiving, crystallises in the freedom of choice/action we draw out of this relation.

We trust our friends and do not have to treat them as tools which we can control, or need to control, indeed we want our friends to be uncontrollable, for tools, i.e. as controllable, can be used by anyone, and in this sense cannot be trusted. We treat our refusal to do as we are told if being told is being controlled, not as a sign of weakness but of strength. For those, if any, who do what they are told merely because they are told would be reducing themselves to the status of being tools. However, the notion of tool is not totally out of place, for man's place as a thinker, as a committed actor necessitates that he/she offers his/her person in the service of his/her commitment. We choose to use our persons in our search to be producing better notions of self and society.

But by now you our reader will be waiting for us to address an issue of great importance which surfaces through that paragraph. We refer of course to the section on 'questioning'. Here is where the hypothetical worrier's shallowness, as disintegrated man, is clearly visible, for by resting with apparent differences between self and other selves she refuses to hear how questions are not ways to differentiate but ways to display our sameness. Whilst the worrier produces a version of questions as tools of manipulation and then seeks both to avoid being questioned, and also seeks to avoid asking others questions, we seek to continue raising ourselves and other selves above unthoughtful distinctions through and by our questioning. Our commitment to continued questioning,, to continuing inquiry, i.e. to dialogue/speech is the antithesis of the hypothetical worrier's commitment to a version of questions as forcing submission. Questions do not force for they are liberating, i.e. they liberate those who hear them who could otherwise remain imprisoned by unthoughtful, and in that sense indefensible modes of speech.

Analysis of Paragraph 6

The idea of submission here brings out the forceful nature of the serious as that which has an impact, and reminds us that the serious is unlike the unserious in being something which can instil fear. The absent minded professor appears as an example of someone with no fears i.e. he doesn't care above survival, caring about survival can mean then being present rather than absent. For the absent minded professor time simply passes, nothing seems to have any impact upon him, at least nothing other than that which totally absorbs him, whatever that might be. Perhaps though the worrier is much closer to the absent minded professor than it originally appears, i.e. she is absorbed by her worries and recognises little else, or better, her worries involve her in trying to recognise absolutely everything. The difference between the absent minded professor, the worrier, and Socrates, could then be one of subject matter i.e. of what matters to them, or how things come to matter for them. Somehow the absent minded professor seems to me to be a pretender (I don't trust him) so I'll forget him; the worrier and Socrates seem to differ greatly on their versions of the serious, for the worrier what matters is that which is causing trouble i.e. the bad, evil, whereas the only concern to be treated seriously by Socrates is the pursuit, in an active, productive sense, of the good.

Response:

We are reminded by this paragraph that if we had chosen to formulate the serious as having a forceful nature, i.e. as instilling fear, we would not also think of our activity as serious, for we are concerned to produce social action as liberating i.e. as that which frees actors from the force of thoughtlessness by facing up to fears. So where you speak of caring about survival as indicating presence we would have said that it was careless, for that interest absents those it engages from the truly social, hence careful, activity of friendly collaborative inquiry. The absent minded professor might or might not be a good friend but the hypothetical worrier whose sole interest is in her own survival needs to do a great deal of thinking if she is to act in a friendly manner.

Where your speech chose to concentrate on differences between those characters we would rather have concentrated on what they share, and upon what we share with them, and you, i.e. upon our place as thinkers/speakers and the potential that accrues from it. You would do well to notice what the speech you were using allowed you to do with the absent minded professor, i.e. the one you do not trust! This could indicate the terrifying answer to our earlier question about what the worrier would do with inventors (cf., p101), i.e. about what you would do with those you could not trust, i.e. ultimately with all if you continue to resist questions. We choose not to forget any in our actions by orienting to that which speakers share. Your hypothetical worrier could have been absorbed by her fears and have become deformed by them, and yet we choose not to dismiss her, as she might us, but to trouble her to trouble her person. Where she seeks to be free of troubles, for she sees troubles to be the result of evil, we, like Socrates, trouble ourselves and other selves to think about what we do. For whilst we cannot get beyond good and evil i.e. whilst we always have to trouble ourselves, i.e. to remain uneasy, we know that good characters are not products of nature but of continuing trouble and effort. Whilst your hypothetical worrier is permanently pained by her failures to get beyond her worries, we can console ourselves by remembering our unnatural efforts, the troubles we go to, to act more thoughtfully. By not going to the trouble of actively pursuing the good because she cannot see it, the hypothetical worrier is forever closely pursued by her worries, for she fears the bad whether she can see it or not. The worrier thinks she is naturally good and ought not to be troubled by evil, yet we remember that good only arises in the effort to combat bad, and that is a situation peculiar to man's place, i.e. he/she is a thinker and would not reduce him/her self to the natural for to do so would be to brutalise him/her self, and no speaker would, or could choose that option without engaging in self destruction.

Analysis of Paragraphs 7 and 8

The worrier sees taking something seriously as trusting, yet she seems to equate trust with knowledge, or to see knowledge as a prerequisite for trust. She thinks that being truthful (i.e. trustworthy) involves knowing whilst at the same time she feels/knows that both others and herself do not know. The result of her confusion is that she sees taking other seriously as being a slip into laziness i.e. as being seduced. An example of this would be how she is unable to feel pleased or glad about another's acceptance of her work for more than a few moments, before she starts to worry again about whether she is right to allow her own opinion of her own work to be changed so easily.

For the worrier then, unserious becomes untruthful and she equates untruthful with dishonest, at the same time she sees the unserious as something you need not be afraid of, i.e. as something you can enjoy. We can see how in this way she comes to see enjoyment as bad.

Response

With the help of your speech we achieve a version of trusting others such that we do not equate trust with knowledge, or see knowledge as a prerequisite for trust, for why should we? Rather we think of the trustworthy as those characters who continue to question, i.e. who refuse to be corrupted by apparently forceful conventional usage, i.e. as the characters who through their consciousness of their own ignorance about matters of good and evil come to desire knowledge and to make thoughtful decisions in the light of this desire. We think of trustworthy characters as honest characters and by doing so are better able to raise ourselves above the seductions of the 'knowledgeable'.

As to your 'example, we do not choose to measure our opinion of our work upon such arbitrary scales as acceptance or non acceptance by other for that is too contingent upon other. Rather we do what we think is for the good and trust other to engage in a dialogue with us and to provide arguments which progress beyond our speech and can instruct us. We have no desire to resist arguments, questions, i.e. to defend our speech as if it was complete. We do not want to be accepted as we are but to be engaging in relationships that call for, and display our continuing willingness and ability to be deepened, and in this way to become dependable. So, we do not set out with a low opinion of our work in the hope that other will be impressed by it, for that would be to have a low opinion of other. Rather we do as best we can, and through our doing make the effort to achieve a conversation that can be instructive, that does extend ourselves.

The deeper, i.e. the more profound, the better, i.e. the more enjoyable, for thinkers/speakers in their search display their desire to move, to be becoming less superficial, and to be better able to hear the depths of others' speeches. For where the thinker seeks the truth the worrier imagines that escaping the truth provides a temporary expedient. The worrier, who imagines she is pursued by what she fears, cannot rest, she fights off fatigue so as to keep her guard up, so as to keep safe. Whereas the thinker who is in pursuit of the good is always at rest for he knows that he has nothing to fear i.e. that he need not fear what might happen to him for he knows that only his intentions matter. The hypothetical worrier fears that she herself is dishonest, for she equates honesty with truthfulness and is aware that she is not full of the truth, but the thinker by thinking of the honest man not as one who is full of the truth, but as a character who seeks the truth, need not hide himself, but can expose himself as a character who shares with others the profound place of the social actor. That is the place of a character who enjoys acting with integrity, i.e. who enjoys overcoming, rather than being overcome by, his fears, who risks openness rather than opting for a life behind bars wrought out of thoughtless fears of what might happen.

Analysis of Paragraph 9

Somehow now we must see whether worry could be serious, i.e. whether worry could have an impact, which would be like saying that it wasn't merely a failure to do, as it did do something. The point here is that if worry has no impact it is unserious given this version of serious as having an impact. This sounds odd now though, for, having an impact really does sound like a worrier's negativistic version of action i.e. it has no sense of direction or progress/purpose. This suggests then that the versions of serious i.e. re having an impact and being final are still too shallow, in the sense that talk of stopping and starting only really make sense in the context of a recognised direction. Indeed being too shallow is like coming to an end too quickly. Being serious still then means to the worrier something bad, also being unserious means something bad to the worrier, in this way the worrier shows us that her versions of serious and unserious activity still fail to provide any help in her choosing of what to do. The point here is that her version of herself as a tool requires her to deny her ability to choose, and given this denunciation she does need help about what to choose. She needs to be reminded that in seeing the bad she is in a way exercising her choice.

Response:

Through this paragraph you help us to remember that we would not allow the worrier's version of the serious to have an impact upon us as you appear to have done, i.e. we would not orient to it as given, but would seek to recognise our part in its production. Your speech reveals that you forget that it is you who are doing, you say 'Somehow now ...' as if the work which preceded this paragraph was description that does not call for questions about how it is arrived at. We also think of an impact as having no sense of direction; and we think that worry stops speakers rather than starts them, for it imagines others have been seduced into going where they are going. The worrier wants to remain where she is and if possible to keep others with her. She seeks a direction she can recognise, where we seek not to recognise our direction, but to produce it, i.e. we want to collaborate, converse, and choose where we go not to be told where to go. We want to start talking together not to stop each other, but to seek signposts is to seek to be sheep and that is shallow. We collaborate and take responsibility for producing our direction out of directionlessness, the myth of rebirth. Where the worrier denies her ability to choose because she imagines she needs knowledge before she can choose, we display how by not knowing, and knowing we cannot know, we provide ourselves with room to collaborate and choose. It is through our willingness and ability to choose that we help ourselves and we do not need the sort of help to choose that would reduce our freeedom. And yet the worrier's denunciation is an achievement for it reveals the desire for social relationships by rejecting the notion of disintegrated man as a human possibility, for choice involves thought and thought involves social relationships. However, we do not seek to remind others, but at most through our actions to encourage others to remind themselves, for we remember that we cannot be given more liberating relationships with our thought/speech by others, but have to be achieving them ourselves. The worrier's denunciation lacks passion, desire, for it asks too much of other and too little of its self. Thoughtful others would not offer her the help she imagines she wants, for they are aware that that help would be no help at all.

Analysis of Paragraph 10

Somehow on rereading what I have said it seems to me that the shallowness of this version of seriousness needs to be emphasised for it does seem as if whilst it does tell us more about the worrier, it still falls far short of telling us anything about a strong version of seriousness. Somehow this speech in spite of its remarks on finishing off as reifying still looks like fishing or searching for something complete, i.e. a good version of seriousness. Somehow the idea of fishing whether methodically or not seems lazy, whereas being serious seems to involve something much more like effort or work, even if because of the seductive nature of the serious it is bad work. It seems now that something which is serious is something which is unfinished i.e. something that required work more like the future than the past. The worrier would then be right to see the unfinished nature of things but wrong to see this as being a fault, at least as a fault of the things, for she must see her own responsibility for what she produces before she can see choosing as an activity she can take part in.

Response:

Here your speech reminds us of the weakness of our prior notion of caricature, for we have not merely been emphasising shallowness, for we have been raising and emphasising in our responses the good of human possibility, i.e. our speech no doubt does fall short, but we would say that not falling short, i.e. being perfect, is not a human possibility, and would not enhance our human character. We would emphasise that the good of falling short is that at least it has over come the fear of starting, and once started, i.e. once we do expose ourselves, we can begin to engage in instructive dialogue.

We are not fishing or searching for something complete, but are engaged in unending inquiry which requires commitment for its own sake and not for future rewards or approval. We would rather have said that things may or may not be finished, but that thinking/speaking, i.e. our ability to respond thoughtfully, never is, and that we are all the better for that. Your speech helps us remember that we would not treat our own or others' speeches as finished objects and then look for their faults, but that we allow our relationship to others' speeches to waken us up to our own limitations and to continue working to overcome them. However, whilst you speak of working as being better than laziness even if it is bad work, we would opt for enjoyment, and by doing so realise that our work is good for ourselves and other selves, and in this sense is profitable.

7 Thought, speech and self

Original Speaker:

> But aren't you afraid of making a fool of yourself? I imagine you must be as I think of those who aren't afraid as being fools.

Response:

But you seem to speak as if foolishness is something men degenerate into, or fall into accidentally, as if it is a pitfall rather than something we all begin in.

Original Speaker:

> But there, you see how easy it is! I made a fool of myself as soon as I opened my mouth. I wish I thought more before I spoke/acted, and I have a feeling that if I was left to myself to think I would not be diverted and could then speak less foolishly!

Response:

Now this is interesting for you do speak and act as if you always want to think before you speak or act, but what you seem to be forgetting is that our speech is involved in our thoughts. We cannot think before we speak for our thought is speech. However, where you speak of opening your mouth as making a fool of yourself, i.e. where you commend silence, we propose that by opening our mouths, and our ears, we can converse in such a way as to make our actions more thoughtful. In your forgetfulness you come to imagine that you could remove bias/distortion by removing other, rather than, as when bias is conventionally understood, by removing your self. But we say that it is only through conversations with others that we can come to better understand how our thoughts could have been constrained, but are being liberated by our modes of speech. We would not seek to separate ourselves from other selves as you appear to do, for we imagine that by doing so we could never be becoming less foolish.

We imagine that you are afraid of appearing foolish for you fear it will lead to you being dismissed, for you produce other as an icon of yourself and anticipate that he will dismiss the unserious, i.e. the fool as being dispensible. Yet we have been reminded through Section 6 that we would not dismiss the unserious but try to deepen it.

Original Speaker

> But I would like to be able to speak in such a way as to show you that I can meet your demands. I would like to produce a finished article for I imagine it is lack of finish that makes room for rejection. I seek through my work/speech to display that I am competent, i.e. not foolish, and I would like to be remembered for the finished article I produce, I guess that is how I'd like to leave my mark.

Response:

Still you appear too ready to distinguish between self and other, for why treat our speech as demanding? Why subordinate yourself to it as if to an employer? By doing so you come to conceive of work as forced labour where we as thinkers/social actors see our work as the collaborative effort of freeing ourselves from the force of thoughtlessness. You treat your hearing of our speech as a finished article and by doing so you become engaged in an effort to compete with us, to free yourself from what you imagine encages you, i.e. our questions. But we are not interested in a competition with you, for that would be foolish. Your speech could be seen as revealing an effort to dispense with companionship in favour of differentiation, but we are seeking to display how that 'commitment' would have involved us in remaining superficial. You want your finished product to set you aside as special, perhaps as that which cannot be marked. You want to be left alone where we as thinkers/speakers remind ourselves that we want and need to be with others, with other thoughtful interlocutors, for we see your wish to have nothing more to do as the urge to have a dead life. We want to continue extending and deepening our relationships, and can only do so by seeking to collaborate and move beyond any impulse to use our speech to mark each other, and to be remarked upon for the differences these abilities to mark, and avoid marks, make. These efforts to differentiate between self and other selves do not attract our attention/our efforts for our analytic concern is to engage in friendly relations, and they do not rest in superficiality. We do not produce other's speech as making demands upon us, but think of ourselves as engaging in an activity with other selves in which, and through which, we choose what we do. By risking displaying our incompetence, and our uncompetitiveness, we encourage ourselves to continue with our collaborative work. By producing ourselves as unfinished we do not seek to act in order to be remembered by others, for we remember that we are still acting to produce better versions of ourselves. We do not seek to be remarked upon, for we are not remarkable, and do not seek to be remarkable, for we understand dialogue to be more than a series of remarks. We seek to develop our community not to raise ourselves in comparison with other selves.

The thinker does not want an audience, i.e. he doesn't want applause, as perhaps the musician might, for clapping has no depth, i.e. it is simply the collision of different surfaces[1] that are not changed by that collision, but revert to what they were. Thoughtful social interaction is such that it is heard in a manner that makes the move to revert to what we previously were a conscious decision. And, through having become more thoughtful, more moral, social actors are aware of the foolishness of choosing to revert rather than to continue developing. Socrates' speech is engaging for it shows his interlocutors that it is they, as well as he, that must and do choose.

We imagine that you, qua worrier, choose to worry because you conceive of worry as less banal, i.e. as more reflexive, than other forms of speech, and that by differentiating yourself in this way you come to imagine that it takes extra effort on your part to engage in ordinary social interaction for you begin by placing yourself outside. You imagine that worry is like stopping and thinking and by doing so choose to prevent yourself from moving/acting thoughtfully. Your speech is always stopping yourself and others from speaking for you imagine silence is safer. We imagine that you treat life/conversation as problematic/demanding, and death/silence as unproblematic, i.e. that whereas you could fear nothingness, you imagine nothingness as nothing to fear. But perhaps you would even worry about death, i.e. fantasise that even in death you will be called upon to respond thoughtfully? But we call upon you to speak now, i.e. to respond, for by now you should hear that our intent is to appreciate and deepen our understanding of your speech, and by so doing, to raise our community by resisting lazy/shallow versions of our speech that depreciate/underestimate its possible value/virtue. Please go on, and whilst we will not take back what we have said we will work harder to offer formulations of your speech that display how it could be thoughtful.

Original Speaker:

I will go on as you request, for perhaps I could better formulate my wish to produce a finished product as the desire to contribute to the conversation, and yet, my problem is that I don't know how to start! This is what worries me about stopping. Others act as if things start them off, e.g. good topics, good art, good music or whatever, and yet these leave me cold, and I only get going when problems arise. I treat good things as complete, i.e. as finished articles and whilst I wish that these could start me off I cannot see how I can add anything to them. I can't see appreciating as contributing, i.e. as adding anything.

It seems that worry is like stopping and thinking (yes-but), however, its version of thinking becomes a problem already because it is, or wants to be thinking when you have stopped about starting/speaking. Movement is conceived of as the problem, for worry tries to see all the places you might go wrong before you begin, and this involves realising that you need to know where you are and how you got there (i.e. which way you are facing) in order to begin. My inability to start, i.e. to become part of things places me outside and I see others, i.e. those who have started, as those who have been taken in.

Response:

But of course you must realise that you have already started. You say your problem is that you don't know how to start, but this reveals that you have started to inquire into what is worth doing/starting whereas those, if any, who imagine they know how to start are those who choose not to inquire, not to think. You say it is having to start that worries you about stopping, and by saying this remind us of the good of stopping, for stopping is alright if it isn't finishing. For instance, each section in this work has stopped, though like any conversation, each is far from finished, if that is, by finished is meant complete, rather than polished. They may or may not be finished in the latter sense. The good of stopping is that we can and always are, always recontinuing.

You say others act as if things start them off, and you show your sameness with them by saying how problems are like good topics for you. Now we could have heard you as bringing yourself down to their level, but we choose to hear your speech as raising yourself, as pointing to the fact that thinkers/speakers do what they choose/decide is good, and that this is what we, and all speakers share and this is why conversation/dialogue is always worthwhile. You go on to talk about good things but by doing so remind us that we would rather speak about good people, good intentions. So, precisely by not orienting to other people as things, or as themselves good, but as thinkers about the good we can appreciate their good intentions. But, by appreciating, we do not mean merely applauding, for the addition of applause adds to a performance in only the shallowest manner. Appreciation for us is the active effort to resist any temptation to underestimate other; it is the effort to offer a reading of others' actions/speeches as being those of thoughtful, social, moral actors. So you are right, appreciating is not merely adding to, for thoughtful formulations appreciate others' speeches by deepening them through dialectical development.

Your second paragraph reminds us that our notion of appreciating could be spoken of as stopping and thinking, for what we are continuing to stop are thoughtless readings, that is, if thinking when you have stopped means being continually prepared to question and in this way deepen. But, we would rather say that the thinker refuses to finish thinking. Your expressed wish to think before you start need not indicate that movement is your problem, but can direct us to seeing that thoughtless starts aren't real starts at all, i.e. that the movement they bring about is directionless. So you remind us that starting to move before inquiring about where you are and where or why you are going is thoughtless. But, we engage in conversations/thought, we have started in such a way as to prevent ourselves being sucked into thoughtlessness. We are engaged in locating ourselves such that these questions are placed essentially in our actions and are not jettisoned like unwanted ballast if we begin to move. They always remain with us. So, now we hear your speech as saying that the places where we might go wrong are precisely those situations where we might have forgotten to think about what we are doing and why. What you refer to as your inability to start, i.e. to become part of things, is your ability to continue being more than a thing, i.e. to be continuing to free yourself. You, and we are outside things, and by being outside, i.e. by being speakers we are able to hear how other speakers are also with us, how our dialogue enables us to stay outside the world of things. Our ability to read raises us above the world of things and places us in a social, thoughtful, moral community.

Original Speaker:

But still I fear for you, perhaps for us, as I am also involved in the conversation, for whilst in the last section I was worried about falling short, it seems to me now that foolishness can also be going too far, over stepping the mark. I fear that your speech will make fools of us; where making a fool of oneself is different from acting the fool, i.e. where making a fool of yourself is seen as showing what you really are when you aren't intending to. I suppose I don't want to appear foolish because I respect those who instil fear, and in some way those who feel fear, but I cannot respect those who neither feel nor instil fear. So I take precautions against appearing foolish, and I have to admit this is no easy matter for I am perhaps too cautious about precautions, i.e. I don't trust them. Now you speak in the manner of those who take no precautions and it is in this sense that you seem to overstep the mark. I presume that you don't take precautions either because you feel so secure about dealing with problems, or because you don't really care what you do. So your behaviour seems analogous to that of the fool, and yet I am puzzled, for I cannot see how your speech sustains you? Perhaps I am wrong to imagine you are concerned with sustenance for perhaps your very ability to not care what you start with, consume, (i.e. to not take precautions) enables you to sustain yourself very well. Sustenance is much more of a problem for me as I am particular about my food (i.e. what I consume). I am concerned about what I digest for I see what I produce as dependent upon what I consume.

Response:

Thank you for your concern, i.e. that which you speak of as fearing for us, but whilst we could have heard your speech as revealing very quickly the shallowness of that interest, i.e. how it was a veneer that soon gave way to reveal your own self protectiveness, we will not do so. Rather we hear you as taking on responsibility for leading our conversation into danger, and by doing so as making the effort to get us out again. You need not fear that our speech will make fools of us (including you) for in a way that is our intention; for it is only when we are aware of our own foolishness (that which we referred to much earlier as being at a loss) that we can grasp the conceit of knowledge that fears rely upon. If by a fool you mean one who is ignorant of important matters but seeks to know, then we are fools, but it is only by acknowledging our foolishness that we can converse and decide upon, not subordinate ourselves to, versions of the good. The fool is the philosopher, i.e. is the thoughtful social person, i.e. is the speaker/thinker, and it is only those, if any, who pretend to some higher status, i.e. who pretend to know, rather than collaborate and decide upon the difference between good and bad, just and unjust, who need to hide their ignorance. We are intending through our speech to display what we all already really are, i.e. that we are those who have no need to fear exposure.

On first reading we heard your statement about respecting only those who instilled fear or those who felt (succumbed?) to fear as illustrative of your failure to move beyond a restrictive notion of social relationships as comprising merely of dominator and dominated, i.e. we could not grasp why you had no respect for friends, i.e. perhaps those who neither instil fear nor succumb to it. However, if we are to befriend your speech we must bring into question our impulsive reading for no thoughtful actor could deny the place of friendship. We imagine that you must by 'respect' be implying 'treat with deference', and be calling us to remember that deference has no part to play in true social relations. So you are not commending those who instil fear nor those who succumb to fear, but are commending that we remember how respect as deference is not worthy of friends.

We, like you, do not trust precautions for we are aware how protectiveness can so easily encage. However, your speech differentiates here, i.e. you refer to yourself as being too cautious about precautions, and to us as taking no precautions, but that precaution, i.e. of differentiating between self and other selves, is one that we would do away with, for our interest is showing our deep sameness with other selves. Ironically it is at this point of differentiation that you appear to overstep the mark, for instead of speaking about yourself, you choose to make presumptions about why we do not take precautions, and neither of your accounts does our behaviour justice. If we appear not to take precautions we can say that this is neither because we feel secure about dealing with problems, in the sense of controlling what happens, nor because we do not care what we do. Far from it, it is our way of caring what we do and not merely about what may happen to us. We cannot control what will happen, but we can be making an effort to free ourselves from thoughtlessness that could control us. We have no need to fear other's remarks for we act with good intentions and can be instructed by other's responses to our actions. For instance, we have no need to be angered by what we could read as your careless hesitant accusation of us, i.e. that we are fools. For through your speech, we help remind ourselves not to accuse others, but to make the effort to see how their speech could be a product of thoughtful good intentions: that you aren't accusing us but trying to help us.

As to the issue of sustenance that you raise, this is important for whilst we agree with you that you are wrong to imagine that it is our ability to not care what we start with (consume) that sustains us, you help us to remember that when we use something, i.e. start with something we don't consume it but work with it to make more/better out of our relationship to whatever it is. We form what we hear through our thoughtful work. So, we formulate your need to be particular not as being the result of a fear of poisoning, nor as being a result of fears of other's remarks if you made a weak choice, but as your desire to use, select from the possibilities around you in such a way as to act most humanly. You remind us to recognise the active part we play in our relationships, i.e. you remind us not to forget that we are all always theorising, and that it is through our theorising that we form our relationships with other, whether other is another person or a thing. By remembering this we are reconstituting ourselves as social/moral actors rather than as those who can only be acted upon.

Original Speaker:

But the way you use my speech makes me feel that for you anything that fits will do, whereas I can't respect that which I feel comfortable with, i.e. that which fits (that which is easy/tempting), and can't be comfortable with what I respect. I need tension. I only trust my fears (i.e. my distrust) and I view fear as my strongest feeling, and respect the strong rather than the weak. I see weakness as succumbing to temptation, but I don't treat succumbing to temptation as the danger for I treat temptation as that which prevents you seeing the danger. I see fearful thought/worry as strong minded and see a lack of fear as indicating weak mindedness. In this way I come to see seriousness in the sense of awareness of dangers as the highest form of life. More than this though I have a specific version of dangers as pitfalls, i.e. as things that can be avoided if I keep my wits about me. I suppose I treat my life as Popper treats scientific theories, i.e. as being in danger of falsification.

Response:

Here you appear to try to take advantage of us, for you begin yet again by making a presupposition about what we are doing and then on the basis of that presupposition, i.e. that anything that fits will do, you indulge your worst impulses, and we note that we do not refer to this as self indulgence for you are much better than those impulses. So let us think through your speech. You say we use your speech and you say this as if it is your possession, and as if by using it we consume it (in your sense), and yet we would say that our effort to think about your speech[2] is our effort to contribute to it, and so it is not a question of whether it fits or not, whatever that might mean, but of whether our efforts can produce formulations that are harmonious (i.e. that fit) in social relations, i.e. in friendly relations. But, we, like you, perhaps, do not treat friends like easy chairs, i.e. there is tension in our friendships, but it is not the tension of fear or distrust, but of desire, and it arises in the continuing collaborative effort to make these relationships more profound, more moral, more social, more free. We are reminded by your speech that we distrust our fears; that we view our desires as our most trustworthy feelings, and befriend neither the strong, if by that is meant those who instil fear, nor the weak, if by that is meant those who succumb to fears, but those whose thoughtful desires enable them to act freely not fearfully.

The tension we feel is enjoyable for it accompanies thoughtful actions in the face of dangers. Avoiding dangers can at best only lead to momentary relief and this is why the worrier's life is stops and starts, whereas the thinker's life has rhythm and development as does dialectical development. The thinker's virtue lies neither in failing to see dangers nor in orienting to dangers as something to avoid but in seeing that the true danger is the difference between a principled committed thoughtful life, and what you refer to as the highest form of life, i.e. a strong awareness of dangers. Speeches which orient around the latter commitment would deform man, they would preclude social development, and the fact that we can engage in this conversation indicates that we all do do better than that.[3]

You go on to speak of pitfalls and we will, no doubt, have more to say on that issue as we proceed, but before you speak again we would ask you to notice how you speak of using your wits, i.e. you speak of keeping your wits about you! You use your thought/speech as a shield to protect yourself, but here is revealed the weakness of your notion of the relationship between self and speech, for they appear as separate, the one protected by the other, but for us as speakers/thinkers our selves cannot be separated from our speech. So whereas in an 'emergency' you would perhaps consider discarding/sacrificing your speech/thought in favour of your person, we cannot understand what you think your person is. Perhaps you think of our speech as threatening to falsify your life, but we would say that it was a false life anyway.

Our readers will be aware that though we may be using strong words our speech is not extremist but moderate. It is an effort to stretch ourselves beyond unthinking talk, and if it appears clumsy that is because moderation is not the same as restriction; the moderate man is not restricted by the weight of convention.

Original Speaker:

> Oh yes, that is all very well but everybody has limits, and this is why worriers fear falsification, failing or falling. The man you speak of seems complete, he is good alright, but the danger of speaking about him is that by doing so you demand too much of us. Perhaps this is what worriers' fears consist of, i.e. the awareness of the difference between your ideal and their reality.

Response:

Yes, bodies do have limits you are right, but it is your surface commitment to the body, to life at the price of speech which tempts you to limit your self (i.e. you speak of everybody). You can offer no argument to support your commitment for you are aware that any argument reconstitutes you as a

speaker/thinker and brings you back into our community. The difference you
refer to between ideal and reality helps us, for the reality is that we are
speakers/thinkers and as such do not need to invoke vague beliefs in some
mysterious correlation or coincidence between self and body which cannot even
be spoken of without paradoxical results.

The man we speak of is you, and us, and what we are doing with our speech is
encouraging ourselves to act thoughtfully, and to resist the demands of silence,
thoughtlessness, which are, in any case, beyond us. We don't need to be
complete to act well, we only need to say what we think; where thinking is
deciding what thoughtful men, i.e. what we would do, and then doing it. We
have bodies yes, but have no way of thinking of ourselves as being our bodies,
we use our bodies thoughtfully, and do not conceive of ourselves as used by our
bodies. As thinkers, if we eat, run, make love, speak honestly, or whatever,
these actions are matters of decision and as such can be enjoyed. We choose
not to reduce our enjoyments to being the necessary inputs for the satisfaction
of bodily needs, for if we did, we would be denying our social character, we
would be denying ourselves.

Original Speaker:

> Alright, for the moment we will forget the body, but don't you fear the
> ridicule that may be heaped upon you when this work is read? It is not
> writing or speaking that troubles us, but being heard, and what that
> can entail! Won't the laughter you hear when your speech is heard hit
> you in the same way that the ground would hit you at the end of a
> fall? I seek to avoid that pain by speaking more cautiously.

Response:

But did you laugh? Oh no, you choose to formulate other as less trustworthy
than yourself, i.e. as more likely to laugh, as a way to hand over the blame for
your silence to them. You begin by imagining the worst possibility and
orienting your actions to that. But, whilst we cannot imagine a worse way of
proceeding than yours, we can imagine plenty better. For instance, others may
not laugh, but may show us how our arguments are faulty; if so we will have
profited by speaking, as you can be doing. Alternatively, we may find that we
are not laughed at for others may think as we do, if so we can then continue to
converse about how our society, our lives, should be built around our place as
thinkers/speakers, and not as bodies/things. Even if we are laughed at that
would not be the end of matters, for the analogy you draw upon, i.e. that of
falling can be instructive. For, whilst it reveals your orientation towards
prospects, versions of the future, as something to fear, couldn't we welcome
hitting the ground as the point at which we may be able to begin to move of our
own accord. We cannot stop ourselves if we formulate ourselves as falling, but
we can pick ourselves up by risking grounding our speech, i.e. by thinking about
how we speak.

We imagine that nothing could be more profoundly painful than for a
thinker/speaker, i.e. a man/woman, to choose to live an unthoughtful life, i.e.
to pretend he/she wasn't free.

We suspect that your fear of hitting the ground is not that you may be
laughed at for falling but that you may be laughed at because of your pathetic
efforts to get out. But we remember that it is you who begins by construing
your future efforts as pathetic, not us, for we appreciate human efforts, i.e.
true suffering. Speakers/thinkers excite collaborative efforts not pity, for pity

rests in difference, and perhaps reveals indifference. Your fear of having to get out, of having to raise yourself, bring yourself up, is closely intertwined with the fact that you have always avoided situations where you needed to learn to climb or jump precisely for fear of falling/failing and not being able to get out. You don't want your incompetence to be seen, and the manoeuvres in which you indulge in order to screen it from others could eventually have resulted in your own blindness. You never try to learn to climb, or live well, but instead learn how to avoid situations where it will be required. You have learnt how to be avoiding pitfalls, i.e. how to tip toe round with your talk, e.g. your 'perhapses' and ' yes buts', but you secretly view your tip toeing as grovelling, which is like acknowledging to yourself that you are in a hole. Grovelling is like appearing to walk in a hole and refusing to try to climb out. But, it is not your position in the hole that disturbs you, you would happily stay there but for the fact that you fear other's glance, for you fear that other can see through, or over your excuses to your fearfulness.

What a pleasant surprise it must be for you when you relate to an other who looks through your speech in such a way as to uncover a thoughtful character whose dignity resides in the fact that she must always be choosing to act in such a way as to display a refusal to decline into thoughtlessness. And how much pleasanter a surprise still when you remember that that other is yourself!

We do not begin by thinking we are perfect and have no need of other speakers, i.e. that we are remarkable, complete, for the inevitable result of this beginning, i.e. this conception of self is that it acts as a contraceptive, for it turns any reminders of our social character, i.e. of our dialectical relationships with others, into signs of imperfection. Whilst you construe needing other speakers as a weakness we construe it as our strength, i.e. as essential to our character.

Original Speaker:

But now your speech reminds me that the notion of pitfalls I was using was too passive, for your ability to see through or over my excuses is far from being a pleasant surprise. On the contrary, if I might be permitted a metaphor, your speech is like the lion that sometimes sees through the zebra's stripes. But the metaphor is not adequate, for man's mental faculties are such that he can see invisible lions when they aren't there.

Response:

Your metaphor is instructive for it displays an inability to concentrate, for your impulse to differentiate between self and other is such that you apparently do not notice the lion's camouflage. You imagine that the only form of camouflage is stripes in the same way that you imagined the only dangers were pitfalls. But we achieve an understanding of your metaphor as camouflage.

Your worries prevent concentration, what they call for is a very wide range of vision, i.e. the zebra and the worrier are continually looking round and the effort involved tires them and places them in danger as a result of their fatigue. By reducing thinking to keeping your wits about you, i.e. by being constantly on the look out for dangers, you can't concentrate in the manner that the climber needs to do. And yet perhaps it isn't that you can't concentrate, but that you see concentrating as dangerous, e.g. the zebra really getting into a piece of grass as the lion approaches. You are always stopping and starting in order to ensure that your activity is not that of a foolish zebra, i.e. your 'yes buts' are your reminders to keep looking round.

But we are reminded by this that getting into the difference between a man and a zebra is different from the zebra getting into a piece of grass, for it is only inquiry grounded in this difference that can produce social action/moral action.

Perhaps you see concentration, like rhythm, as being something you get into, carried away in, in a word as tempting? If this is so it can only be by having allowed your self to be reduced in such a way that you treat what you want as what you are tempted by. Deeply you know that the version of the good around which you organise your life, i.e. the good as your own personal safety, is not that which thinkers/speakers would want/desire to commit themselves to: you know it isn't you. But the 'commitment' you rely upon prevents you from inquiring any further and displaying that safety for man rests in the decision not to treat self as natural/as animal. That is, the decision not to draw analogies, and rely upon analogies, between men and zebras for instance, but to choose to display through our speech/actions how we are all always seeking to be achieving social character as those who think about their relation to nature, and do not subordinate themselves to what is, after all, only a conception of nature.

We imagine that you treat life as a pit into which you have been dropped (borne), which is full of problems. We imagine you are fixated upon problems for they remind you that you were brought into life, i.e. forced into a situation where you are called upon to act, when you were absent. We imagine that you see birth as analogous to falling into a pit, i.e. it merely happened to you. Now if you persist in choosing to equate your life with that of the zebra everything fits naturally enough. But that is not a thoughtful choice, for the thinker's notion of birth is not restricted to the natural event, but is related to our continuing willingness and ability to be bringing ourselves up into thoughtful social relationships. Once birth is conceived in this way we have reason to carry on, and to bring our efforts, however clumsy, to bear on our situation.

For instance, perhaps we can take what may appear to you as a liberty, and remind you of some notes you wrote earlier which began by making reference to the issue of making a fool of yourself. We will as in certain previous instances present the notes complete so that our readers can work upon them independent of our analyses, and we shall then proceed to make an effort to draw out of ourselves a thoughtful, social reading, i.e. we will work with your notes to deepen our understanding of our speech. Our interest is not in dismissing your notes in favour of something we already know, but in working with your notes to be achieving more thoughtful conversation.

APPENDIX D

Para. 1   Earlier I began by suggesting that the worrier was afraid of making a fool of himself, and we found as we progressed that the worrier relied upon a version of foolishness as incompetence. Perhaps this could be deepened if we began to think about the fact that it might not be that the worrier is afraid of making a fool of himself, but that he can't make a fool of himself, i.e. he imagines that people treat him seriously even when he is being unserious. Initially it sounds here as if the worrier is merely being rigorous and extending the idea of his own incompetence to 'making a fool of himself', i.e. if he could make a fool of himself he could make something and would not be 'completely' incompetent. However the point is a stronger one, it is that nobody can make a fool of him/her self, i.e. others are involved in making fools of people, and so the worrier was afraid of something which could not happen. This can be strengthened even further in two ways (a) when we remember that the fool isn't taken as being responsible for his actions, and so the fool doesn't make or create anything other than by accident; and (b) when we see that this point doesn't only apply to fools, i.e. nobody can make anything of themselves without others (perhaps friends). To return to the first way (a) above the fact that the fool is held not to be responsible for his actions (let alone himself) tells us why the fool can often have an impact, i.e. remark in a very pointed and stunning way. The reason is that the fool can be fearless, or is fearless, i.e. can do anything, because he isn't held to do anything; he is neither deserving of praise nor blame, i.e. he isn't responsible for his irresponsibility.

Para. 2   The worrier either worries about the fool because the fool doesn't worry, or dismisses the fool as unworthy of worry. In both instances worry is seen as good, however, the fool also acts as a reminder of our own cautiousness, i.e. he acts in such a way as to point out what is bad about worry, i.e. its cautiousness or lack of action. The fool appears to treat caution as cowardice and the worrier knows that there is something in what the fool says, for this reason the worrier as worrier is uncomfortable in the presence of a fool. And yet when we remember the worrier's mode of discourse (i.e. his yes-buts) we find that the worrier could only make remarks followed by mumbling, or stuttering, i.e. that the worrier speaks like a fool. The point here is that the worrier treats speaking as sticking his neck out, and treats this as something you do quickly, i.e. if you get away with it you sigh a sigh of relief and feel you need to relax until you try again. It is almost as if your neck needs time to stiffen again in order to stick out. Somehow the worrier's version of his own speech as a climax, i.e. as short and sweet, leaves him unable to speak again. His version of himself as working better under pressure treats his own speech as something which cannot be followed. (It is the idea of forced confession again!) The worrier doesn't really want to be spoken to once he has spoken, for he would see this as asking him to do more, and he had to use up all of his reserves to speak in the first place. He wants others to stop and start when he does, this is the closest he can get to rhythm. Before leaving this theme of speech as climax we can see how the worrier might develop a love/hate relationship to his own speech for perhaps it is precisely this tension which makes a sexual climax have such an edge. The idea of tension as an edge seems to take us back into the oscillation topic, i.e. life and death. Also perhaps it can account for why the worrier is always looking for 'good' topics, i.e. each occasion is different somehow, i.e. one is not in any straightforward way built upon the other because the other has been taken to a climax, i.e. as far as it can go.

Para. 3   The worrier's problem then is that he treats life or others as anticlimatic and hence treats life as a problem. He tries to excite other with his speech but doesn't see how his speech/remarks finish both him and his listeners off.

Para. 4   What I am trying to say here is that the worrier doesn't notice that his remarks can be tempting to others, i.e. they could provide easy ways out - stops. It is as if his remarks leave other with nothing to say, i.e. they strangle other by speaking for other, saying what other should have said. The worrier steps into silences, sticks his neck out in order to offer a sense of direction, but doesn't realise that from the silence nobody can be heard. He intends his remarks to be used as sign posts but finds that they fall down and are used as road blocks as soon as he has erected them. He wanted to help but was treated as a hindrance, and perhaps he was, or is, because remarks, like the remarkable, i.e. miracles, do not help because they too easily create lazy pointing. They can be entertaining but so can the fool and this was what the worrier was trying not to be. Miracles and remarks make an audience of man and this suggests the worrier's arrogance for it is as if he feels that observers (i.e. the audience), i.e. those who concentrate, are taken in by what they see/hear in a way that he manages to avoid. By not concentrating he could see what might pop out from behind the theatre. The place for the remarker then is outside, i.e. you can only remark if you are outside, i.e. unmarked, immaculate and one way to remain unmarked, or so the worrier thinks is to avoid contact. Avoiding is like putting yourself in a void, i.e. making yourself scarce, I can't say it clearly but perhaps the best way of doing this is by becoming a fool, i.e. empty headed, carrying your own void around with you. The fool is not held to be responsible for his actions because he is empty headed, has a diminished self. The worrier's conception of his own speech as a climax is the means by which he tries to reduce his own responsibility, i.e. his speech was forced by pressure, time limits or whatever, and anyway once he has spoken he is in the same situation as the fool, i.e. he is empty, and hence cannot be taken to account for what he said. So the worrier becomes a fool not when he speaks but when he has spoken. Perhaps the emptiness which the worrier feels once he has spoken can also be related to his sense of relief, i.e. he feels light headed.

Para. 5   The worrier's remarks are starts which seem to be designed to stop other, as if the worrier sees stopping and starting as helping other to keep awake. He seems to bang his head against a brick wall to let himself and others know what it is like, rather than to show them what a waste of time it is. He builds walls with his 'yes-buts' (i.e. they are like blocks) and he is still surprised that he doesn't get on, and that others try to discard the blocks he provides them with. Remarks stun in the same way as walls can, i.e. they can stop you going where you were going.

Para. 6   The worrier does increasingly start to sound like a martyr now, and funnily enough starts to sound even more tiresome the more martyr like he sounds! The dilemma for the worrier or the martyr is that by their actions they point to what is bad about life, and given that life is bad their own deaths hardly seem so courageous. By sticking his neck out the worrier is seen to devalue his neck, and this is how other can come to view him as a fool: for the fool is one who doesn't know what is valuable, i.e. good or bad, and other in this instance is sure that necks are good! That this conception of the fool is foolish, i.e. that we were wrong to find the notion of the worrier as a martyr both funny and tiresome above, is what we now need to show. What is foolish about this conception of the fool is that it, or its holder, doesn't yet know whether fools or anything else are good or bad. This would be another way of saying that we are already sticking our necks out even if we pretend we don't know it. The point being that that which is tiresome need not be bad. Hence the fact that the worrier finds life tiring shouldn't lead him to think it is bad.

Para. 7   The fact that the worrier as a remarker needs to separate himself from others seems to contradict his own view of his actions as attempts to help other, however we can see more clearly that this is not so when we realise that the worrier thinks he must perfect himself before he can help others (or do anything good), and he treats separating himself from others as a means of perfecting himself. He treats responsibility as pressure and sees the taking on of responsibility as being irresponsible unless it is done by someone who knows he can fulfil his obligations. He further thinks that nobody can know this and as a result tends to equate the acceptance of responsibility with arrogance, or a lack of humility. He justifies his own inaction by pointing at the lack of justification others have to act rather than by showing how a lack of action is just. He uses 'yes-buts' to try to produce inaction, i.e. if his 'yes-buts' were heeded everybody would be reduced to waiting for miracles. Perhaps this would get rid of arrogance but it would get rid of responsibility as well, i.e. it sounds like throwing the baby out with the bath water, or in another way like having a version of the highest form of life as the serious, i.e. as being watchful for imperfections. The worrier tends to treat interventions as imperfections, i.e. actions as bad, and this shows us how he prefers the serious, i.e. that which proceeds in a series.

Para. 8   The worrier treats actions, or interventions, like viruses, i.e. whereas with children pain is normally taken as an indicator that something is wrong, the worrier sees a lack of pain as an indicator that something is going to be wrong. That is he sees lack of pain as producing ease or carelessness, i.e. as failing to produce the necessary precautions, and on the other hand as producing careless actions, and it is these that we need to take precautions against. He treats ease as a doctor would treat a contagious disease, i.e. as a danger and hence as something to be avoided. The worrier then can be treated as a sophisticated child, i.e. he sees not only that pain is an indicator that something is wrong, but also that things can go wrong as a result of a lack of pain, i.e. carelessness. Somehow both seem like functionalists in their failure to question the fact that the goal of the system is taken to be efficiency, i.e. a lack of pain, or of friction! Here we see then that the worrier doesn't really want tension in itself, as we earlier thought, but that he wants tension now as a sign that the future will lack tension!

Para. 9   Perhaps the medical analogy above can be carried a little further if for a moment we consider the 'yes but' as similar to immunisation, i.e. the acceptance of just a small amount of the disease (not enough to have lasting effects, i.e. to leave a mark), but enough to prevent the disease occurring again. The worrier then accepts in a small way what other says only to know it and be able to reject it more forcibly as a result of this knowledge. The worrier then treats the person who doesn't use 'yes buts' as he would the person who doesn't get immunised, i.e. as a fool.

Para.10   Somehow talking to yourself, or thinking before you act seems like the same sort of precaution as immunisation, and the fool does seem like a person who never talks to him/her self. That is the fool is reckless, i.e. doesn't reckon. However the worrier is foolish in this way, in the sense that he fails to take account of (reckon) other's view that thinking out loud is foolish. What other's, the manipulator's, view here presupposes, is that our thinking is foolish, and as a result that it is something to hide with our speech. The fact that this is not possible escapes both the worrier and the manipulator here, who both try to separate speech and thought.

RESPONSE TO APPENDIX D

This appendix, like all speech, is stimulating for us, through our reading of it we help recreate conditions which enable us to further our thoughtful inquiry.

Analysis of Paragraph 1

Earlier I began by suggesting that the worrier was afraid of making a fool of himself, and we found as we progressed that the worrier relied upon a version of foolishness as incompetence. Perhaps this could be deepened if we began to think about the fact that it might not be that the worrier is afraid of making a fool of himself, but that he can't make a fool of himself, i.e. he imagines that people treat him seriously even when he is being unserious. Initially it sounds here as if the worrier is merely being rigorous and extending the idea of his own incompetence to 'making a fool of himself', i.e. if he could make a fool of himself he could make something and would not be 'completely' incompetent. However the point is a stronger one, it is that nobody can make a fool of him/her self, i.e. others are involved in making fools of people, and so the worrier was afraid of something which could not happen. This can be strengthened even further in two ways (a) when we remember that the fool isn't taken as being responsible for his actions, and so the fool doesn't make or create anything other than by accident; and (b) when we see that this point doesn't only apply to fools, i.e. nobody can make anything of themselves without others (perhaps friends). To return to the first way (a) above the fact that the fool is held not to be responsible for his actions (let alone himself) tells us why the fool can often have an impact, i.e. remark in a very pointed and stunning way. The reason is that the fool can be fearless, or is fearless, i.e. can do anything, because he isn't held to do anything; he is neither deserving of praise nor blame, i.e. he isn't responsible for his irresponsibility.

Response:

You begin by speaking of 'suggesting', but you could not desire either to have a suggestible audience, i.e. you could not wish to talk in such a way as to bring others under the sway of your talk, or to be easily brought under the sway of another talker. A thoughtful formulation of suggestion could not mean the wish to produce unquestioning acceptance, rather our notion of suggestion would involve the hearer being stimulated to think, i.e. to doubt and question.

You go on to say 'Perhaps this could be deepened if we began to think about the fact that it might not be ... etc.', but your 'Perhaps ... if' cannot mean to display only a shallow commitment to deepen, i.e. as if you could choose to leave matters as they are: rather it displays the depths of your commitment even in the face of difficult odds. You decide to ' ... think about the fact that ... etc.' and by doing so remind us that we can never deepen our activities by merely thinking about facts, in the sense of observing them, for facts as such are such that they become estranged from thought. By 'think about ...' you must mean think about, in the sense of turn about, switch around, rather than in the sense of observing, i.e. subordinating your self to facts by pretending the facts are first. Indeed your speech proceeds to exemplify thinking about in the sense we are commending. We choose to contemplate what it is good to do, and not think about what the facts merely are.

When you say that the worrier can't make a fool of himself you cannot mean that he wants to but fails, for that you could never know. Rather you must mean that selves cannot be made fools of, i.e. that thoughtlessness is no longer self, i.e. it is the absence of self. (We are formulating the fool as the clown here, and not as the man who whilst recognising his own lack of wisdom still seeks wisdom.)

Your speech on the worrier 'merely being rigorous and extending the idea of his own incompetence ... etc.' reminds us of the thoughtlessness of that rigour, for what is the purpose of diligently extending the domain of an idea to draw in other items prior to contemplating the place of the idea? For thinkers/speakers ideas necessarily exercise great power, and though this power can be harnessed in the service of the liberation of men/women, the thoughtless usage of ideas must always encage for it is to be used by the ideas, it is to rule out dialectical development/social development.

When you say that 'nobody can make a fool of him/her self ...' you must mean that no body can make a fool of a self and this is true if make is being used in a strong sense of design, for bodies cannot design without thought. Also when you say others are involved in making fools of people you cannot be referring by others to thoughtful interlocutors, for thoughtful interlocutors are aware that we can only have a better society, i.e. better lives, by working to make ourselves thinkers out of our foolishness. The thinker could be formulated as the social climber in the profound sense of one who seeks to elevate society. We imagine by others you must be referring to those who pretend to be already knowledgeable.

You say 'the worrier was afraid of something which could not happen' and we hear this as meaning not that it is impossible, but that it could not happen if the worrier prevents it, i.e. if he overcomes his irrational fears of others, other speakers, for these fears could force him to make a fool of his person unless he deepens his involvement with other speakers.

Your speech reminds us that by the fool we mean all men, and not the clown, but perhaps the worrier seeks to be a fool in the latter sense, for he could formulate the clown as meaning no harm, and as such, as free from blame, i.e. as merely letting things happen. But we know that the circus audience's laughter at the clown is always half hearted, for to laugh whole heartedly would be to have made fools of ourselves. To laugh at the clown is to empathise with an attempt to become thoughtless, and deeply we all know that the clown cannot be thoughtless. The sadness which is conventionally postulated as underlying the clown's make-up displays the audience's discontent with its own response, i.e. with its laughter, and reveals the beginnings of its search to reach a more human notion of enjoyment.

When you say the point is a stronger one you must mean it directs us towards more profound questions, for the realisation that men cannot make fools/clowns of themselves is very important for it reveals that we can never be suited to be slaves, that we can never be thoughtless, for as speakers, i.e. as social, we always display thoughtful character. We choose not to remain as fools by claiming response-ability for our actions, i.e. by being willing to think about what we do, and only in this way can we be freeing ourselves from thoughtless lives. Unlike the fool your speech does not merely have an impact, i.e. remark in a pointed and stunning way, for it stimulates not stuns. You could not want to stun us, for what use would we be to you in your dialogue in a stunned condition? You seek to stimulate/to goad others into actions that deepen relationships/society with your speech. Thoughtful speakers never seek to stun others, for that is to produce silence rather than continuing conversation. If our speech is to stimulate ourselves, or others, it must get beneath the surface, it must have penetration. Analytic speech incites selves, it does not deaden into submission in the manner that a systematic straight jacket might. Socrates' speech is not intended to stun others, but to play a part in stimulating dialogue.

You speak of the fool's remarks as pointed and stunning, as we have intimated, this is to us, a misleading juxtaposition of concepts. However, perhaps the fool points in a stunning way because he is fearless. He has no sense of direction so his speech has no penetration, it can only bounce off the surface of speakers, for speakers have depths which the fool's remarks cannot reach. The fool remarks in a random fashion, and if, now and then he hits a target he cannot claim or be offered any credit, for he is merely the vehicle of chance, rather than a thoughtful deliberate actor. And this is why any reduction of man to nature could have had tragic results.

We are, and desire to be, responsible for all that we do, and we did not say for 'everything' we do, for we want to resist forms of speech that reduce thoughtful, intentional, actions to the status of things. We are claiming responsibility for our reading of your speech and by doing so expose ourselves, and show our willingness to continue deepening our ability to respond. Your speech reminds us that we are not responsible for irresponsibility for our version of self is as response-able.

Analysis of Paragraph 2

The worrier either worries about the fool because the fool doesn't worry, or dismisses the fool as unworthy of worry. In both instances worry is seen as good, however, the fool also acts as a reminder of our own cautiousness, i.e. he acts in such a way as to point out what is bad about worry, i.e. its cautiousness or lack of action. The fool appears to treat caution as cowardice and the worrier knows that there is something in what the fool says, for this reason the worrier as worrier is uncomfortable in the presence of a fool. And yet when we remember the worrier's mode of discourse (i.e. his yes-buts) we find that the worrier could only make remarks followed by mumbling, or stuttering, i.e. that the worrier speaks like a fool. The point here is that the worrier treats speaking as sticking his neck out, and treats this as something you do quickly, i.e. if you get away with it you sigh a sigh of relief and feel you need to relax until you try again. It is almost as if your neck needs time to stiffen again in order to stick out. Somehow the worrier's version of his own speech as a climax, i.e. as short and sweet, leaves him unable to speak again. His version of himself as working better under pressure treats his own speech as something which cannot be followed. (It is the idea of forced confession again!) The worrier doesn't really want to be spoken to once he has spoken, for he would see this as asking him to do more, and he had to use up all of his reserves to speak in the first place. He wants others to stop and start when he does, this is the closest he can get to rhythm. Before leaving this theme of speech as climax we can see how the worrier might develop a love/hate relationship to his own speech for perhaps it is precisely this tension which makes a sexual climax have such an edge. The idea of tension as an edge seems to take us back into the oscillation topic, i.e. life and death. Also perhaps it can account for why the worrier is always looking for 'good' topics, i.e. each occasion is different somehow, i.e. one is not in any straightforward way built upon the other because the other has been taken to a climax, i.e. as far as it can go.

Response:

We begin by being reminded not to respond to your speech or to any speech as that of a fool or a worrier, and when you said that the worrier either does this or that, we were unsure whether to read this as an expression of doubt on your part as to your knowledge of the worrier, or whether you were asserting that the worrier does (i.e. that you know he does) either this or that. Now you are a thoughtful speaker, and we know that you are aware that you cannot know what one who is other than yourself, i.e. different, would do, so we assume that your either/or displays your own doubts. But our assumption is the expression of our attitude of doubt and not of feigned certitude, i.e. we are as you are. An assumption for us does not remove questions/doubts rather it is the effort to raise ourselves by continuing questioning. Our effort is to assume, to take upon ourselves, thoughtful character, we do not orient to assumptions as being that which block inquiry.

Had we heard you to have been commending the view that the worrier either does this, or that, we imagine you were trying to alert us to extremism, for either/or shows little grasp of moderation.

You say that worry is seen as good, and then proceed to speak about how the fool points to the worrier's cautiousness, but, if the worrier were one who imagined he was good, we could understand his protectiveness. And yet what we want to commend is that thoughtful selves, i.e. friends, are those who seek the good and are not those who imagine they are good. So thoughtful characters recognise other's actions as displays of caution about the good but not about self. We imagine that the cowardly are those who have committed their persons to survival on the surface, and forget that we only truly protect our selves, our characters, by acting with character, i.e. by acting thoughtfully. You speak of the worrier being uncomfortable in the presence of a fool, and remind us that we would welcome the fool's presence, for he could help us maintain our uncomfortableness and maintain our ability not to degenerate into thoughtlessness/silence. Here is why we seek continuing conversations with thoughtful interlocutors, for they help us not to overvalue our persons, for the product of that presumption, if it is left unquestioned, is ultimately cowering characterlessness. The manner in which we hear you speak of the worrier being uncomfortable in the presence of the fool leads us to view the worrier as one who is uncomfortable in the presence of the truth, and that could only be a thoughtful response if uncomfortableness was being commended, for the truth need never be feared.

The transition your speech makes now from the worrier's uncomfortableness in the presence of the fool, to the discussion of the worrier's discourse, is stimulating, for it reminds us that the usage of 'And yet' is thoughtful, for it indicates unease, continuing thought, i.e. unsettledness, uncomfortableness. It illustrates your commitment to the rigorous maintenance of unease, of thoughtful inquiry, and your continuing willingness to bring your own speech/thought into question. You remind us that we do not need to rely upon specific embodied others to remind us to be uneasy, for we need only listen to, rather than dismiss, our own thoughts.

We hear the version you offer of the worrier's speech as stimulating, as calling for our thoughtful efforts, for it is only with effort that we can be becoming more than a suggestable audience, i.e. it is only with effort that we can contribute to the conversation/inquiry. We want to say that if we had accepted the version of the worrier's speech you describe we would have placed a wedge firmly between the worrier's speech and our own, i.e. we would have allowed ourselves to be reduced to silence. However we attempt to offer a deeper reading of the thinker's/worrier's speech which is moulded from your speech, and should be regarded as a deeper version, and not as an alternative, for we would not have achieved it without hearing your speech. Dialectical development is deepening not dismissing, it is the exercise of friendship which is human freedom.

When we remember the worrier's mode of discourse (i.e. his 'yes-buts') we remember that we heard him to be risking asking questions that he could not answer (the only questions worth asking), and this is why they were followed by mumbling and stuttering. Indeed perhaps it was not mumbling and stuttering, but responsible muteness, i.e. the non assertiveness that encourages other also to make the effort to respond. Unlike the version you offer we appreciate the worrier's effort as intended to stimulate and not to stun, and we hear his sigh not as a sigh of relief at having got away with it, but as a sigh of disappointment at this failure to stimulate other to respond thoughtfully. We hear the worrier as risking sticking his neck out so as to stir up a conversation that has become still/silent, and that in its stillness becomes brittle, fixed, and less likely to develop, bend and grow, and much more likely to snap.

You speak of the worrier's speech as climax, and remind us that speech is a constant feature of our lives, not an exceptional feature. We are always speaking/thinking except perhaps when we are not ourselves. So we would not hear speech as climax unless the notion of climax were stretched in such a way as to enable it to encompass duration. The thoughtful character is always moving/proceeding never completing/accomplishing. Perhaps we do better to formulate speech as providing the climate for friendly relationships?

You speak of the worrier working better under pressure but to have reduced stimulation to pressure would have been narrow minded, constrained. We heard the worrier as pressing for stimulating relationships and your reading displays how he wasn't forcing other. Likewise our speech cannot be followed by any who rest with force as the only form of stimulation.

We do not use up all our reserves when we speak, for we formulate our readers as our reserves, i.e. we are not alone for we offer and seek other's help. You heard the worrier as trying to make the perfect speech, and this is why you imagined he would have had to have used up all of his reserves. But we hear his speech as asking us to be less isolated, more friendly. It is interesting that you even say ' ... he had to use up all his reserves to speak in the first place' for this reminds us that speakers are never first, we are always responding.

We trust that you do not want us to stop and start when you do, for if you did you would be very disappointed with us! More seriously conversationalists, dialecticians encourage others to take up the argument when they fade, i.e. friends don't try to do everything themselves but to collaborate, i.e. they enable others to start and stop when they stop and start, and that is closer to a sense of rhythm.

When you spoke of the worrier 'wanting' other to stop and start etc. you could not have meant merely wished other would stop and start etc. for that would have displayed no awareness of how his speech relates to/with others, i.e. of how by speaking we alter alter. Self and other develop through conversation, they do not remain the same.

You go on to say 'Before leaving the theme of speech as climax' and we hear this as your acknowledgement of our place, i.e. it is you saying 'before I leave the theme of climax for you to take up'. And we take it up by showing how we can take it further, how to have rested with an idea of the worrier as one who 'develops' a love/hate relationship to his own speech is to rest on what you produced as the edge. By refusing to rest there we display our commitment to continue seeking for a version of speech that is stronger, more profound, than the notion of climax we might have relied upon.

So we hear deeper issues in your speech for you are using the notion of sexual climax as a metaphor for the edge between life and death, between thought and thoughtlessness and by doing so are orienting our speech to the difference between free moral human lives and thoughtless/enslaved reactions. We imagine that eroding eroticism by ignoring all but the sexual climax would reduce preorgasmic activity to the status of a waste of time. Similarly we imagine that an impulse to spend life orienting towards the moment of death would reduce conversations/life to the status of a waste of time. But, by seeking to act more freely, more morally, we seek to be freeing our speech from such alienating notions and we recognise others as those who assist us in our active inquiry.

We do not hear your concluding sentence on why we do not build in any straightforward way upon our past work, as if this was intended as an explanation of our failings, for we do not use the analogy of climax to rationalise our failures, but seek to stretch ourselves beyond past achievements. For instance, whilst simply to move from one climax to another could express the shallowness of a repetitious journey, i.e. of one who uses all his resources every time he speaks such that he has no energy left to listen and develop; whilst one who speaks in order 'to get away with it' is likely to see himself as having no need to learn/listen if he imagines he has escaped, you are intending to remind us that our future is not built upon our past in any straightforward fashion. That dialectical development is different from determinism as it involves selves, productive thinkers, and not merely things. Thinkers/speakers can and always do go further than the past would have allowed, for it is not us to stay the same.

Analysis of Paragraph 3

The worrier's problem then is that he treats life or others as anticlimatic and hence treats life as a problem. He tries to excite other with his speech but doesn't see how his speech/remarks finish both him and his listeners off.

Response:

When you say the worrier's problem is that he treats life or others as anticlimatic you remind us to formulate the anticlimatic as that which does not allow us to end. Throughout our lives we generate occasion after occasion for social, thoughtful, activity none of which is oriented to finishing, whereas we imagine the version of life offered by a shallow worrier would be that life generates worries, that life is harder than death.

By treating other as anticlimatic we recognise other's efforts, speech, as intending to keep our relationship moving, developing, i.e. to prevent our conversation from ending. We recognise that others could not be making remarks designed to strangle us. To rest with a version of speech as climax, is to reveal a wish to produce a silence out of which no further development can be achieved, and that wish could not be social.

You say that the worrier tries to excite others, but some may imagine that the only reason to get excited is the presence of dangers. If these are the worrier's listeners they reduce his speech to the sounding of an alarm rather than appreciating how it was intended to incite others to join in collaborative action. Once a speech is reduced to the status of an alarm it is only heard as a noise, for the desire to analyse, to befriend the speaker by thinking about the grounds of his speech, is lost. If we had heard your speech as a warning against worry we might have heeded it, but by doing so would have failed to think about it, i.e. to develop our relationship through it.

Analysis of Paragraph 4

What I am trying to say here is that the worrier doesn't notice that his remarks can be tempting to others, i.e. they could provide easy ways out - stops. It is as if his remarks leave other with nothing to say, i.e. they strangle other by speaking for other, saying what other should have said. The worrier steps into silences, sticks his neck out in order to offer a sense of direction, but doesn't realise that from the silence nobody can be heard. He intends his remarks to be used as sign posts but finds that they fall down and are used as road blocks as soon as he has erected them. He wanted to help but was treated as a hindrance, and perhaps he was, or is, because remarks, like the remarkable, i.e. miracles, do not help because they too easily create lazy pointing. They can be entertaining but so can the fool and this was what the worrier was trying not to be. Miracles and remarks make an audience of man and this suggests the worrier's arrogance for it is as if he feels that observers (i.e. the audience), i.e. those who concentrate, are taken in by what they see/hear in a way that he manages to avoid. By not concentrating he could see what might pop out from behind the theatre. The place for the remarker then is outside, i.e. you can only remark if you are outside, i.e. unmarked, immaculate and one way to remain unmarked, or so the worrier thinks is to avoid contact. Avoiding is like putting yourself in a void, i.e. making yourself scarce, I can't say it clearly but perhaps the best way of doing this is by becoming a fool, i.e. empty headed, carrying your own void around with you. The fool is not held to be responsible for his actions because he is empty headed, has a diminished self. The worrier's conception of his own speech as a climax is the means by which he tries to reduce his own responsibility, i.e. his speech was forced by pressure, time limits or whatever, and anyway once he has spoken he is in the same situation as the fool, i.e. he is empty, and hence cannot be taken to account for what he said. So the worrier becomes a fool not when he speaks but when he has spoken. Perhaps the emptiness which the worrier feels once he has spoken can also be related to his sense of relief, i.e. he feels light headed.

Response:

You remind us that we do not stick our necks out in order to offer directions for others, but in order to join with others and be seeking better directions. We are rerouting our speech/action, and if this involves pulling down signposts, rewriting and reusing them, we will do so. Whilst you say the worrier finds his remarks when used as signposts fall down, we hear his speech, as we hear your speech, as occupied in pulling them down, i.e. as bringing our direction into question, as encouraging us to think about what we do. If he wanted to help then it is those who would reduce his questions to remarks, i.e. those who treat his speech as remarkable, who make him into a hindrance, for they treat his speech as a ready made signpost, and what a close analogy you provide for the authoritarian nature of ready made signposts with your notion of lazy pointing! Whilst you speak of the worrier as one who resists being taken in, we would radicalise that notion, and say that we, and our readers, are not taken in by what we read, but take it in and make what we say with it. So, when you say 'The place for the remarker is outside, i.e. you can only remark if you are outside ...', we do not hear you as commending remaining outside but as commending that we get involved, for what you are saying is that if we remain outside, the most we can do is make remarks. Analytic work is the effort to bring self and other selves into friendly social relationships, it is the effort to go further than remarks, for remarks, like worries, appear to happen to us, i.e. they seem as if they can't be helped, and aren't related to our intentions. It is this appearance they have of being beyond our control, i.e. of coming from outside that can make them appear oppressive/weighty.

Your discussion of the emptiness that follows the worrier's speech helps us to remember that we are all much better than the version you describe of the worrier, for we are not ourselves if we are empty headed. We do not feel light headed when we have spoken, for our interest is not in merely passing our burden, perhaps our worries, from ourself on to another, for that would be to rest with a weak version of society as consisting of discrete, separate, but similar, individuals who cannot progress through social relationships, and who remain essentially the same. Our interest is in speaking in such a way as to continue developing our relationships. We enjoy speaking not because it gives us a sense of relief, but as our way of deepening our characters, and so of leading our lives more thoughtfully/more enjoyably.

Analysis of Paragraph 5

The worrier's remarks are starts which seem to be designed to stop other, as if the worrier sees stopping and starting as helping other to keep awake. He seems to bang his head against a brick wall to let himself and others know what it is like, rather than to show them what a waste of time it is. He builds walls with his 'yes-buts' (i.e. they are like blocks) and he is still surprised that he doesn't get on, and that others try to discard the blocks he provides them with. Remarks stun in the same way as walls can, i.e. they can stop you going where you were going.

Response:

You remind us not to orient to your speech as a brick wall, that is if a brick wall is oriented to as a constraint. But perhaps we can still orient to it as a brick wall if we offer a formulation of a brick wall as a metaphor for man's constructive capability. By doing so we will lead ourselves not to concentrate our attention upon the surface of your speech which may appear impenetrable, but upon your intention in constructing your speech in that particular fashion. You cannot be speaking in the way you do in order to block our inquiry for such an action is out of character, so you must have written that paragraph to help us continue our inquiry, and you do help us for you remind us that we don't want to 'get on' in the sense of climb on top of our wall (our speech), i.e. we are not orienting towards success as finishing, i.e. as reaching a climax, for we are committed to continuing. When you speak of the worrier as one who bangs his head against a brick wall, you remind us that our activity involves us in working at the limits, and in stretching those limits, and that whilst to some this may appear to be banging our heads against a brick wall, we are aware of the depths of the changes our work does bring about. It is only those who risk extending themselves to their limits, who can proceed to extend their limits, and be becoming less constrained. To deformulate philosophy as banging your head against a brick wall, is to opt for an existence walled in, or sheltered by thoughtless/untouched constructions, i.e. it is to remain worried. By engaging in our activity we let ourselves and other selves see what we are, and we do commend what we do as other than a waste of time. We keep ourselves and others awake and do not do so merely in order to stay safe, but in order that we can continue conversing and developing our relationships, our society. Thoughtless, unreflexive, activities would take on the mantle of sleep, and by doing so, would reduce speakers to silence, i.e. individuals to isolates. Perhaps we can talk in our sleep, but we can't hold conversations in our sleep, and this tells us something about what alienated talk would be, i.e. about what speakers who imagined they had no need of other, of friendship, would sound like.

Friends stimulate each other, they do not speak in such a way as to stun as if from a position of superiority, for they speak to and for themselves, as well as to and for other selves. Friends are those who keep each other moving towards more thoughtful forms of speech/life by continuing to question current forms of speech/life.

Analysis of Paragraph 6

The worrier does increasingly start to sound like a martyr now, and funnily enough starts to sound even more tiresome the more martyr like he sounds! The dilemma for the worrier or the martyr is that by their actions they point to what is bad about life, and given that life is bad their own deaths hardly seem so courageous. By sticking his neck out the worrier is seen to devalue his neck, and this is how other can come to view him as a fool: for the fool is one who doesn't know what is valuable, i.e. good or bad, and other in this instance is sure that necks are good! That this conception of the fool is foolish, i.e. that we were wrong to find the notion of the worrier as a martyr both funny and tiresome above, is what we now need to show. What is foolish about this conception of the fool is that it, or its holder, doesn't yet know whether fools or anything else are good or bad. This would be another way of saying that we are already sticking our necks out even if we pretend we don't know it. The point being that that which is tiresome need not be bad. Hence the fact that the worrier finds life tiring shouldn't lead him to think it is bad.

Response:

The effort to respond thoughtfully to this paragraph is perhaps more necessary for our task than all that has preceded it, for how we hear the paragraph reveals whether we are prepared to raise ourselves in such a way that we hear the martyr's speech, or whether we choose to fail to raise ourselves above the din of the audience, which is voluminous not because it consists of speakers who wish to be heard, but because many are involved in talking in such a way that they need not be heard, i.e. in such a way that they may on this occasion slip away and remain unnoticed. If this were not the case there would be no execution.

We began by hearing your speech as that of a member of the audience, i.e. as miserably failing to achieve a hearing of the martyr's speech that did yourself credit. We heard your speech as the whispered rationalisation of your own silence that each member of the audience has to whisper, if only to convince their own persons. We heard your speech as degrading the martyr's act by failing to empathise with it, for to hear the martyr as pointing to what is bad about life can hardly be called a hearing at all, for the martyr is one who has such a commitment about the good of a good life, i.e. about being honest and human, that he is prepared to sacrifice his own personal life for it. To hear this as pointing to what is bad about life is to be trapped in thoughtlessness that fails to hear the irony of the martyr's death, for the martyr provides a supreme example of the good of human life.[4]

However, no doubt our readers detect the irony here for the reading we have offered of your speech shows little effort, for it reveals an understanding/an empathy with the member of the audience that could have displayed our own failure to hear the martyr's speech. If we are to preserve your speech, and hence our own, as the speech of a thoughtful man, we can only assume that there is more than a touch of irony here, for how else in the same paragraph could you commend the worrier for finding life tiresome, and, at the same time, appear effectively to reduce the martyr's act to an accusation of life?

So, if we are to be achieving a thoughtful reading of your speech, we must hear it as that of a martyr, and perhaps we are beginning to do so by seeing that what is tiresome for the martyr is not his recognition that his act can

146

always be misunderstood, but that it so frequently is! By reminding us that that which is tiresome is not bad, you do provide an opening for us to get back on track, for those who are prepared to do what might at first sight seem tiresome, are those who are prepared to make sacrifices, and though small they are a start, and do differentiate speakers from the laziness of talk that wishes to make no effort, i.e. from the audience's whispers, i.e. the whispers of those who only make an effort when they are forced.

So, yours is a good speech for it really does enable its readers, i.e. us, to choose for ourselves. Perhaps our speech could be criticised as being too forceful, i.e. as leaving readers little to do for themselves, but of course mere criticism is not an activity in which thoughtful interlocutors will engage.

By speaking of humble beginnings, i.e. of making small sacrifices you show us how to begin to create our social context where martyrdom is not called for, where the many are those who speak honestly not knowingly. Indeed perhaps a readiness to perceive the situation as other than this would reveal a failure to resist the temptation to paint others in the form of the most extraordinary, i.e. degenerate versions we have of ourselves.

Analysis of Paragraph 7

> The fact that the worrier as a remarker needs to separate himself from others seems to contradict his own view of his actions as attempts to help other, however we can see more clearly that this is not so when we realise that the worrier thinks he must perfect himself before he can help others (or do anything good), and he treats separating himself from others as a means of perfecting himself. He treats responsibility as pressure and sees the taking on of responsibility as being irresponsible unless it is done by someone who knows he can fulfil his obligations. He further thinks that nobody can know this and as a result tends to equate the acceptance of responsibility with arrogance, or a lack of humility. He justifies his own inaction by pointing at the lack of justification others have to act rather than by showing how a lack of action is just. He uses 'yes-buts' to try to produce inaction, i.e. if his 'yes-buts' were heeded everybody would be reduced to waiting for miracles. Perhaps this would get rid of arrogance but it would get rid of responsibility as well, i.e. it sounds like throwing the baby out with the bath water, or in another way like having a version of the highest form of life as the serious, i.e. as being watchful for imperfections. The worrier tends to treat interventions as imperfections, i.e. actions as bad, and this shows us how he prefers the serious, i.e. that which proceeds in a series.

Response:

As always we choose to stir ourselves for only by doing so are we able to offer more than an indolent reading of your speech. Through our reading of your speech we have recognised the fertility of the soil you have provided but we have needed to plough it up and often to turn it right over to make use of it in our efforts to think through and extend our forms of speech/life. Indeed, our brows became so riddled with furrows that had we not paid close attention we might have mistakenly imagined your speech was already ploughed, i.e. ready. We are only able to repair that initial reading by saying how it has played a part in our work to overcome the impulse to differentiate between self and other selves, i.e. the impulse to offer indolent readings of other's speeches as thoughtless, i.e. as mere surface. That is the impulse to hear self as deeper than other speakers by only going so far as to acknowledge that self speaks uneasily, i.e. thoughtfully; that one's own speech requires effort, but not going far enough to extend this version of self to other speakers also. To settle in this way for lazy understandings of others' speeches would have been to begin to drift apart, i.e. to separate, and to settle for defectiveness which could have done no more than give voice to utopian wishes. Your speech in this paragraph calls for our ploughing, our effort to bring to the surface that which might have remained covered over.

Through our work with the first sentence of para. 7 we have helped ourselves remember that by refusing to differentiate between selves we enable ourselves to speak and act in such a way as to be helping ourselves when, and as, we help other selves. We seek to continue improving our versions of self and by doing so hear your speech as reminding us that separation from others, i.e. thoughtful interlocutors, can only leave behind defectives. We are social and continue to improve our characters, and our society, only as long as we engage in dialogues with others which display by their very being the defective nature of any separatist notion of self. We do not seek to perfect ourselves before we can help others but to collaborate with others in such a way that we are together achieving more thoughtful notions of self. To seek to perfect oneself as if that was a prerequisite for helping others would have been thoughtless utopianism, it would have been to seek to be a leader or teacher rather than a companion or friend. To seek to be a leader or a teacher is, we imagine, to seek to differentiate between self and other selves as if good actions can only be done by those who are different, perhaps better than others. But we are all aware that our actions are neither good nor bad, but that we all decide how we want to live, and by acknowledging our place as makers of communal decisions we are becoming ourselves as companions/friends. Indeed we are reminded that one who was perfect could never act well for by knowing everything that one would be denied the freedom that not knowing and yet still deciding requires. Social relationships and moral action are inseparably intertwined. We choose to involve ourselves with others in such a way that we can reflect upon, and continue developing and deepening our relationships.

Alternatively we could only hear your expressed desire for self's separation from other as thoughtful/social/moral by hearing the other you were referring to as weak anti social notions of self. By working to improve our readings of others' speeches we provide the ways forward that utopian wishes of perfecting self alone could never do.

In your second sentence you speak of responsibility as pressure, that is not new, but to speak of all who respond as being irresponsible surprised us a great deal. And yet as we work more closely with your speech we are able to achieve a more profound understanding of human action for you remind us to bring into question the relationship between obligation and responsibility, for we remember that actions designed to fulfil obligations are always irresponsible: they are acts of resignation, for by subordinating self to other in that way an actor would relieve him/her self of response-ability. We are never obliged to do anything, if by obliged is meant bound, or rather if we conceive of ourselves as obliged that is our own choice. So, obligations are only binding if we choose to orient to them as binding. The thinker/social actor/free man does not do whatever he does because he is obliged to, for that would be a deeply tragic misreading of the moral 'ought'. Those, if any, who hear what they ought to do as an imposition, a duty imposed by other, society or whatever, forget their true characters as producers of social relationships. Those who would only act when they know they can fulfil their obligations would irresponsibly throw away their ability to act response-ably without obligation. Response-able actions are those which work to free men from thoughtless adherence to rules that bind.

But still we must listen more carefully for what you say is that actions are irresponsible unless they are done by someone who knows he can fulfil his obligations. We were too ready to hear 'his obligations' as imposed duties. By reading in such a way as to emphasise that the obligations are 'his', i.e. the actor's, we hear how he can know he can fulfil them and by doing so fulfil himself; the moral/social actor acts in such a way as to retain or regain his own self respect. The only obligations he would seek to fulfil are those oriented to maintaining his respect for self.

Now those who hear obligations as imposed by other would also acknowledge that nobody can know they can fulfil obligations of that sort and would rightly see those who acted as if they could as claiming too much, i.e. as arrogant and lacking humility. But, by hearing our obligation as being to doing/deciding what we think is for the good we hear how truly response-able actions are humble, but by being so do not arrogate their being to others, e.g. employers, tradition, history or whatever.

As to your fourth sentence, here your speech helps us to achieve a reading of the worrier's 'inaction' as arrow-gant for this is what pointing or accusing always is! How could an actor imagine that he justified his own inaction by pointing at the lack of justification others have to act rather than by showing how a lack of action is just? What we are saying is that those, if any, who imagine that pointing is inaction are those who arrogantly refuse to reflect upon, think about, their own speech/action, and are constrained by thoughtless adherence to rules. By merely adhering to rules they would be denying their character as those who decide what is just. But your sentence is important to us, for it displays how those who used the knowledge they imagined they had to bolster up what they imagined were themselves, might retort to the speaker who risks reminding himself and others that our actions are free decisions, and are not knowledgeable reactions. They might retort in this manner rather than openly acknowledge that they cannot justify their own actions.

Thoughtful interlocutors do not hear speech which brings to the surface the lack of justification they had for their speech as pointing at them, i.e. as separating speaker and listener but as directing attention towards the direction in which their conversation can thoughtfully proceed. Our actions are not and very likely can never be justified, if by justified is meant secured within a perfect system of knowledge, but what we are saying is that an acceptance of that version of justification degrades men who are those who do not opt for closure/completion, but are taking a place in the production of their lives. Obedience is not the stuff out of which social/moral relationships are born. We are not disposed to obey friends. We befriend your speech by showing our character as those who hear it as other than commanding submission: as those who hear it as requesting a thoughtful friendly response.

As to sentences five and six, right! As we have said if speeches are treated as warnings and merely heeded those who hear them in this way do reduce themselves to waiting for miracles, but we hear the speaker who uses 'yes-buts' as helping us to direct our dialogue, and not as claiming prior knowledge about dangers that he is ahead of us in observing.

Yes-buts, i.e. questions, do play a part in reducing arrogance if they are situated in the context of friendly relationships. That is of relationships between selves who recognise what they have in common. To speak of throwing the baby out with the bath water, as you do, is to provide an extremely illuminating though here inappropriate, analogy for worry, for it is to invoke an extremely unlikely outcome in order to 'justify' a specified decision not to act. Imagine never bathing a baby for fear of that happening! How absurd, and yet this is the immobilising tendency of the worrier's form of speech/life.

We said the analogy was inappropriately placed for as we have said we wish to encourage yes-buts, i.e. the effort to question and deepen and in this way to act more response-ably and less arrogantly.

The analogy of the baby and the bath water provides an acute illustration of alienated 'thinking' as the impulse to be watchful for imperfections. An intimate and comfortable scenario is transformed by an orientation towards imagining what might happen into a tragedy, when it could have been used to display the profundity of human action by concentrating upon the thoughtful good intentions chosen by the character doing the bathing. The analogy orients to bathing the baby as an intervention and seeks to point out the imperfect nature of that action. It forgets that not bathing the baby would be more dangerous.

You conclude this paragraph by proposing that the worrier prefers the serious, i.e. that which proceeds in a series. The unbathed baby would presumably be an instance of proceeding in a series, but to prefer that would be to resist response-ability without acknowledging that that resistance, that that preference, was itself a response. To prefer the serious is to exercise a preference and to intervene, we always intervene, we cannot do otherwise, and by acknowledging and grasping this we can come to live more thoughtfully. Perhaps the unbathed baby could be read by us as representing forms of speech/life which have not been reflected upon! We have to risk active intervention if we are to prevent the onset of decay. We could only merely leave things as they are and hope we wouldn't be brought to light if we were thoughtless, i.e. if we did not reflect upon what we ourselves do. But, as we have said that is not a human possibility, it is not a course of action which is either desirable or open to us. We proceed by conversing, and as a result of our conversations deciding not to turn back, but to commit ourselves to going on.

Analysis of Paragraph 8

> The worrier treats actions, or interventions, like viruses, i.e. whereas with children pain is normally taken as an indicator that something is wrong, the worrier sees a lack of pain as an indicator that something is going to be wrong. That is he sees lack of pain as producing ease or carelessness, i.e. as failing to produce the necessary precautions, and on the other hand as producing careless actions, and it is these that we need to take precautions against. He treats ease as a doctor would treat a contagious disease, i.e. as a danger and hence as something to be avoided. The worrier then can be treated as a sophisticated child, i.e. he sees not only that pain is an indicator that something is wrong, but also that things can go wrong as a result of a lack of pain, i.e. carelessness. Somehow both seem like functionalists in their failure to question the fact that the goal of the system is taken to be efficiency, i.e. a lack of pain, or of friction! Here we see then that the worrier doesn't really want tension in itself, as we earlier thought, but that he wants tension now as a sign that the future will lack tension!

Response

Again you adopt the form of speech of the worrier and we can only maintain our version of you as a thoughtful interlocutor by hearing your speech as the exercise of irony, for you could not be commending worry by your speech, but are encouraging us to think about our own actions.

By refusing to be turned upside down, i.e. by resisting the persuasiveness of your speech we display how to make progress through it. Let us rewrite your paragraph and substitute ourselves for the worrier and in this manner expose what we do, i.e. what we choose to do and not rest with pointing at a hypothetical other.

We treat inaction/thoughtlessness/silence as an intervention, or better as an interruption to our mode of action/life. That is inaction/thoughtlessness/silence is the virus, it is painful to us. As thinkers/speakers a lack of pain is thoughtful for us, and a lack of thought is painful. The thinker/speaker recognises that a lack of thought not only indicates that something is going to be wrong, but always brings it about. We see a lack of thought not as producing carelessness but as carelessness, but not as easy, for we are at ease in our thoughts/speech, for we orient to our thought/speech as caring for selves, (i.e. both our own selves and other selves). Our interest is not limited to protecting our persons from careless actions by taking precautions, but in thinking about what we do so that we do not act carelessly. If any imagine that being easy is being thoughtless/carefree, we would say that they cannot do any good for their actions are products of either carelessness/accident, or are tinged by their efforts to avoid their own pains. If we settled for a formulation of ease as thoughtlessness we would treat ease as would the doctor you mention, i.e. as a contagious disease, as a danger, but we are pleased your worrier is not your doctor for the good doctor is better formulated not as avoiding disease, but as seeking a cure, and to do this involves contact with the disease, and the risk of contracting the disease in order to produce remedies. So the doctor would want to separate the uninfected from the infected but by doing so places himself precariously in the middle. Similarly the analyst/speaker has to risk considerable contact if he is to come to grips with and help to remould social practices, indeed as we are showing he must always be working from and on the inside. From the outside the worrier appears as one who avoids social contact as your doctor avoids contagious diseases for he imagines others put him at risk.

The worrier's conception of the child that you offer, i.e. as less sophisticated, i.e. as only treating pain as an indicator that something is wrong and not yet realising that a lack of pain indicates that something is going to be wrong, reminds us that if our children treat pain as an indicator that something is wrong this would have been because we had taught them to do so. But we would rather encourage our children and our selves to remember that we must continue to take pains with ourselves, i.e. make an effort, for that is the only way that speakers, social actors can lead better/more thoughtful and more enjoyable lives, and that this effort is always necessary for all. By formulating a lack of pain as thoughtfulness, i.e. as carefulness we show how we are moving so as to deepen the shallow version of worry as conceiving of thinking as unpleasant, i.e. as something to be stopped. What we are uncovering is that thoughtlessness, i.e. the refusal to bring our own forms of speech into our inquiry would have left us paying a very heavy penalty, i.e. the penalty of a dead life, and that would be deeply painful to any who thought/spoke, i.e. to all. But, we need none of us suffer that penalty if only we think about, converse about what we do. We are pro lack of pain, i.e. pro thought, but we remind ourselves not to treat this as a goal, but as a condition we are maintaining by making the effort to continue thinking about how we act, i.e. to continue producing more thoughtful versions of self and society. We do not reduce tension/our desires/our liveliness to the status of friction for to do so is to set out upon a search for lubricants (funny, perhaps that is why solutions could sound so comforting to some!). We seek to sustain our desires by thinking/conversing about them and, by doing so, making them more thoughtful. We will have more to say about the future later, but we are reminded by your final sentence in this paragraph that we do not know what we want, we have to decide, and we do decide more thoughtfully by conversing with thoughtful interlocutors. To refuse to engage in conversations of this type would be to settle for thoughtless wants, and as we are thinkers/speakers, to settle for thoughtless wants could, we imagine, be one way of speaking about alienation.

Analysis of Paragraph 9

Perhaps the medical analogy above can be carried a little further if for a moment we consider the 'yes but' as similar to immunisation, i.e. the acceptance of just a small amount of the disease (not enough to have lasting effects, i.e. to leave a mark), but enough to prevent the disease occurring again. The worrier then accepts in a small way what other says only to know it and be able to reject it more forcibly as a result of this knowledge. The worrier then treats the person who doesn't use 'yes buts' as he would the person who doesn't get immunised, i.e. as a fool.

Response

What a testing but instructive time we are providing for ourselves with the help of your speech!

You speak of the analogy being carried a little further as if you recognise its weakness, and ask your reader to join with you in carrying it, as if on a stretcher. But we want analogies that stretch and strengthen our selves, our relationships, i.e. we want friendly speech, for unless we keep ourselves fit we will not be able to help others or ourselves to move. So when you speak of carrying that analogy further you are asking us for more effort, but as we move so we bring it into more light. 'Yes but' as like immunisation! It no longer sounds that way to us. We hear it as closer to the beckoning of a researcher who is daringly entering into unmapped and possibly dangerous territory. Not to join him, i.e. not to raise questions and try to stretch ourselves beyond conventional boundaries is to succumb to the virus of silence/thoughtlessness that we are exposing as we also expose ourselves. Had we kept both hidden, the former would work to corrupt the latter. The inquirer listens to what others say and weighs how far he can stretch the conversation without being the one to break it down. He listens and speaks so as to play a part in extending understanding for self and other selves. He has no interest in rejecting other, for an interest in rejection is the voice of silence/thoughtlessness. The inquirer cannot accept in a small way what other says only to know it and be able to reject it etc. for the inquirer isn't able to begin by understanding other or himself. The unmapped territory of which we speak is self and self's relationship with other selves. Your speech reminds us that our effort is to hear other's speech as 'yes-buts', i.e. as questioning that stretches us, we don't seek immunity but community.

Analysis of Paragraph 10

Somehow talking to yourself, or thinking before you act seems like the same sort of precaution as immunisation, and the fool does seem like a person who never talks to him/her self. That is the fool is reckless, i.e. doesn't reckon. However the worrier is foolish in this way, in the sense that he fails to take account of (reckon) other's view that thinking out loud is foolish. What other's, the manipulator's, view here presupposes, is that our thinking is foolish, and as a result that it is something to hide with our speech. The fact that this is not possible escapes both the worrier and the manipulator here, who both try to separate speech and thought.

Intervention by Original Speaker:

Perhaps I can display my commitment to community rather than immunity here by responding to the final paragraph of those earlier notes myself in the light of what I have heard you to be saying, for I am disturbed and unsettled by my reading of your responses, but with their help I will make the effort to think about what I said, for I am aware that not to do so is a possibility no longer.

By responding to what I previously said I will be displaying how talking to, or with, our selves which is not limited to observing our imagined beginnings, is our way to be achieving society. So I would now speak of talking to myself not as immunisation but as communisation; not as thinking before I act but as acting thoughtfully; not as a precaution but as social development. By talking to myself I mean engaging in dialectical development, questioning, deepening and not mere repetition for I produce a version of myself as developing not as static. I do not and cannot reify myself for I recognise the freedom I have to extend myself through thought/conversation.

When I spoke of the fool as reckless, i.e. as not reckoning, I was stretching myself in such a way that we could understand how the reduction of thought to reckoning would deformulate men/women. It was too mathematical a notion, and would if left unanalysed have reduced us to numbers.

When I spoke of the worrier as failing to take account of (reckon) other's view that thinking out loud is foolish I was providing a way for us to achieve a reading of the worrier's speech that does us credit, for it is not that the worrier fails to take account of other's view, it is that through his speech he displays how he achieves social character by refusing to be oppressed by silence. If any other did view thinking out loud as foolish that other needs to remember to reflect upon his view and perhaps the worrier's speech could have helped him to remember to do that.

What could be more absurd/more destructive of speakers/thinkers, i.e. of human potential for social development, than an oppressive idea that thinking out loud, talking to ourselves is foolish! I begin to detect, in what I imagined was my disturbed and unsettled condition, that something is going on here and I want to continue to be part of it. So we hear the conventional expression that talking to yourself is the first sign of madness as itself an expression of the dangerously alienating tendency oppressive forms of speech/life have to reduce speakers/thinkers to the status of automatons, clean machines, and we need to fight that tendency if we are to preserve our sanity; if we are to continue developing socially. Yet even the notion of sanity has been rerooted by conventional usage in a notion of bodily health, and hence bodily survival, and needs to be rooted in the realm of decision making if we are to develop social practices which truly recognise the freedom we have to decide whether and how we continue to live. So, if we are to preserve our sanity, i.e. our place as thinkers, as producers of our society, we must resist practices which persuade men/women that their behaviour is acceptable/justified because it is natural, for it cannot be justified on those grounds. We choose how we act and must continue questioning and deepening our manner of choosing if we are to pursue thoughtful/social/moral response-able lives.

But I am weary now for I feel I am being turned upside down, so perhaps I can now take a liberty and rest a while before we proceed.

Response:

You say that it is time you need, and whilst we have doubts about this we have no desire to force you to continue, but will for the present merely remind you that you are not being turned but are yourself doing the turning, as are we with ourselves, i.e. we are not ahead of you but are collaborating with you, so do not imagine you are alone in your efforts for that would be to ground our relationship in a difference your work, and ours, seeks to be outgrowing. When you say 'I want to continue to be part of it' you must intend to include others. One means of proceeding might be for us to think of the worrier as seeing things upside down because he is falling?

NOTES

[1] Left hand and right hand, audience and performer

[2] And what does it matter whose speech it is? i.e. Perhaps we should remind ourselves that we are working upon/with forms of speech not particular embodied persons!

[3] The worrier is after all only a hypothetical construct which is being used to show the importance of our continuing speech/thought about how we can be improving our ways of speaking/thinking.

[4] Of course we are not by martyr referring to the religious type who does devalue human life by an acceptance of a dogmatic belief in an afterlife, for by subordinating himself to myths in this way he does devalue his own act: rather we refer to the truly moral character who does not pretend to know about that which is beyond his life/speech. This is of course only a surface reading of the religious martyr which needs to be deepened but this is not the place to begin a different task.

8 Falling

Original Speaker:

I have written the notes that are here presented in Appendix E as my way of taking issue with your notion that the worrier sees things upside down because he is falling.

APPENDIX E

Para.1   For some reason writing is proving even more difficult than before (this is the eighth first page!) and yet far from this being because I have nothing to say it is because I feel I have made progress from our recent discussion on several different issues. Perhaps it is because I think it is progress that I am hesitant to write about it - now I begin to see a more easy way to write which would be to treat this progress as merely being seeing what was wrong with what we said before, or better what was missing or hadn't yet been said. I shall take this easy way to begin with for perhaps all beginnings are merely ways of easing ourselves into good work. To begin then I will offer work I have done on the following issues in the endeavour to produce the material for some better work to follow:

(A) Haste

(B) Complaining

(C) Falling - (1) regarding upside down and better as downside up.

(D) Falling - (2) and its relationship to manipulation

Section (A)

Perhaps it is no coincidence that haste comes first; however, we have seen in our previous work that the worrier has frequently seen hasty actions as being those which can inflict pain, e.g. the angry man's actions, the careless action, or the foolish action. Even the worrier's own actions, i.e. sticking her neck out, seem to be characterised by haste where haste would mean a lack of preparation, a lack of thought! The worrier's view is that you should think before you act or speak and that hasty actions are simply those which do not allow time for thought. She tries to stop others being hasty, or at least going on being hasty with her yes-buts. She always thinks you should think more before you act or speak, and her yes-but is there even if she thinks better than (i.e. yes buts it) to say it for any reason. She sees an action beginning or perhaps a beginning as a sign that problems have not been remarked upon, and that there are consequently either matters of which the actor is ignorant or matters he is choosing to ignore. Either way the worrier feels obliged to speak even in her somewhat hasty manner. None of this seems to sound new but what will perhaps be new will be the realisation that the worrier, who on the face of it would seem to be the last person we would suspect of or charge with being hasty, is indeed hasty, and hasty in a way, and on an issue which is crucial in understanding how she comes to act (or not act!) as she does. The worrier is hasty in her definition of hasty, i.e. she starts with a definition and works from it. (I have a feeling that I ought to say this more slowly rather than simply repeating it in different ways but perhaps the outcome will be the same.) The worrier is hasty because she chooses not to talk or think about whether her decision that inaction (for her thought) is better than action (for her speech) has any foundation. To say this in one other way the worrier is hasty because she starts by thinking that you should think before you speak (act), and she doesn't see how this is a bad start! That this issue is crucial can be emphasised if it can't be already seen by saying that it is this unconsidered beginning (i.e. finish!) which makes the worrier see all actions as inconsiderate. Indeed it may be this that forces her to see life, i.e. actions (whether her own or others) as falling short: i.e. as falling/failing.

Section (B)

Para.1   A hasty decision is a suitable subject for a complaint; and the worrier's version of speech could be treated as a one sided version of remarking - in the sense that it merely points out the marks, i.e. the worrier's remarks can (and often are) treated as complaints. Given this, some consideration of the grammar of complaints may help us understand the situation within which the worrier speaks. There is something about complaints which suggests they are a last resort (perhaps this is the worrier's version of any action!) i.e. you don't complain if you can act in any other way. The worrier however, as we have seen, tries to restrain herself from acting in any way, and the result is that when she does act/speak, her actions/speech share similar characteristics to complaining. The point about a complaint is that it asks others to act to correct their own error, i.e. it suggests that all the responsibility lies with other, and that the complainer after complaining need only wait for action. The complainer then is relieved of responsibility and it is this that suggests the complainer's superiority - or feeling of superiority. What I am saying is then that complaints issue forth from complacency, (perhaps that is why the elderly complain so much, i.e. they feel they have fulfilled their responsibilities). The person who complains is satisfied that she has done all she could do. Now I feel that this view of the worrier as a complainer underlies hints in your remarks both about the worrier unloading her burden on another and about the worrier stunning from a position of superiority; I also feel that the worrier may be being misjudged here and this I should show in my discussions on falling - more specifically in (C) falling regarding upside down.

Para.2   But before leaving complaining it seems worth saying that this version of a complaint makes it sound like a climax, i.e. you complain when you can't take any more (pressure for example) i.e. you complain when you reach what you perceive to be breaking point.

Para.3   Also somehow the difference between a complaints box and a suggestions box seems to suggest (? complain) that whilst complaints do seem arrogant (i.e. as if from a pseudo superior) suggestions seem humble (i.e. as if from an underling).

Para.4   I have a feeling that the worrier thinks you can or should only complain if you are suffering whereas the complainer feels you should complain whenever you see there is something wrong. But now I have a feeling that it is precisely when there are things wrong that the worrier suffers!

'Yes but' does sound like a complaint unless the but becomes a suggestion!

Section (C)

On falling, regarding your suggestion about the worrier seeing things upside down because he is falling. What I am trying to say is that this is upside down, i.e. because the worrier is falling he sees downside up: up in the sense of above like a ceiling. Without being too fanciful it is as if the problems which underlie others' apparently solid surfaces only come into view as you drop beneath them. (It sounds too neat to be true but perhaps that is why we talk about understanding [understanding] things.) This then could begin to show us why the worrier is miscast as a complainer, it is as if the worrier needs to be falling beneath others in order to point at the weaknesses which he feels they should be aware of. The worrier doesn't look down from above then as a superior or judge would, but looks up from below, and perhaps this also fits with the idea of

157

the worrier as a groveller which has previously been suggested. The problem for the worrier (and perhaps for the others!) is that he doesn't really know why he is falling and this fact combined with the very fact that he is falling provides others with a reason to shelve his advice until a later date. (Again I feel as if I should make more of this section.)

Section (D)

Para.1   On falling, and its relationship to manipulation. Now this seemed like news to me at the time and seemed worth reporting as a result, but is beginning to sound less interesting as I try to say it again. (Perhaps that is what is interesting about strangers and is usually uninteresting about the news, i.e. its newness. This is odd, for the worrier was always wanting to start with what she knew and risked losing interest even if she succeeded, whereas the quality of the new is that it is what you didn't know!)

Para.2   The point here is that though we seem to have been occupied with the idea of falling our attention, or mine at least, has been drawn away from what would seem to be a very important consideration. This is that the notion of a fall presupposes that the falling object is totally dependent upon the environment within which the fall takes place, e.g. for its length, duration, direction and, perhaps because it isn't a jump even for its beginning. The fall then is outside its object's control. The reason why this seemingly obvious consideration is important is because it can bring home to us the way the worrier produces his environment as manipulative. In a fall then you are totally at the mercy of your environment, there is nothing you can do. To produce yourself as falling is then to produce yourself not as a fool, i.e. one who isn't responsible for his own irresponsibility but as a responsible person who is unable to exercise his responsibility because he is falling, i.e. if only he could stop he could get started.

Para.3   Somehow the worrier thinks you must be outside to avoid being taken in but feels that if you are outside you must be falling, he has no conception of weightlessness.

Para.4   When you are falling you have no way to resist the pressures which act upon you, and at most can only work on different ways of succumbing to them. A fall now sounds very much like the idea of climax we spoke of earlier, and yet perhaps this will be because we had a worrier's version of climax, i.e. as a fall - as being unable to go on - as falling by the wayside - i.e. as being an end. Which reminds me that perhaps to treat life as anticlimatic is precisely to treat it as a fall, i.e. as an anticlimb, whereas a climb is up and in control a fall is down and out of control.

Para.5   Now this is the stage at which I should try to draw together the different issues so as to reach a clear conclusion, however I have no desire to try to tie things together here (perhaps strangle) i.e. I have no desire to finish it off. Perhaps this is because I feel a bit like the king's horses and the king's men when they were faced with Humpty Dumpty, i.e. tired. Alternatively perhaps it is because we all too readily see a new order as chaos because we haven't yet got beneath it, i.e. perhaps it doesn't need to be tied together.

Response

Your speech reminds us that we do not take issue with what others say rather we choose to work with what we hear, we are not taking issue with you/against you, for we are not interested in argument/accusation, but in dialogue/movement and development. So what do we hear/remember as we read this Appendix?

Prior to working on/with specific sections of it we can say that our work upon it has led us to deepen our understanding of the notion of 'praxis'. Up until now when we have heard this notion being invoked it has been as a method to encourage apparently non practical theorists to relate to the 'real world', to try out, test their theories, or whatever, as if ordinary conventional social practices were first, and were untheoretical. But that was an indolent reading, for now we hear praxis as reminding us that all social practices are necessarily theoretical, and that it is only when we ground them by exposing their theoretical foundation, their place as possibilities, that we provide ourselves with the means for preserving or altering them without force. So the loud belch we heard on the platform at Slough station was the expression of a theoretical orientation, and as such is in need of the same analytic exposition as is Parsons General Theory, both are social practices which call out for analysis, and we mean neither any disrespect by the juxtaposition. Analysis is a process through which we continue to liberate our social practices by hearing how they/we were, and are, grounded in theory/possibility about which we can converse and decide in a friendly manner. A commitment to analysis is a commitment to continuing exposure which helps us to grasp how deeply impractical 'theories' are, which are designed to bring conversations to an end. Analysis is always possible, and is always desirable, and our readers will exercise its practice on our speech by making the effort necessary to deepen and liberate their hearing of this speech. In this way our readers move ahead of us and we will need to listen hard to their responses if we are to continue together. However we continue to expose ourselves by our reading of your speech for through our reading of it we are uncovering much that we had almost forgotten, such is our need for continuing conversation. Your speech helps us to stimulate so many formulations now that the format of our writing seemed to be bursting at the seams, not from over indulgence, from exercise/development. By our writing we display our intention to be promoting a social situation in which seams are stretched and moved rather than burst. For whilst the urge to end rather than to continue conversation/thought will always remain, threatening to burst in upon us and interrupt, we need not listen to it. We turn to your speech and this is what we hear, this is what your speech helps remind us to say:

Analysis of Paragraph 1

For some reason writing is proving even more difficult than before (this is the eighth first page!) and yet far from this being because I have nothing to say it is because I feel I have made progress from our recent discussion on several different issues. Perhaps it is because I think it is progress that I am hesitant to write about it - now I begin to see a more easy way to write which would be to treat this progress as merely being seeing what was wrong with what we said before, or better what was missing or hadn't yet been said. I shall take this easy way to begin with for perhaps all beginnings are merely ways of easing ourselves into good work. To begin then I will offer work I have done on the following issues in the endeavour to produce the material for some better work to follow:

(A) Haste

(B) Complaining

(C) Falling - (1) regarding upside down and better as downside up.

(D) Falling - (2) and its relationship to manipulation

Response

Having something to say would be oppressive to us for we do not have to say anything, perhaps those who imagine they must have something to say before they speak display a possessiveness which prevents speech. They display an orientation to speech as statements like bank statements that reveal what they own, but forget how they can only continue to develop by involving their speech in conversation/action rather than trying to save it/protect it. We, none of us, have to say anything, we always choose what we say, so having nothing that we have to say is the only way for dialogue to proceed. So, we do not write or speak because we have made progress, that would have been bragging which treats listeners with disrespect. We are writing/speaking as our way of continuing to make progress possible. Indeed how could we make progress/become more thoughtful before we speak/think? That would have been to commit ourselves to the deeply anti social notion of inspiration which underlies the restrictive view of art as being the prerogative of the gifted few. We make progress possible through speech/thought and we all of us speak. Our discussions bring us up, perhaps they whirl us forward as if on a discus. We have not made progress from them, we don't have to leave them behind, but we make progress on them, and can only continue to do so by continuing to discuss/to engage in conversations.

You say that was your eighth first page and we do not hear you as asking for our pity, or admiration, but as reminding us that reworking/thinking about what we write/say is what social action is about; you are not saying you have rejected/dismissed the previous seven first pages, but that you learnt from writing them, they helped you rather than hindered you, as your writing is helping us.

Writing about things whether progress or whatever, i.e. description, can be boring, for it seeks to secure a special place for the writer as privileged, and by doing so disengages the reader. Description treats the reader like a conscript. It can leave the reader with nothing to do but listen, or at best later to decide to step in the writer's footprints, and to try to relive his experiences. We do not write about things in that descriptive way, we write for our friends, for our selves.

You remind us that we are at ease in our writing, that we do not seek an easy way to write, for our writing is our effort to deepen our selves through what we hear. We formulate our efforts as uncovering what we missed, not what was missing. We do not add to what was said as if from our own mysteriously inherited private store, but stretch ourselves by admitting how thoughtless indolent readings are. We do not seek the easiest way to overcome our hesitation, our doubts, but proceed in the most honest/friendly way available to us, and by doing so may well increase our doubts, but we do not deny our characters in such a way that we leave ourselves unemployed: i.e. with nothing to do.

You remind us that we do not ease ourselves into good work as if it is already there waiting, we ease ourselves out of bad work, i.e. out of oppressed/constrained modes of speech/thought.

You remind us that our current work uncovers/reveals and instructs us as to the depths of past speeches or other's speeches. Progress for us is a deepening of understanding, of the ability to understand. It is not a product of time or travel for our future work is not necessarily an improvement on our past work for we can make mistakes, take wrong turns. If our work is to improve it is we who do the improving. The material we work with is immaterial for it is the condition of the worker that matters. So, when you speak of producing the material for some better work to follow, by material, you must mean workers/thinkers, for these are the stuff from which better work is derived.

Analysis of Section (A)

Perhaps it is no coincidence that haste comes first; however, we have seen in our previous work that the worrier has frequently seen hasty actions as being those which can inflict pain, e.g. the angry man's actions, the careless action, or the foolish action. Even the worrier's own actions, i.e. sticking her neck out, seem to be characterised by haste where haste would mean a lack of preparation, a lack of thought! The worrier's view is that you should think before you act or speak and that hasty actions are simply those which do not allow time for thought. She tries to stop others being hasty, or at least going on being hasty with her yes-buts. She always thinks you should think more before you act or speak, and her yes-but is there even if she thinks better than (i.e. yes buts it) to say it for any reason. She sees an action beginning or perhaps a beginning as a sign that problems have not been remarked upon, and that there are consequently either matters of which the actor is ignorant or matters he is choosing to ignore. Either way the worrier feels obliged to speak even in her somewhat hasty manner. None of this seems to sound new but what will perhaps be new will be the realisation that the worrier, who on the face of it would seem to be the last person we would suspect of or charge with being hasty, is indeed hasty, and hasty in a way, and on an issue which is crucial in understanding how she comes to act (or not act!) as she does. The worrier is hasty in her definition of hasty, i.e. she starts with a definition and works from it. (I have a feeling that I ought to say this more slowly rather than simply repeating it in different ways but perhaps the outcome will be the same.) The worrier is hasty because she chooses not to talk or think about whether her decision that inaction (for her thought) is better than action (for her speech) has any foundation. To say this in one other way the worrier is hasty because she starts by thinking that you should think before you speak (act), and she doesn't see how this is a bad start! That this issue is crucial can be emphasised if it can't be already seen by saying that it is this unconsidered beginning (i.e. finish!) which makes the worrier see all actions as inconsiderate. Indeed it may be this that forces her to see life, i.e. actions (whether her own or others) as falling short:

161

i.e. as falling/failing.

Response

Your speech helps remind us that we do not take Ordinary Language Philosophy at its word if it claims its authority arises from its decision to restrict itself within the confines of usage. For ordinary usage is not confined. Analysis seeks to hear ordinary language as philosophy, and by doing so frees speech from the constraints of pedantry by making room for continuing dialogue; by treating speakers with the respect social/moral actors, i.e. thinkers, deserve. But how has this reminder been drawn from your speech? Well, listen to part of what you said.

> The worrier is hasty in his definition of hasty, i.e. he starts with a definition and works from it.

Initially we heard this as criticism of the particular definition but we were confused by the fact that you appeared to rely upon the same meaning of hasty in your description of the worrier, for you offer no alternative. But now we hear that it is the notion of definition which requires thought, for those, if any, who hear definitions as decisive, i.e. as closing discussions, and yet still rely upon definitions as starting points, deny themselves the possibility of dialectical development, in effect they would deny the possibility of social change. So, we choose to formulate definitions not as means of closure, but as possible ways forward, we formulate definition as against/opposed to finishing, and by doing so remind ourselves not to treat definitions as starting points or finishing points, indeed not to treat them as points at all, but at most as pointers. The step from your speech to the preceding paragraph was then only a short one and without your speech as stimulus might not have been taken. So let us turn to listen more closely to your speech.

You say 'Perhaps it is no coincidence that haste comes first' and remind us that we achieve readings of human actions/social actions that elevate: that begin to do them justice, by not allowing them to be reduced to happenings, to coincidences, to being first in the sense of prior to thought. It was no coincidence that haste came first, for you decided to place it first. And our way of reading your speech is our decision, we are not forced by your speech to read it in a certain way, for that would be to hear speech rather than silence as violent, that would be to forget the possibility of friendship.

You speak of haste as a lack of preparation, a lack of thought, and by doing so must mean to remind us to formulate preparation as concern about what we are intending, and will intend, to do, and not as fantasising what may, or is likely to happen and preparing ourselves for it. Such a notion of preparation as the latter reveals a lack of thought for it forgets how involving ourselves in preparation is acting, it is producing, we are always acting rather than subjecting our selves to happenings. So we would formulate the actions of the angry man, the careless man, and the fool as thoughtful, i.e. as theoretical, not as lacking thought, for to reduce them in that way to products of thoughtlessness would be to subject our selves to happenings, coincidences, i.e. to force. But when you spoke of those actors as lacking thought you could not have meant they were thoughtless for that would have been to deny those actions theoreticity: that would have been to dehumanise, i.e. to differentiate in such a way as to rule out conversation. You must be seeking to help us remember for ourselves that all social actions are incomplete, i.e. can be becoming, and always will be able to be becoming, more thoughtful.

As we proceed we hear your speech as reminding us that we cannot act or speak without having thought for we are thinkers. So, by saying that we should think before we act/speak, you remind us that we could not do otherwise without denying our characters. But, we must resist the inclination to hear your notion of before in too concrete a fashion for the thoughtful action might require speed, i.e. thinkers act thoughtfully, but it does not follow from this that they need to be presented with time, i.e. that they can be deprived of it; that their actions are contingent upon it. Rather it is that thinkers/speakers make time for thought and it is in this sense that we spoke of Socrates as having a full life. So we do not hear your speech as commending actions that allow time for thought, for that would be to leave thought contingent upon things, it would be to deny the possibility of liberating social action, we hear you as commending thoughtful action, i.e. that which does not begin by being allowed, but by freely deciding.

Where you speak of the worrier as trying to stop others being hasty we hear her as stopping others stopping, i.e. as keeping others and herself moving in the same manner that our reading of your speech keeps us moving. She wants to stop them in order to engage with them in conversation which would be productive for both, and for others, rather than letting each remain unknown/superficial to the other. Conversations of this sort require commitment which, if it is present, provides time. They do not require uncommitted time for they bring apparent commitments into question. Dialogue is not hasty for it is not oriented to accomplishing.

You remind us that the worrier's 'Yes but' does encourage us to 'think better than' for it chooses not to let speakers, whether self or other, settle in the quicksand of conceit of knowledge. When you say 'she thinks better than to say it for any reason' you remind us that we do not speak for 'any reason' for that would be to reduce the serenity of social life, of moral action, of continuing dialogue, to serendipity, and what would be the virtue of that reduction?

You remind us that our problem is never that of starting for we have all already started, but of finishing too soon, our problem is not that of awareness of ignorance, but of a too ready wish to ignore the benefits that ignorance, as a knowledge of that which we cannot know, can bring, i.e. the freedom to decide. So you are commending continuing inquiry as a form of action/research, for you could not be commending non action for you are aware that we are all always acting.

You remind us that the worrier, and each of us, would have been acting with conceit of knowledge if we settled for versions of others' actions as thoughtless, for how could we know that they were? Indeed the thought filled character of our own action is enough to remind us of the absurdity of settling for indolent readings of others in that way. So, when you say '... the worrier feels obliged to speak even in her somewhat hasty manner' you have not forgotten already what we said about obligation, you are saying that the worrier is a thinker, i.e. she does/says what she wants to say, and risks the accusations of hastiness that might be hurled by those, if any, who continue to restrict themselves to the weak notion of preparation we have moved from.

Your remark that 'None of this seems to sound new ...' can only be read by us as an expression of fatigue, for as we will show when we come to analyse your Section (D) (i.e. where you speak of an interest in news) we do not rely upon happenings for our news. But more of this later.

163

You go on to speak of suspecting or charging the worrier with being hasty, and in doing so remind us not to settle with suspecting, or charging other's speeches for how could that be the exercise of friendship? But we misunderstood you for by speaking of the last person we would suspect or charge, you sought to remind us to think of ourselves, i.e. to reflect upon what we ourselves are doing, and not to be so ready to speak of those who may appear before us, i.e. superficial versions of self as taking the place of other.

Your parenthetic comment about speaking more slowly reveals to us how speed has little to do with the matter, for if your speech was oriented around the idea that 'perhaps the outcome will be the same' and you were relying upon a version of outcome as mere happening, your speech would have been hasty whatever the speed of delivery. However, we hear your speech as revealing a commitment to a dialectical notion of conversation in which outcome might mean drawn out by analysis. Furthermore, our notion of self as developing dialectically displays how repetition is no longer a possibility for us, for we do not remain the same.

You say 'The worrier is hasty because he chooses not to talk or think about etc. etc.', but what we are saying is that she would not choose not to commit herself if she had remembered that inaction is not necessarily to be preferred to action. She could only not talk or think about her decision for as long as its character as a decision evaded her. Once we remember that that division is grounded in a surface commitment to thought as safer than speech, that surface itself becomes as safe a place as the sun's surface. We would not turn back, we would not opt for silence rather than conversation.

You go on to speak of the worrier's start; and perhaps you will permit us to say that we imagine you can only propose that she starts in this way for you have imagined you have started this way yourself, as have we; and you speak of that start as a bad start, but how could it be bad if it helped us to begin? We imagine that only one who continues to fear action would speak in such a way as to find fault with starts rather than to deepen them, to be moved by involvement with them.

You emphasise that this is crucial as if you do not trust your reader to read well, but we must misunderstand for you are a thoughtful interlocutor, and would not orient to your reader as being less thoughtful than yourself, i.e. you must be reminding yourself that unconsidered beginnings, i.e. finishes could finish you off. Also you remind us to address the unexplicated notion of crucial, for we would say that analysis of speech is always necessary if speeches are to be formulated as considerate actions. So what we are saying is that if we began by imagining we needed to know what was crucial before we began we would never begin for we decide, but do not know, what is crucial for us. We could have decided to treat as crucial, issues of life and death, or of happiness and unhappiness, or of honesty and dishonesty, or of originality and traditionality, and so on, but what we are deciding to make crucial is remembering that it is we who decide. So, we would not speak of an unconsidered beginning making the worrier see all actions as inconsiderate, but we might say that thinkers, by considering their own beginnings seek to act more thoughtfully, seek to develop. Our reading of your speech encourages us to lay stress upon our possibilities so as to subvert oppressive forms of speech. You speak of unconsidered beginnings as forcing the worrier to see life, i.e. actions (whether her own or others) as falling short, and by doing so you remind us that it is we who subvert oppressive forms of speech/life by remembering/by considering our beginnings and not by refusing to reflect upon them.

Analysis of Section (B)

Para.1   A hasty decision is a suitable subject for a complaint; and the worrier's version of speech could be treated as a one sided version of remarking - in the sense that it merely points out the marks, i.e. the worrier's remarks can (and often are) treated as complaints. Given this, some consideration of the grammar of complaints may help us understand the situation within which the worrier speaks. There is something about complaints which suggests they are a last resort (perhaps this is the worrier's version of any action!) i.e. you don't complain if you can act in any other way. The worrier however, as we have seen, tries to restrain herself from acting in any way, and the result is that when she does act/speak, her actions/speech share similar characteristics to complaining. The point about a complaint is that it asks others to act to correct their own error, i.e. it suggests that all the responsibility lies with other, and that the complainer after complaining need only wait for action. The complainer then is relieved of responsibility and it is this that suggests the complainer's superiority - or feeling of superiority. What I am saying is then that complaints issue forth from complacency, (perhaps that is why the elderly complain so much, i.e. they feel they have fulfilled their responsibilities). The person who complains is satisfied that she has done all she could do. Now I feel that this view of the worrier as a complainer underlies hints in your remarks both about the worrier unloading her burden on another and about the worrier stunning from a position of superiority; I also feel that the worrier may be being misjudged here and this I should show in my discussions on falling - more specifically in (C) falling regarding upside down.

Para.2   But before leaving complaining it seems worth saying that this version of a complaint makes it sound like a climax, i.e. you complain when you can't take any more (pressure for example) i.e. you complain when you reach what you perceive to be breaking point.

Para.3   Also somehow the difference between a complaints box and a suggestions box seems to suggest (? complain) that whilst complaints do seem arrogant (i.e. as if from a pseudo superior) suggestions seem humble (i.e. as if from an underling).

Para.4   I have a feeling that the worrier thinks you can or should only complain if you are suffering whereas the complainer feels you should complain whenever you see there is something wrong. But now I have a feeling that it is precisely when there are things wrong that the worrier suffers!

'Yes but' does sound like a complaint unless the but becomes a suggestion!

Response:

You say '... i.e. you complain when you reach what you perceive to be breaking point" but our reading of your speech reminds us that we are always speaking at the breakin point. To complain in the manner of Ivan Illyich Pralinsky, i.e. to sink into our chairs saying 'we were not able to stand it' is not the way of genuine inquiry which does not settle for what it imagines it already knows it can stand, but which chooses to seek to extend itself.

So, we cannot read this speech or any speech whilst we rely upon a conventional notion of complaint, for that would lead us either to accept what you say, i.e. to have no complaints, as if we imagined your speech was perfect, or to reject your speech as if we imagined its imperfections meant it wasn't worth hearing. But you could not be resting with a notion of complaint as accusation, for accusation has no place in friendly relationships. So by complaint you must mean the taking up of our place with/beside the defendants. We say this, for the plaintiff, by resting in accusation, reveals how he settles for social difference, how he imagines he needs no companions for he seeks to free himself from other by imprisoning other, rather than by liberating other and providing himself with a colleague. So, we seek to read your speech as in the service of liberation, for by doing so we will be revealing how those, if any, who continue to rest with indolent readings allow their pliability to be placed in the service of oppression/of silence: how the compliant can only complain when it is too late, and are then not heard. So, let us read your speech closely and seek to uncover how we can instruct ourselves through it.

'The hasty decision to which you refer is the decision to accuse other, ...'. The hasty decision to which you refer is the decision to accuse other, and an act of accusation always places the thinker over with the defendant/the oppressed. '... and the worrier's version of speech could be treated as a one sided version of remarking - in the sense that it merely points out the marks, i.e. the worrier's remarks can (and often are) treated as complaints.' So the worrier is heard as advocate for the oppressed by the accuser for he points to the weaknesses in the accusation's argument. '... Given this some consideration of the grammar of complaints may help us understand the situation within which the worrier speaks. There is something about complaints which suggests they are a last resort (perhaps this is the worrier's version of any action!) i.e. you don't complain if you can act in any other way.' The worrier is speaking not only for herself then, but for all who are accused, and as the advocate of the oppressed she does act as the oppressed's last resort, for we don't need advocates if we can speak for ourselves. '... The worrier however, as we have seen, tries to restrain herself from acting in any way, and the result is that when she does act/speak, her actions/speech share similar characteristics to complaining.' Yes, the worrier/thinker does restrain herself from acting in any way, for she seeks to act well, and acting well for her is speaking with/for the oppressed. No wonder Nietzsche sees Socrates as spokesman for the rabble! 'The point about a complaint is that it asks other to act to correct their own error, i.e. it suggests that all the responsibility lies with other, and that the complainer, after complaining, need only wait for action.' Right again, for all the responsibility for an accusation does lie with the accuser, and the complainer need only wait after complaining for she has nothing to fear from an accusation and by waiting allows the accuser to decide. 'The complainer then, is relieved of responsibility'. The complainer in our sense is relieved of responsibility for she has shown the thoughtlessness/the conceit of knowledge from which accusation derives, i.e. she is relieved of any responsibility for a thoughtless act by her own claiming of response-ability, for thoughtful actions are those that raise themselves above/out of the thoughtlessness of accusation. '... and it is this that suggests the complainer's superiority, or feeling of superiority.' We, the complainers, are superior if you wish, but our superiority rests in our refusal to degenerate and settle for/with dehumanising differences, and it ought not to need saying that there is room for all who choose to sit and converse at a table grounded in friendship. '... What I am saying is then that complaints issue forth from complacency, (perhaps that is why the elderly complain so much, i.e. they feel they have fulfilled their responsibilities).' Yes, if complacency means being aware of our place, our speech on behalf of, or with the oppressed does issue forth from complacency, but, as this work displays, complacency of this sort is not self satisfied, but is intent upon achieving social character. It is never satisfied with itself, for it always has more to do. 'The person who complains is satisfied that she has done all she could do. Now I feel that this view of the worrier as a complainer underlies hints in your remarks both about the worrier unloading her burden on another ...' So now the worrier is not unloading a burden upon another but choosing to share other's burden. '... and about the worrier stunning from a position of superiority;' and her remarks are not intent upon stunning from a position of superiority but upon sharing in the task of elevating/liberating social life. 'I also feel that the worrier may be being misjudged here, and this I should show in my discussions on falling - more specifically in (C) falling regarding upside down.' So when you speak of the worrier as being misjudged you remind us to say that we are not judging your speech or any speech as if it is not our own, we are making the effort to improve social relationships by improving our means of relating, our speech/thought. Your speech cannot be read as a complaint, in the conventional sense, about our earlier response to your earlier speech, for that would have been for us the readers to have misjudged you.

So now, when you say in Para. 2 '... you complain when you can't take any more (pressure for example) ...' you are reminding us not that we should allow ourselves to be pushed and pulled and only begin to make a fuss when we break, but that free men/women/social actors/thinkers are those who formulate the very slightest amount of pressure/oppression as too much to take, and so you are reminding us to be joined together thoughtfully against oppressive conventions so as to deal with them as soon as they begin to be heard, and not to have to start when we cannot hear ourselves for the din.

Re Para. 3, the skilful way in which this speech upon suggestion and complaint boxes conjures up the image of the partition between the factory floor, and the office, almost persuaded us that you would be content to remain servile, i.e. to act as an underling to the forceful man but we know you better than that. You must be using understatement in such a way as to allow us, your readers, to detect the emptiness of the social situation your speech purveys. There is no friendship to be found, no conversation, no room for social development, only at most for corrections/practical suggestions (sic) and all they can do is keep the silence tidy.

As to Para. 4, and more specifically its last sentence, we can see how you could not be intending 'complaint' and 'wrong' to be read in an indolent fashion for if they were the worrier would be one who always suffers, for there is and always will be something wrong. This would be to have heard the worrier as one who has no sense of the good of imperfection, the good of liveliness, the good of not knowing but deciding. This hypothetical worrier would be led to grumble about her life by noticing things like: she has to die, she can't have everything, she can't do everything, and that would be to fail to see that grumbling doesn't do any good, that it merely mirrors the hypothetical worrier's image of the world as being that which fails, that which is faulty. Instead of repairing faults she restricts herself to finding faults, for she faults her ability to do repairs. She doesn't see (in her restricted/blinkered vision) that she is responsible for faults, that by worrying about imperfection, e.g. death perhaps, she allows herself to be strangled by her form of speech/life. If this was worry it would always be counter productive, for by seeking protection rather than understanding that hypothetical worrier would be discarding her productive potential, when she could, as we are showing, be working to discard the blinkers.

However, as we were saying you could not be intending complaint and wrong to be read in that fashion. We have already offered a formulation of complaint, and as to wrong it is oppression of whatever kind, for instance, a version of the good life as free from imperfection is oppressive for its very inconceivability could lead those committed to it to objectify themselves as failures that nothing/anything can be done with.

Furthermore, you remind us that those, if any, who hear 'yes buts' as complaints in the weak sense, would be those who sought suggestions, i.e. would be those who did not want to have to think for themselves. They would avoid questions they could not answer, and would also look for others to rely upon rather than choose to think.

Perhaps you hear our speech as extremism, as shouting, but our readers know that if you do, this is because your hearing has become accustomed to the oppressive silence that can surround us if we start to forget to think.

Analysis of Section (C)

On falling, regarding your suggestion about the worrier seeing things upside down because he is falling. What I am trying to say is that this is upside down, i.e. because the worrier is falling he sees downside up: up in the sense of above like a ceiling. Without being too fanciful it is as if the problems which underlie others' apparently solid surfaces only come into view as you drop beneath them. (It sounds too neat to be true but perhaps that is why we talk about understanding [under-standing] things.) This then could begin to show us why the worrier is miscast as a complainer, it is as if the worrier needs to be falling beneath others in order to point at the weaknesses which he feels they should be aware of. The worrier doesn't look down from above then as a superior or judge would, but looks up from below, and perhaps this also fits with the idea of the worrier as a groveller which has previously been suggested. The problem for the worrier (and perhaps for the others!) is that he doesn't really know why he is falling and this fact combined with the very fact that he is falling provides others with a reason to shelve his advice until a later date. (Again I feel as if I should make more of this section.)

Response:

You speak of the worrier as having been miscast as a complainer and by doing so remind us to cast our speech into deeper/more profound water. You remind us that we need to, and do, cast ourselves into our versions of other. You remind us to take a step further back and to recast and this time to cast the worrier as a thinker/speaker for only in this way can her speech come to life for us.

Your speech reminds us that we are lifting ourselves by our speech by hearing deepening not as dropping down, for to deepen our understanding is to elevate social action, it is to make our selves less shallow, to give ourselves depth. So whilst your speech may have been an attempt to defend the worrier as she appears, i.e. whilst your speech seemed to befriend the worrier as she appears, it would have been restricting yourself to a superficial reading: it would have displayed a lack of understanding, for you would have been claiming to know more than you knew. We have no need to be fanciful for we are talking about what we can be getting to know better, i.e. about our forms of speech/life, and by making this effort we raise ourselves above the apparently solid surfaces of our beginnings by choosing not to treat our selves as things. By our decision not to be redirected by usage we provide ourselves with room to continue moving, our environment is no longer heard as merely a limitation/a ceiling. Not only do we not drop beneath surfaces but we decide not to be kept down by them.

We help ourselves to proceed more thoughtfully by calling into question the worrier's decision to claim to know she is falling, i.e. to treat that as a fact which calls for explanation: it is not a fact but a possibility which she decides upon. So, if this hypothetical speaker is falling it is because she too readily settles for a version of herself as a worrier rather than a thinker, and we imagine she is too ready to clutch at this straw because she takes her stand/position from danger rather than from doing what she decides is good to do. So, once having adopted this position, i.e. this stance, the worrier formulates questions as designed to dislodge, upset, damage, rather than befriend. No wonder she imagines she is fragile, for she imagines her surface is brittle, thin, and that these aspects of it are transparent, but also essentially her. However, by beginning to see how self is not adoptable but is adaptable we are displaying how we all do better to formulate our selves as developing through friendly social interaction, and not as standing still, for that can only lead to stagnation.

Our readers will doubtless orient to our speech as advice for they will formulate advice not as grounded in superior knowledge but in friendly good intentions. They will join with us in calling into question the grounds of speech and in doing so will not seek to shelve questionable advice, for that would be to care only for their own persons and to reveal a failure to hear how thoughtful actions care for self and other selves. So with our speech we are seeking to do what you say you feel you should have done, i.e. to make more of that section, and by doing so to achieve a more thoughtful notion of productivity than more of the same.

Analysis of Section (D)

Para.1   On falling, and its relationship to manipulation. Now this seemed like news to me at the time and seemed worth reporting as a result, but is beginning to sound less interesting as I try to say it again. (Perhaps that is what is interesting about strangers and is usually uninteresting about the news, i.e. its newness. This is odd, for the worrier was always wanting to start with what she knew and risked losing interest even if she succeeded, whereas the quality of the new is that it is what you didn't know!)

Para.2   The point here is that though we seem to have been occupied with the idea of falling our attention, or mine at least, has been drawn away from what would seem to be a very important consideration. This is that the notion of a fall presupposes that the falling object is totally dependent upon the environment within which the fall takes place, e.g. for its length, duration, direction and, perhaps because it isn't a jump even for its beginning. The fall then is outside its object's control. The reason why this seemingly obvious consideration is important is because it can bring home to us the way the worrier produces his environment as manipulative. In a fall then you are totally at the mercy of your environment, there is nothing you can do. To produce yourself as falling is then to produce yourself not as a fool, i.e. one who isn't responsible for his own irresponsibility but as a responsible person who is unable to exercise his responsibility because he is falling, i.e. if only he could stop he could get started.

Para.3   Somehow the worrier thinks you must be outside to avoid being taken in but feels that if you are outside you must be falling, he has no conception of weightlessness.

Para.4   When you are falling you have no way to resist the pressures which act upon you, and at most can only work on different ways of succumbing to them. A fall now sounds very much like the idea of climax we spoke of earlier, and yet perhaps this will be because we had a worrier's version of climax, i.e. as a fall - as being unable to go on - as falling by the wayside - i.e. as being an end. Which reminds me that perhaps to treat life as anticlimatic is precisely to treat it as a fall, i.e. as an anticlimb, whereas a climb is up and in control a fail is down and out of control.

Para.5   Now this is the stage at which I should try to draw together the different issues so as to reach a clear conclusion, however I have no desire to try to tie things together here (perhaps strangle) i.e. I have no desire to finish it off. Perhaps this is because I feel a bit like the king's horses and the king's men when they were faced with Humpty Dumpty, i.e. tired. Alternatively perhaps it is because we all too readily see a new order as chaos because we haven't yet got beneath it, i.e. perhaps it doesn't need to be tied together.

Response to Para.1

Here is where we raise the issue of news, as we earlier intimated we would; your first paragraph of this section ends with you saying that ' ... the quality of the new is that it is what you didn't know.' But we remember with the help of our reading of your speech that we need not restrict what we didn't know to what happens to us for such a restriction would deny our productive character. So, if conventionally the media relies upon a version of news as happenings, e.g. plane crashes, falls in the value of currency, etc. etc., and the media's interest both reflects and regenerates this superficial version of news in which its public may ground itself, and yes we do here mean ground down in the sense of reduce; we, as thinkers/speakers/inquirers say that there is a far more important sort of news and this is production/development. Only by grasping this can we grasp our potential to develop and resist oppressive forms of speech/life, i.e. the silence, that seeks to persuade us that thoughts occur to us, that ideas come from out of the blue. We seek to remind any who have come to believe that ideas occur to them that they need not allow themselves to be oppressed by forms of speech such as that. By remembering that our ideas are products of our activity as thinkers/speakers we are beginning to pull ourselves together, to understand how convincingly the ideas we have, if we rely upon them, and take up a position from them can leave us disjointed and merely subject to contingency. Whilst chance does play a part in the production of our social relations those relations only truly develop when we grasp their non contingent character; when we grasp that they are dialectical developments. So now we hear why news as happenings is only worth reporting/repeating, when news as development is worth reporting in the sense of bringing back into our lives, into how we proceed. Reporting of the latter sort is deeply interesting, i.e. it is engaging.

So here we are liberating ourselves from forms of speech/life that would have us forget that we produce ideas, that they do not happen to us. This writing is a product of our work and it displays how dignified labour does not subordinate itself to current conventions, it has to risk doing more than career.

Response to Para.2

When you speak here of being occupied with the idea of falling you remind us not to treat ideas as secure permanent homes. If we occupy an idea it is with a view to liberating its use, and not with a view to domesticating ourselves, i.e. we are not interested in orienting our actions to becoming merely house trained, that would be boring.

Now what you say about the falling object all sounds very correct but for all its correctness it is hollow,[1] and of little other than marginal interest to us, for we are not objects. And yet, perhaps your speech can help remind those, if any, who are tempted to worry that if they orient to their environment as that which might befall them, as that which might cause them pain, they are bringing 'it' upon themselves in the profound sense of objectifying themselves.

Furthermore by saying that 'In a fall (then) you are totally at the mercy of your environment there is nothing you can do', you not only remind us of the weakness of anthropomorphism, but you remind us that we might be able to do nothing only if doing something is limited to saving our persons. Yet we might shout to warn others of the hole, we might sing to cheer ourselves up, or we might feel sorry for ourselves. So you remind us that whatever we choose to do we do do something not nothing. So now we hear how even one who is falling can and does act response-ably. How the hypothetical worrier of whom you speak would strangle her life, if she were a possibility, which fortunately she is not, by settling herself within this limbo like state of wanting to stop in order to get started, without noticing that whilst she can perhaps choose to stop, she does not need to stop in order to get started for she is, as we are all of us, already moving.

Response to Para.3

What you say about weightlessness is interesting and we presume that by saying that the worrier has no conception of weightlessness you direct us towards the ambiguous notion of gravity which can perhaps draw together the notions of falling and seriousness, i.e. as heaviness. However how do we think of being outside as being weightlessness for our movement is towards stretching ourselves out of oppressive usage? As theorists/inquirers, i.e. as speakers oriented to reflecting upon, rather than habitually repeating, superficial versions of self, we have no need to let ourselves settle/solidify, so ourselves are not heavy. Our commitment to our inquiry is such that we do not fantasise versions of our selves that hold us back, that drag us down, why should we? Perhaps the hypothetical worrier would imagine that her outsideness, i.e. the fact that she is outside nature means that she is worse than nature. She might even fantasise that she alone was in this condition, i.e. that other persons had no problem acting 'naturally', i.e. that others were inside. We however choose to view our unnaturalness/our deliberateness, i.e. our social achieving of thoughtful character, as raising us above, rather than lowering us below nature. We cannot be natural but we do seek to be social, i.e. to act thoughtfully.

Response to Para.4

How can we hear this paragraph such that our method of hearing improves? Well, we hear how it directs us not to settle for what something may sound like, i.e. it reminds us that to hook our attention upon sounds/appearances could be to clutch for the first 'thing' to come to hand as if we were falling, i.e. that would be to settle for the first thing that stands out rather than to make the effort to act more deliberately. Your speech reminds us not to hang our place in the present upon the most apparently convincing idea from our recent past, for that would have been to display a version of good ideas as finished, i.e. as means to secure, rather than as ways to release, ourselves. So when you say 'perhaps this will be because we had a worrier's version of climax etc.' you are not relating an old idea to a new topic, i.e. a fall, but you are bringing the idea of ideas as climaxes into question, i.e. you are reminding us to think about how we think. If we do hang our persons from past ideas something has to give/collapse, either the ideas or our persons. So, your speech helps us to remember not to treat our ideas as hooks, unless by hooks are meant those we might carry with us and manipulate to aid our climb. So, when we spoke of life as anticlimatic we intended that what would be heard was that it does not let us end, but your speech reminds us that it could have been heard otherwise, but by doing so you show us how life does not let us end/complete: how we will always have more to do.

Yes, our work/life can be heard as a climb, i.e. as up and in control but if it is heard in this way 'up' must be being formulated as upbringing, as elevating our society/our lives and control must be being formulated not as restricting but as against merely rolling, i.e. as deliberate movement, for merely to roll along with the tide, of convention for instance, is to do no more than fall, it is to be restricted/subject to force. Also, we must be extending the conventional notion of climb so as to release it from a connection with the notion of summit or end, for ends are not essential to us. Our work is rewarding in itself, as is all true labour, we do not degrade our activity by orienting to its end as being desirable, for we desire to continue.

Response to Para.5

You say you have no desire to tie things together here, no desire to finish it off, and yet you say it is the stage at which you should try to reach a clear conclusion. You are seeking to remind us not to orient to conclusion as the stage at which to tie things together, as the stage at which to finish things off, but as clearing the way for us to proceed with our inquiry. You speak of all the king's horses and all the king's men being tired when faced with Humpty Dumpty and remind us that Humpty Dumpty's fate is the fate of the soldiers, unless they refuse to be treated like chattels, i.e. unless they differentiate themselves from the horses. Perhaps the king was behind the wall from which Humpty Dumpty fell? He is certainly not in evidence where the work needs to be done! The soldiers' problem is not Humpty it is their refusal to think about their relationship to the king. If any orient to their work as something they have to do, i.e. something they are forced to do, then they also are likely to be tired rather than stimulated by it.

Your last sentence reminds us that current chaos could all too readily be seen as order unless we seek to rise above it, to be hearing how social order does not rest upon orders/oppression, but develops in and through friendly relationships.

NOTES

[1]   That is a constant feature of correctness.

9 Hurrying

•

APPENDIX F

Original Speaker:

Para.1   I have reread Appendix E which was a forgetful piece of work
for I forgot that I was in the main only worrying about worry,
i.e. producing worry's faults rather than trying to do better than
just worry and to see some good as well (in this instance the
good of worry). The result is that the somewhat more confident
appearance of the paper was like an ill chosen turn of phrase,
i.e. it was hasty, because it could have led us to think that the
worrying had been replaced by confidence. In fact I think it did.

Para.2   The point here then is that if producing faults is not enough, it
is not enough to say this; or better it is foolish to merely find
fault with fault finding. The set of notes was full of itself then
in more ways than one. But now this is starting to sound like an
encore and we are hardly likely to be impressed by that if we
weren't impressed by the performance itself.

Para.3   My forgetfulness in the last set of notes could be treated as
merely one example of the worrier's hurry to get out (i.e. it is
when you are in a hurry that you forget things). In an odd way
this factor in the worrier's make-up shows us how she can
become the non worrier, for she can forget anything, even on
occasions her worries, (i.e. like the drunk, or when she is
drunk). I think this may be why she sticks her neck out, though
later she forgets that it was through forgetfulness, and may

even be tempted to think it was courage!

Para.4   One reason amongst others why this movement (if such it can be called) is no real help is that she may later stumble into them, the worries again, and this is what might have been expected as she didn't know where she left them or why!

Para.5   Hurrying, like worrying degrades the present, i.e. you hurry what you are doing because you want to do something else, or because other exerts pressure upon you to move on to something else, and you treat other's approval as more valuable than what you were doing. In both cases what you are doing at present takes on a secondary role as something to be rid of or finished off. Hurrying becomes what you are doing and it is this that causes forgetfulness for knowing how to hurry is knowing how to forget things, e.g. worries. When the worrier acts her actions are hurried because she wants to get what she is doing over with, because she doesn't think it is worth doing, and this can make her appear unworried. Whereas, perhaps all hurry should be taken as a sign of worry, i.e. if you think what you are doing is worth doing why hurry it?

Para.6   The worrier has a version of herself as hurrying, she has to hurry because her action is always a last resort. By doing this she gives herself a holiday from responsibility by seeing the environment as producing the limits, i.e. as exerting the pressure. For example, these notes aren't as good as they could have been because I haven't had time to reread Candide or whatever. The worrier thinks she needs to hurry, and she does, but not for the reason she gives, for she forgets that she produces her own time limits. She hurries to get away from her own products, i.e. it is blame or guilt that she seeks to escape from. The worrier wants to think that accidents can happen when you are hurrying, and that because accidents 'happen' she need not feel responsible. The worrier lacks self control, i.e. hurries, because she produces herself as lacking self, i.e. as acting accidentally, not deliberately, i.e. as not knowing what she is doing, e.g. not knowingly worrying. The fact that she sees herself as not acting deliberately when she does act shows us why the worrier is very close to the angry man; for it shows us that worry produces unthoughtful actions, i.e. precisely those it is critical of. When these accidents do occur all that they produce in the worrier is the feeling that the best she can do is not act in the future, for she doesn't see that she could act deliberately. Perhaps, more strongly, she is critical of deliberation on other's part for she treats it as tacticalness, i.e. as mere usage. She reduces deliberation to tacticalness and sees tacticalness as the exercise of self control in the interest of self protection, and, because she has a bad version of her own self she doesn't see self as worthy of protection/preservation.

Para.7   The worrier tires herself by hurrying and then thinks and says that she can't work well because she is tired. Tired work is yet another version of the last resort, i.e. all you can do when tiredness really takes a grip is nothing, and this is what the worrier wants to do, but she also wants to guard against it

175

because she sees it as full of dangers, (e.g. like drinking after arranging a business deal and messing it up!). By hurrying the worrier produces her situation as dangerous, but she needs to remember that perhaps she and others work best when they are tired, i.e. off guard (forgetful of their self protection). When she is tired she can no longer use her speech to protect herself. In this way we can see that good work reveals self and doesn't call for a version of self control as self protection. (Revealing self need not be revelling in self.)

Para.8   The hurrier sees what she is doing as a waste of time, i.e. she has, like the revolutionary, a version of prehistory - if I could get this finished I could get started. Perhaps both the hurrier and the revolutionary come to waste time because they see the present as something which has in effect to be thrown away, i.e. wasted. So the worrier, like the manipulator, could at best only leave dead bodies behind with her yes-buts, her stopping of starts. Your speech suggests that the challenge is to stay alive, i.e. lively, i.e. not to become dull, without worrying. In the manner of speaking of this paragraph this would seem to be to be now, i.e. not to consider the present as a waste of time. Which, whilst it says other things as well, still shows us that worrying about now isn't enough. That sentence even made me yawn, i.e. dullness can be the present, and this seems to be the problem raised by forms of anti philosophical realism which say that things are as they appear to be. Somehow being now must involve a conception of possible presents rather than that of alternative futures which rely upon a version of the present as a waste of time. To see the present as waste in terms of the future, or the past, or vice versa, is merely another version of stopping and starting, and the problem this raises is one of routine, i.e. it sounds like clocking in and out. The problem with mere routines is they both are dull and produce dullness. To just go on talking as a matter of routine would both be dull and produce dullness. In the same way to just go on worrying is to settle for routine, i.e. to become dull, thus to see worrying as enough is to allow worry to produce ease. To be satisfied with merely satisfactory performances is to be dull, i.e. it resonates .with playing safe, and this resonates with the worrier's version of the good life as staying on the ground. To settle for usage seems like just going on for the sake of going on, and seems like a rather pointless exercise, or perhaps as mere exercise as a result. Routine then, like usage or worry has no sense of the good of anything. Acceptance of routine is the refusal to acknowledge other possibilities; to go on worrying is the refusal to acknowledge possibilities other than worry. Somehow teasing or cajoling seem to make more of these possibilities than worry. The worrier tends to stop other's starts whereas we can get people started by teasing or cajoling but even this involves openness or some revealing of self by the one being teased. If the worrier could come to treat problems as teasing and not merely as faults she might arrive at a different version of the good from the good as safety.

Para.9   The worrier uses her yes-buts to disarm others, i.e. they are like safety catches but she seems to resist all efforts to get her to

176

face up to what she does know: which is that not facing up to things can be a very unsafe practice. Staying alive without worrying is produced by the worrier as being beyond her, i.e. worrying produces life as routine and provides room for worry in this way. My problem is that I can't help (says I!) feeling that the last set of notes is better than this, which is perhaps saying that I am easily taken in by usage, which might be just another version of the worrier refusing to see that what she tries to escape is the fact that escaping does rely upon some notion of the good, i.e. as safety.

ANALYSIS OF APPENDIX F

Our readers will no doubt be making the effort, as we are doing, to be achieving a reading of this one of your speeches that does our communal commitment to continuing conversation justice, but our efforts, whilst increasing our desire too attend carefully to what you are saying, are also increasing our awareness of the limited level of ability we have to hear. However we know, as our readers know, that we are only able to stretch these limits if we are aware of them. So our continuing committed engagement with your speech is as necessary for us as ever.

Analysis of Paragraph 1

I have reread Appendix E which was a forgetful piece of work for I forgot that I was in the main only worrying about worry, i.e. producing worry's faults rather than trying to do better than just worry and to see some good as well (in this instance the good of worry). The result is that the somewhat more confident appearance of the paper was like an ill chosen turn of phrase, i.e. it was hasty, because it could have led us to think that the worrying had been replaced by confidence. In fact I think it did.

Response:

Your speech reminds us that we are thinkers/speakers not worriers, and by remembering this we are able, through our conversations, to reflect upon worry and to display how it could only be a possibility for us if it was formulated as a thoughtful activity, for if it is not a thoughtful activity it is beyond/beneath us. Our reading of this paragraph reminds us to think about what we are doing now, for this is what you are doing when you think about what you were doing, i.e. it is not merely an exercise in history but your way to improve your current mode of speech/action. Your speech also reminds us that our speech is more confident, for we are able to confide in others, for we have no wish to orient our choice of turns of phrase with a view to how we appear, for we are well aware that as thoughtful interlocutors we spend only as little time and effort as is necessary on the surface, i.e. with appearances. As thoughtful interlocutors we seek to rapidly cut through superficial make up in our efforts to be achieving and displaying true human character. For us, confident speech displays its awareness of its place in dialogue, in friendly relationships, it displays, through its openness, its awareness of its need and respect for other speakers.

Analysis of Paragraph 2

The point here then is that if producing faults is not enough, it is not enough to say this; or better it is foolish to merely find fault with fault

177

finding. The set of notes was full of itself then in more ways than one. But now this is starting to sound like an encore and we are hardly likely to be impressed by that if we weren't impressed by the performance itself.

Response:

We begin by hearing how quickly you perceive that a shallow reading of our speech in Section 8 could have heard it as commending mere disobedience and unruliness. When you speak of finding fault with fault finding you are reminding us how we are in our speech/action, doing more than accusing the law/the state of being oppressive: i.e. as in the main restricting its energies, or concentrating its resources upon seeking out those at fault, rather than hearing how it could do better by seeking out and extolling those qualities that help lead us towards more social lives. So, when we spoke of obedience and orders as anti social we were referring to their place in oppression, disorder, silence, and not to our formulation of obeying which is as being open to listen to, i.e. to converse with, others. True social order is always understood as continuing engagement in conversation. So the law as continuing conversation elevates social life for being its producers we can willingly submit to it or change it, we cannot be oppressed by what we submit as being the way we choose to live. But, what if the notion of law has degenerated, and become so closely identified with oppression by those, if any, who are tempted to worry? Then we do better to speak of the lawless state as desirable, i.e. as being the condition in which free men/thinkers/all men abide, and proceed to decide upon how they desire to live rather than to let the indolent rest content to settle for a version of continuing oppression as an evil but a necessary evil. Your speech reminds us that our commitment is to a version of law as liberating, i.e. as the expression of a communal commitment, to prevent our society stagnating within the confines of thoughtlessness. Whether that thoughtlessness takes the form of (1) a commitment(!) to law as that about which we need not think, i.e. question, or (2) a commitment(!) to lawlessness as that about which we need not think. Both of these extremes seek to deny our character as speakers, i.e. as those who can choose/decide how we want to live.

Perhaps you, our original speaker, will invoke your notion of not enough here, and say it is not enough to say this. Of course in a sense you are right/correct, but the notion of not enough could be grounded in the idea of an imaginary goal that has to be accomplished, and this could distract its users in such a way that they never do anything. We, as speakers, are concerned with engaging in the ongoing work of improving our conceptions of self and society, i.e. of intending to do good, and the fact that we can never do enough always leaves us more to do, and where is the harm in that? It is only a problem for those oriented to completion, to finishing, rather than to continuing development.

We seek to be liberating our selves through our speech by displaying how it does not contain us, i.e. we seek to be filling it out by hearing how we can continue to be instructed by it. So our speech is not full of itself, but it is full of the desire to continue deepening and extending our versions of self and society. Your speech reminds us not to merely repeat what we have heard for we are aware that thoughtful interlocutors are those who do not set out seeking to be impressed, or to impress, but set out to increase understanding, and increased understanding can only be being achieved in the context of friendly relationships.

So, when you speak of it being foolish to merely find fault with fault finding you are not commending that we dismiss fault finding, but that we befriend it by seeking to understand it as an instance of that speaker's effort to do what she thinks is good. So, whilst revenge, as conventionally understood, is not an activity in which we would engage, we call upon ourselves to offer a formulation of the possibility of revenge so as not to limit ourselves to a speechless opposition to an apparently thoughtless activity. Perhaps revenge could be formulated as our efforts, as those who could have been accused/oppressed, to lay claim to what is ours, i.e. our freedom to decide how we live, how we speak. If revenge is formulated as an instance of moderation in this way, i.e. as grounded in friendship, not in continuing abuse, this can perhaps help to encourage us to think more about our responses, for then extremism is less likely.

So, we do not orient to your speech as something to complain about in the conventional sense, indeed we do not orient to it as a thing at all, for our efforts are intent upon elevating our readings of others' speeches, for we seek to be rising above contingency/mere thingness, and not to be dragged down into it by settling in versions of our selves as being limited by others' speeches as if they were happenings: as if we did not play a part in the readings we achieve of them!

Analysis of Paragraph 3

> My forgetfulness in the last set of notes could be treated as merely one example of the worrier's hurry to get out (i.e. it is when you are in a hurry that you forget things). In an odd way this factor in the worrier's make up shows us how she can become the non worrier, for she can forget anything, even on occasions her worries, (i.e. like the drunk, or when she is drunk). I think this may be why she sticks her neck out, though later she forgets that it was through forgetfulness, and may even be tempted to think it was courage!

Response:

By listening carefully to your speech we hear how you are commending your forgetfulness, for what you are referring us to is that we do not begin by already knowing, but by seeking to extend our inquiry, and we cannot proceed in this way unless we are able to forget what we imagined we knew, i.e. unless we let loose what we may have imagined were our secure moorings. This is especially necessary for any who seek to call themselves sociologists, i.e. who seek to speak about our social condition. So, we hear remembering as the active awareness of our ignorance/our lack of knowledge that frees us in such a way that we can choose to converse and achieve communal decisions as to what we want to do/to be.

So now the worrier's hurry to get out is not heard as commending escapism but as desiring/risking less unreflexive, less blinkered modes of inquiry. We admit that we do not know what we are doing, so our inquiry is genuine, and yes, we do seek to hurry to forget 'things' for we seek to increase our awareness of the productive part each of us plays in constituting what we may refer to as things.

Your speech reminds us that we do seek to forget our worries, i.e. we seek not to treat them as secure moorings, but to treat them as products of our own activity, and as such as forms of speech/action that we can think about and alter. So, by thinking more deeply about what we are doing we uncover that we have no desire, or need to drink to forget, for we hear our liveliness to consist in thoughtful activity, and not in the movement towards mindlessness. But, we are aware that our enthusiasm and the freedom of our speech/thought might be heard as drunkenness by listeners who could not yet conceive of any other way to be liberating their own activities than a stock of bottles.

The last sentence of this paragraph of yours seeks to tell us how you are aware that courage is less thoughtful than forgetfulness, for the latter is more encompassing, i.e. it involves risking speaking/acting in a committed way that does not rest in the impulsiveness of apparently secure feelings, e.g. rage, but in continuing doubt, i.e. in a continuing commitment to conversation/inquiry.

Analysis of Paragraph 4

One reason amongst others why this movement (if such it can be called) is no real help is that she may later stumble into them, the worries again, and this is what might have been expected as she didn't know where she left them or why!

Response:

Here your speech is heard as the exercise of irony, for it appears to offer us an almost irresistible invitation to worry, i.e. 'One reason amongst others ...' seems to warn us that even if we grasp what you mean here, in an instant we will be confronted by numerous further reasons which lie in wait, though they are better hidden than the one you offer. So if we rested with this reading of your speech we should come to a halt here, and spend ourselves hypothesising about what, and where, the other 'reasons' to which you refer are and might be. But, we will resist that temptation to immobilise ourselves, by choosing not to rest upon the surface of your speech. We proceed by hearing the movement to which you refer as our continuing inquiry So, our mode of inquiry lets loose worries, i.e. makes them less secure, but as you correctly point out this is no real help. Here you are reminding us not to seek help for worries are always and always will be readily available and there is no help for it but to deal with them if they seem to threaten to invade our conversations. True, we may very well stumble into them again, for our inquiry continues to lead us into uncharted territory, but if we concentrate upon the virtue of what we are doing rather than upon what may or may not happen to us, worries will be kept at the periphery of our thought and conversation, where, if anywhere, they belong. If we did know where we left our worries, and why, we would have reduced our freedom of action by reducing the room we have for thoughtful good intention; which is that effort to continue acting in the face of our worries, i.e. without needing the confinement of a completely integrated, closed, finished environment. Philosophy as thoughtful action is only a continuing possibility for us whilst worry remains a probability with us.

Analysis of Paragraph 5

Hurrying, like worrying degrades the present, i.e. you hurry what you are doing because you want to do something else, or because other exerts pressure upon you to move on to something else, and you treat other's approval as more valuable than what you were doing. In both cases what you are doing at present takes on a secondary role as something to be rid of or finished off. Hurrying becomes what you are doing and it is this that causes forgetfulness for knowing how to hurry is knowing how to forget things, e.g. worries. When the worrier acts her actions are hurried because she wants to get what she is doing over with, because she doesn't think it is worth doing, and this can make her appear unworried. Whereas, perhaps all hurry should be taken as a sign of worry, i.e. if you think what you are doing is worth doing why hurry it?

Response:

Here you remind us that we also degrade the present if by the present is meant mere contingency. So, we make the present the servant of our good intentions. The freedom provided by our relationship with the present is such that our pasts and futures become pliable. By deliberating we increase our efforts to use our potential to do what we desire to do rather than to restrict ourselves to merely having things happen to us. We are engaged in resisting the persuasiveness of speech which seems to call us to submit to nature: to contingency, for speech of that kind contradicts itself and would, if it could, deny the possibility of a version of our relationship to the present as liberating. Our desire is to play a part in producing more enjoyable, more liberated lives, for that part is both enjoyable and liberating. We are aware that speech of this kind will sound odd to those who imagine they are committed to nature, for they, if any, may hear it as unnatural. But, through our speech we are seeking to emphasise that as social actors we are not and cannot be natural, and that it is through our unnaturalness that we seek more liberated/more thoughtful forms of speech/life. But, our readers are well aware of this already, and we remember that our speech needs to continue to be stretching us, perhaps by sounding unnatural, if it is to continue to engage their thoughtful efforts.

Your speech reminds us that we do not hurry what we are doing because we want to do something else. If we appear hurried it is only to those who imagine that all seek to finish. In that way our commitment to proceed with the deepening of our speech, i.e. our enthusiasm to continue, may be misheard. Similarly your speech about other exerting pressure seeks to remind us that by producing good formulations of others' speeches we call upon ourselves to continue improving our work/lives. So pressure from other is self induced and is not oppressive but liberating. Other's approval does become more valuable than what we are doing for by orienting to other as a thoughtful interlocutor/as a friend we hear other as trying to get the best out of us, and this involves us in re-evaluating and perhaps no longer doing what we imagined we were doing.

So, when you speak of what we are doing at present taking on a secondary role you are reminding us to think about what we are doing, i.e. you are reminding us that as we are thinking about it we are not allowing what we do to be reduced to what we happen to be doing, for that is allowing our actions to be reduced to accidents, contingencies. But, by getting rid of, or finishing off what we are doing you do not mean dismissing, completing it, but continuing extending/deepening our actions, i.e. acting more thoughtfully, more socially.

Yes, hurrying as we are formulating it, i.e. as enthusiasm/confidence, does become us, and it enables us to continue by not imagining we know things. It displays our continuing movement rather than the immobility of a strategy grounded in the stubborn defence of what a talker might pretend to know. We hear superficiality/stubbornness as that which gives birth to stubs, i.e. as that which rules out development.

Yes, when we act we want to get what we are doing over with, in the sense of turned over, thought about, for unless we are reflecting upon what we are doing in this active way what we are doing is not worth doing, i.e. it is only what we happen to be doing, it is not deliberate. If our speech appears unworried/unthoughtful this is because it is being heard by those who refuse to bring the ends of their own actions into question, i.e. it is being heard by those who assume they know what is good. Whilst they perhaps imagine that the good is what may happen to them, and are disappointed when it doesn't, we remember to think of the good as the standard for our actions and not as a reward. An orientation to rewards degrades labour/human action by encouraging the worker to treat his labour as a means to an end, rather than as a continuing process which is its own reward. Our work is not rewarding in the conventional sense, but through it we are able to bring the conventional notion of rewards into a light that reveals its alienating force. Rewards are the stuff out of which heavens come to be fantasised and lives that are lived around the base of these fantasies are conceptualised by those living them as ways of wasting/using time and effort. Rewards of that kind even if they did satisfy momentarily cannot sustain us, for as thoughtful actors we cannot settle in a condition that seeks to ward off our desire to continue thoughtful production.

But those, if any, who have been swayed by that alienating notion of ends/goals as the good will perhaps reduce their reading of this work to a happening, to at most good fortune,and by doing so will continue to stubbornly persist in treating themselves as things to which other things happen; rather than as thinkers who are collaborating with others in such a way as to act rather than merely be acted upon. What, and how you, our original speaker hear, displays what you imagine you are, and it is what we each of us imagines we are that we must be proceeding to bring into question. What we imagine we are can limit or extend our conception of what we do produce, i.e. our conceptions of good and bad. Whilst we are not responsible for nature, the conceptions we use of good and bad are our responses, and we are becoming more social by contemplating and stretching the limits within which these usages could have confined us.

Analysis of Paragraph 6

The worrier has a version of herself as hurrying, she has to hurry because her action is always a last resort. By doing this she gives herself a holiday from responsibility by seeing the environment as producing the limits, i.e. as exerting the pressure. For example, these notes aren't as good as they could have been because I haven't had time to reread Candide or whatever. The worrier thinks she needs to hurry, and she does, but not for the reason she gives, for she forgets that she produces her own time limits. She hurries to get away from her own products, i.e. it is blame or guilt that she seeks to escape from. The worrier wants to think that accidents can happen when you are hurrying, and that because accidents 'happen' she need not feel responsible. The worrier lacks self control, i.e. hurries, because she produces herself as lacking self, i.e. as acting accidentally, not deliberately, i.e. as not knowing what she is doing, e.g. not knowingly worrying. The fact that she sees herself as not acting deliberately when she does act shows us why the worrier is very close to the angry man; for it shows us that worry produces unthoughtful actions, i.e. precisely those it is critical of. When these accidents do occur all that they produce in the worrier is the feeling that the best she can do is not act in the future, for she doesn't see that she could act deliberately. Perhaps, more strongly, she is critical of deliberation on other's part for she treats it as tacticalness, i.e. as mere usage. She reduces deliberation to tacticalness and sees tacticalness as the exercise of self control in the interest of self protection, and, because she has a bad version of her own self she doesn't see self as worthy of protection/preservation.

Response:

The best we are able to do here with this paragraph of your speech is to hear it as a piece of vicious and biting satire which would be all the more pernicious if it were not that its superficiality calls out for us, its readers, to be continuing to display how we can be continuing to deepen our commitment. And yet, as always our way of hearing your speech involves us in stretching and remoulding the modes of hearing with which we might have rested. So, we hear your speech not as a vindictive attack upon another, the sole intention of which is to draw attention away from yourself, but as a controlled piece of writing which allows us to be achieving a version of self that is worthy of preservation. So, we will do our best to unravel our reading of this paragraph for it is only by doing so that we can proceed to deepen and extend our inquiry.

You begin by speaking of the worrier as having a version of herself, now this manner of speaking creates difficulties for we would rather consider worry as an activity than as a character, for unless we do so we bind ourselves to/in a version of the character as a worrier and prevent any movement. However, perhaps we could hear that, character's acceptance of the version of herself as a worrier as a last resort, i.e. it sounds better than nothing, i.e. than saying we don't know who we are, but we emphasise sounds. For us, the decision is always to remember that we do not know who we are, and the desperateness of this decision, though it remains always with us can make it sound like a last resort. Indeed for those, if any, who decide to claim that they know who they are the conversation is over, they are at their last resort and can move no more unless they are later prepared to question their decision. Yes, those who decide to claim to know what they are do give themselves a holiday from response-ability, but what a thoughtless notion of holiday it is! That is, it rests in the confusion created by speech which hears freedom to decide, to act response-ably, as oppressive.

Of course we could always have done more reading before we began to speak/write, but we know that it is only by listening to, and having others listen to, what we write that we can be learning how better to read. Do we choose to do more reading before we decide to remain silent? Conventionally that is not the norm, but wouldn't it make more sense? Conventionally, or so it sometimes seems, people remain silent if they aren't sure of what they are thinking, but we hear how this prevents development. We speak in order that we might continue instructing ourselves, learning. So, rereading Candide could have been good, but only if we were better readers when we came to it again.

You speak of the worrier hurrying to get away from her own products (one instance which you offer is that of time limits) i.e. of trying to escape blame or guilt. Now blame and guilt are foreign to us, for by recognising that we all always act with good intentions we further recognise that if we are dissatisfied with what we have done in the past, the action in question must have been, or be being formulated as unintentional We 'escape' blame and guilt by recognising that we are all always doing what we think it is good to do. If we make what we later acknowledge was a mistake this was a product of conceit of knowledge/silence for which lack of self/silence can be blamed, but we cannot be blamed or feel guilty, but of course by listening to others we can deepen our version of self such that we do not make similar mistakes again. Continuing conversation with thoughtful interlocutors, and not remaining silent, is the way in which we seek to achieve less oppressive modes of action. Our continuing engagement with others is such that we no longer need the cloak of silence to hide private anti social disintegrating fantasies, for hiding our desires is being oppressed.

You go on to say that the worrier wants to think accidents can happen when you are hurrying, and we confess that we began by hearing your speech as an instance of this, i.e. as you hurrying to get away from the version of self/other that you had produced and for which you felt to blame. But, this would have been a less thoughtful reading for it would have reduced your efforts to improve your version of self, your manner of hearing other speakers, to fearful directionless scurrying, and your continuing presence in this conversation tells us that your actions are more than that. Of course accidents can happen, and we are not responsible for them, but we are reducing their place in our lives by making our actions more thoughtful, less like mere happenings.

We seek control by self not control of self, i.e. self control for us is continuing liberation from contingency, and we continue to increase the amount of our control, i.e. the extent of our liberation by hearing other's speech as reminding us that we have more to do. Liberation/the increase of control by self/thought is a process that need not be conceived of in terms of achieving a goal, an end. We imagine that some, perhaps worriers, may wish they were natural, i.e. seek to act accidentally, i.e. wish to be things rather than thinkers. We imagine that they might treat the fact that they decide what they think is good or bad as a problem that they would be without if they were natural. At most, these, we imagine, would seek to be good natured, but that fantasy leaves them uneasy for they anthropomorphise nature and see it as containing good and bad, perhaps hunters and hunted, or whatever. But eventually if they pursue that path they must degenerate and become anti social for they can neither have, nor see, any reasons for what they or others do, they seek to silence thought. Perhaps they imagine that if they are good natured no harm will come to them, but we know it already has, for they are losing their ability to decide for themselves.

You speak of the worrier as seeing 'herself as acting accidentally, not deliberately, i.e. as not knowing what she is doing, as not knowingly worrying'. Now this reminds us that by seeing we were acting accidentally we would be increasing our potential to act more deliberately, i.e. unless we begin by seeing the accidental nature of non deliberate actions we cannot be beginning to make them more deliberate. But you speak as if by not knowing what she is doing, she is not deliberating, and here you are engaging in satire, for it is only when we do not already imagine that we know what we are doing that we can deliberate and choose. So we hear not knowing as grounds for deliberation where from your speech it could appear that you ground deliberation in knowledge. That would be oppressive, it is the movement to completion, the urge to eliminate freedom, to extinguish desire. Furthermore, you speak of the 'worrier' as not knowingly worrying, now this in a small way is the crux of the matter, for by being thinkers/speakers if we worry it is unknowingly, in a deep sense we don't do it, for when it happens we aren't ourselves.[1]

You speak of 'The fact that she sees herself, etc.' and remind us by doing so that you are engaging in satire for if the worrier herself cannot know she is worrying how could another know? By choosing not to treat others as things, i.e. by choosing not to reduce their speech to a fact we hear that we seek to show how actions could be more thoughtful, and by doing so to increase the possibility of what might otherwise have remained impossible. So, as thoughtful interlocutors we produce versions of actions as thoughtful, and by doing so we always rise above mere criticism. And, by rising above mere criticism we are always showing ourselves better ways to act/speak in the future, for we see that we cannot act, and do not desire to act, accidentally. That is, as social actors, as theorists, our actions are always thoughtful/deliberate, it is not that we could act deliberately, but that we do. We seek to continue developing our modes of deliberation, and not to perform some miraculous transformation of ourselves from accident to non accident, we seek only to develop what we already are. We are not critical of deliberation on other's part; we hear how our version of other does display our version of self. We seek to elevate that tacticalness which disguises and hides bad versions of self in silence, by showing how versions of self are social achievements that develop through deliberation/conversation. By seeking to produce versions of self that are worthy of thoughtful/moral/social actors we are showing why we need not restrict ourselves to bad versions of self, for self is not a thing that can only be changed by force, it is a dialectical development that flows from increasing liberation out of/from force/thoughtlessness.

By hearing that paragraph as satire we hear how it allows us to develop through our relationship with it, rather than to submit to it, and our work with it reminds us that if we had imagined that our selves were natural, perhaps even that it was natural to have a bad version of ourselves, we would have heard no need to work at developing, for we would not have understood what self can do by way of developing. If we restrict our thought/speech to a version of self as natural we reduce our actions to the status of accident/contingency and by doing so rule out any form of liberation by restricting our speech to that of cause and effect.

Analysis of Paragraph 7

> The worrier tires herself by hurrying and then thinks and says that she can't work well because she is tired. Tired work is yet another version of the last resort, i.e. all you can do when tiredness really takes a grip is nothing, and this is what the worrier wants to do, but she also wants to guard against it because she sees it as full of dangers, (e.g. like drinking after arranging a business deal and messing it up!). By hurrying the worrier produces her situation as dangerous, but she needs to remember that perhaps she and others work best when they are tired, i.e. off guard (forgetful of their self protection). When she is tired she can no longer use her speech to protect herself. In this way we can see that good work reveals self and doesn't call for a version of self control as self protection. (Revealing self need not be revelling in self.)

Response:

Whilst your speech in Para. 6 could have persuaded us to submit to a weak version of self, here you speak in such a way as to appear to entice us to discard our commitment to friendship, and to attack, for the surface of your speech seems to reveal your weaknesses. And yet, that degenerate reading of your speech does not detain us for long for we know that your speech seeks to help us to remember not to attack but to befriend. Your speech calls upon us to display how friendship/thought liberates us from any thoughtless urge to protect our persons by attacking and killing or capturing other, i.e. from the urge to differentiate and dominate.

If in the analysis that follows, or has preceded, our speech takes on an aggressive tone, that aggression is not directed at you, but with and for you against an oppressive and constricting version of self. Your speech helps us to remember that as thinkers/speakers we do extend our inquiry by tiring deformed notions of self that might have been heard as secure moorings, but are now revealed as what they are, i.e. shackles. We are bringing ourselves to see and display how the work of liberation consists in the weakening of those shackles and in preventing the din of their clanging from drowning out our conversation.

So, we are saying that speakers who remain tied by/or within conceptions of self (and hence of all selves) as being a worrier can never work well, and can only be beginning to work by wearing that conception of self down. We do not seek to do nothing, indeed we recognise that we can never be doing nothing, we seek to act as thoughtful interlocutors act, i.e. as what we are, i.e. as social/moral/free actors. We do not formulate resting as doing nothing, as you imagine the worrier does, why should we?

However, lifting oppression, liberating ourselves is heavy work, but the penetration of the lessons learnt is such, that after resting our resolve to continue is greater than ever. And, though our work is heavy, by being freely chosen, i.e. by being in line with our commitment it is engaged in willingly, we are not forced to do it, and, we can share it with others. The danger that wanting to do nothing brings for the worrier is a sneaking awareness that her talk is little more than a paper thin mask that hides a death wish, for the urge to stop thinking is the call of silence, and this can only issue forth from a throat already tightly in the grip of a form of speech that is forgetting it is conversation.

But, what of your speech, let us read it and be reminding ourselves through our reading how we befriend other by hearing other's speech as the exercise of friendship. We reveal how conceptions of self are continuing social achievements which display our sameness with other speakers, i.e. which display what we have in common. Whereas, talk which seeks to continue differentiating between self and other selves so as to protect one person from another is always limited to grovelling, for by seeking to speak in a way that will not offend the other's person it degenerates into obsequious bletherings that do none of us any good. Separatist versions of self that seek to deny their need of other selves could degenerate into that sort of noise if it were not that by denying their denial acceptance we encourage them to bring their superficiality into question.

But, what of your speech! You say 'The worrier tires herself by hurrying and then thinks and says that she can't work well because she is tired'. Now as we have said we view any person who chains her speech to/in a conception of self as a worrier as unable to work at all for as yet she does not know what work is. Perhaps she imagines it as speaking to other, her jailer, in such a way that he tortures her no longer and provides sustenance or whatever, i.e. she speaks in order to impress or persuade other. So working well is, for her, gaining other's acceptance and not extending her own and other's version of self and social relationships in such a way that superficial differences are dissolved. So, work designed to impress other where other is formulated as different is alienated work and can never change the relationship between self and other selves such that conversation is elevating and not merely the tiring work of clinching a deal to which neither is deeply committed. Talk which is intent upon clinching deals of that sort is guarded and this is why it is not eloquent, it does not flow. The effort of guarding one's person against other persons is, we imagine, tiring, but that in itself could remind those, if any, who talk in this way, that they need to, and can, find better versions of speech than the effort to maintain difference between self and other selves.

So, you remind us that our best work is when we are off guard, but this is not

186

when we are tired, on the contrary it is when we are most active, i.e. when we are with friends. By speaking openly we are guarding against degenerating into a form of speech that reduces other to worthless objects, or worse to the status of enemies. So, talk which orients to personal protection provides an instance for us of the tiredness that is forced upon those weighed down by oppressive versions of self. You are right when you say that good work reveals self and doesn't call for a version of self control as self protection, provided you are referring to the weak notion of self as known. But, of course, we protect our self (i.e. our version of self as good thoughtful character) by committing our persons to continuing conversations/inquiry, and not by shying away from other for fear of injury to our persons, for the latter course of action detracts from our character.

But, perhaps as earlier you will express fears for us, for you may hear our speech as leaving us defenceless. Now whilst on the last count you may be correct you ought not to fear for us, but if anything to speak in our defence for you will by now be aware that any who would attack us need to engage in conversation for their own good. If what we are saying is mistaken then a thoughtful response from our listeners will help to instruct us, but an attack would be self defeating, for our interest is not in defensiveness but in continuing collaborative inquiry.

Analysis of Paragraph 8

The hurrier sees what she is doing as a waste of time, i.e. she has, like the revolutionary, a version of prehistory - if I could get this finished I could get started. Perhaps both the hurrier and the revolutionary come to waste time because they see the present as something which has in effect to be thrown away, i.e. wasted. So the worrier, like the manipulator, could at best only leave dead bodies behind with her yes-buts, her stopping of starts. Your speech suggests that the challenge is to stay alive, i.e. lively, i.e. not to become dull, without worrying. In the manner of speaking of this paragraph this would seem to be to be now, i.e. not to consider the present as a waste of time. Which, whilst it says other things as well, still shows us that worrying about now isn't enough. That sentence even made me yawn, i.e. dullness can be the present, and this seems to be the problem raised by forms of anti philosophical realism which say that things are as they appear to be. Somehow being now must involve a conception of possible presents rather than that of alternative futures which rely upon a version of the present as a waste of time. To see the present as waste in terms of the future, or the past, or vice versa, is merely another version of stopping and starting, and the problem this raises is one of routine, i.e. it sounds like clocking in and out. The problem with mere routines is they both are dull and produce dullness. To just go on talking as a matter of routine would both be dull and produce dullness. In the same way to just go on worrying is to settle for routine, i.e. to become dull, thus to see worrying as enough is to allow worry to produce ease. To be satisfied with merely satisfactory performances is to be dull, i.e. it resonates with playing safe, and this resonates with the worrier's version of the good life as staying on the ground. To settle for usage seems like just going on for the sake of going on, and seems like a rather pointless exercise, or perhaps as mere exercise as a result. Routine then, like usage or worry has no sense of the good of anything. Acceptance of routine is the refusal to acknowledge other possibilities; to go on worrying is the refusal to acknowledge possibilities other than worry. Somehow teasing or cajoling seem to make more of these possibilities than worry. The worrier tends to stop other's starts whereas we can get people started by teasing or cajoling but even this involves openness or some revealing of self by the one being teased. If the worrier could come to treat problems as teasing and not merely as faults she might arrive at a different version of the good from the good as safety.

Response:

We do not need to be shaken to remember our moral/social response-ability not to orient to this paragraph of your speech, or to any speech, as children might orient to a day excursion, i.e. as something to return from basically unchanged, except perhaps for some sand in their shoes which, sure enough can soon be shaken out. We are working to be shaking ourselves out of indolent oppressive usages. So our work is not designed to move us from one version of the good (e.g. as safety) only on to another, as if that latter was the station platform that signals the end of our journey. Rather we are engaged in a continuing inquiry, a journey if you wish, that carries us out away from our beginnings which could always have become oppressive if we had oriented to them as ends and had not used them as means of departure.

So, we hear settling for usage as a day trip, and yet by listening more closely to your speech we are helped to remember that settling with usage is not pointless for its point is safety. All of the instances you provide, e.g. routine, usage, exercise, can be heard as playing safe, but by playing safe they would be allowing self to be restricted and dulled by continuing oppression, until the abilities of those, if any, enmeshed in these activities, to think/speak for themselves, i.e. incisively, i.e. to penetrate the surfaces of superficial versions of social relationships, and to be liberating themselves had been dulled. So your speech in this paragraph goads us to speak for if we do not we may be ourselves lulled by its surface into the complacency that could lead to us being without a place.

No doubt our readers are aware, as we are becoming aware that the routine you speak of is not merely that of the factory floor, which is perhaps a form of oppression so obvious that we need not here dwell upon it, but the reduction of all of man's activities to cause and effect. So, those, if any, who would reduce the social such that it could be understood as one further topic for natural science would (unwittingly no doubt) be playing a part in the construction of a form of speech/life that could extend the factory floor beyond the factory gates in such a way that clocking out would mean little more than a move to another part of the line.

How we live is a question of how we choose/decide to live, and liberation is oriented to respecting men's/women's freedom to reach communal decisions upon how we desire to live, and our contention is that this involves recognition of other as a thinker/speaker, as a philosopher. To consider men as merely subjects for science is to deny us our possibility as thinkers/moral actors, i.e. as those who are developing and changing in a deliberate rather than accidental manner, as those who choose what we want to do.

So, we choose how we read your speech, our reading is our response, and by responding as we do we are exemplifying our commitment to social relationships as other than cause and effect, as other than routine, i.e. as dialectical developments that respect our special place as speakers/thinkers, i.e. as those who cannot and would not orient to our selves as natural, but as ongoing social achievements.

We do not treat what we are doing, i.e. our work with your speech as a waste of time, we formulate the present as an opportunity, i.e. as the time for us to leave seemingly secure moorings, as the only time in whch we are acting/deciding. Perhaps those, if any, who wish to deny their response-ability would seek ways to avoid the present, for that reason they might deformulate it as pre-sent, i.e. as determined by the past.

In your speech the hurrier and the revolutionary are heard as having versions of prehistory, but your speech helps us remember how as social/moral actors, i.e. as free men we are prehistory, i.e. what we do does become history when we have done it, but to orient to it as history before doing it, i.e. to deny ourselves choice, and lie uneasily in that talk of cause and effect could not be becoming for it is to throw away the possibility of deliberate action by not hearing how throwing away is, or could be, a worrier's notion. The present is neither good nor bad, but, by recognising only its lack of goodness and by not realising that she can use it to make a better future the worrier does as she always will do, unless and until she develops her understanding of self, she throws it away.

Your speech reminds us that we have no reason to carry dead bodies with us, indeed we cannot do so for our speech plays a part in enlivening those who continue with us. Our speech is challenging/lively by not being merely worried, by continuing speaking/thinking we are keeping the dullness/the oppressiveness of thoughtlessness/silence at bay.

Our formulation of the present provides us with the opportunity to act, so whilst you speak of being now in the language of that paragraph, you remind us that we are always becoming by stretching the language we are using, by not allowing it to become languid, inert, a thing. Your mention of yawning helps to reinvigorate us by reminding us how it is through recognising the limits of our speech that we resist restricting ourselves to pedantry, to speech as being no more than a yawn which reveals a gap but chooses to do nothing more about it than conceal it.

Your speech on the issue of alternative futures assists us by reminding us that our present actions can always, and do always allow us to go further than past fantasies of the future would have allowed, for fantasising the future, i.e. as what may happen, constrains us; whereas deliberating about what we are doing liberates us from the impotency inducing world of fantasy. We don't need to be other than what we are, i.e. we don't need to be fantastic, to be improving our selves and our society, we need only continue thinking/conversing about what we desire to be becoming. We do not agree that those who engage in usage have no sense of the good of anything, for that would be to dehumanise, but we do hear routines as oppressive, and yet that we hear this displays how they have not completed their task, that the opportunity to be liberating our forms of speech/life, our social relationships remains with us as long as we can speak/think.

A day trip could be a liberating experience, but not for those, if any, who have decided to return the same as they set out; by orienting to our reading of your speech as an engagement which is not a waste of time for us we are able to learn with it.

189

Analysis of Paragraph 9

> The worrier uses her yes-buts to disarm others, i.e. they are like safety catches but she seems to resist all efforts to get her to face up to what she does know: which is that not facing up to things can be a very unsafe practice. Staying alive without worrying is produced by the worrier as being beyond her, i.e. worrying produces life as routine and provides room for worry in this way. My problem is that I can't help (says I!) feeling that the last set of notes is better than this, which is perhaps saying that I am easily taken in by usage, which might be just another version of the worrier refusing to see that what she tries to escape is the fact that escaping does rely upon some notion of the good, i.e. as safety.

Response:

Yes, our speech may disarm other, but if it does so it is by seeking to make the effort to be continuing to remind ourselves that we do not know, but must always be deciding what are safe or unsafe social practices. We seek to continue intervening, and to be remoulding degenerate routines that would otherwise leave us deadly dull. Whilst we could have indolently read the concluding remarks you make as simply an instance of worry's wish to avoid the insecurity of the present by speaking either of the past or the future, instead we choose to hear your concluding remarks as seeking to help remind us that we always have more to do if we are not to be satisfied with satisfactory performances. That by hearing our orientation to the present as developing through dialogue we display how not to be taken in by usage, i.e. how not to be taken for a ride, by choosing to act deliberately, by collaborating with others in such a way as to be working against oppression. That is, liberating ourselves by not seeking to escape, but to be facing up to, and to be changing oppressive practices, practices which seek to deny us our places as speakers/thinkers/social actors. So, liberation is more than escapism, indeed escapists need liberating but by saying this we do not, of course, intend to deny that escaping might be the right thing to do in certain circumstances, it might be, but we are saying that escaping is never enough.

NOTES

[1] The conventional psychological distinction between consciousness and unconsciousness, we dare say, is topsy turvy. For now we hear how those, if any, whose thoughts are oriented towards happenings, are not conscious of their consciousness, i.e. they reduce their thought to contingency by treating it as natural. The notion of stream of consciousness is instructive here for movement is conceived of as mere repetition of different units of the same substance, there is no notion of real development or increasing control. By reflecting/intervening upon our modes of thought/speech we insist upon bringing our forms of consciousness into consideration, we resist the indolence of an I'm alright jack attitude towards our own thought, for that can only leave us drifting, and far from alright. Could it be that the potency attributed to the psychological notion of the unconscious is deeply an awareness of the way in which we can increase the social potency of our thought, i.e. liberate ourselves, by thinking about

how we think/speak, rather than resting with a version of it as natural?

10 Children and adults

Original Speaker:

Well, I'm intrigued by much that you are saying, and whilst I don't pretend to have understood all that you have said I have no desire to escape, i.e. to leave this conversation, so I will risk offering some more notes. Your reference to childhood (cf., sand in shoe) and your references to nature in the responses you offered to Appendix F are taken further in this next set of notes, i.e. Appendix G.

APPENDIX G

Original Speaker:

Para.1   For the worrier doing good (or bad) is you doing nothing and good (or bad) doing, i.e. she sees good work as good's work (or bad work as bad's), and hence sees man as only a vehicle for good or bad. She sees all men/women as a-responsible for she reduces man to nature, and has a version of nature as child (we will see this more clearly as we go on!). However the worrier draws back at a certain point on this reductionist path for she does not draw the necessary consequence from this, which is that as a result she has nothing to worry about for nothing matters. On the contrary, she carries on worrying about this consequence.

Para.2   What do I mean by suggesting that the worrier treats nature as a child? The question suggests that the reader should now slump back and wait for my answer, much in the way that children do when they are asked if they are sitting comfortably before their story begins. Now the reason why the reader might make a mistake if he did that is because he should hardly expect a child to answer a question like that alone (i.e. without help), and the worrier does tend to treat herself like a child. Unfortunately the worrier seems to be what is left of the child when Peter Pan has gone! However, on to children.

Para.3   When we respond to a child's naughtiness by asking or telling the child to be good we are misled by the worrier's reified conception of good as some 'thing' the child could be, and also we forget what naughtiness is. Naughtiness presumably means doing nought, perhaps doing no good, but when we respond by asking the child to be good we are not asking him to do anything, i.e. we only ask him not to do harm, and so in effect we ask him to do nothing which is what by being naughty he was doing. Now this discussion of children's behaviour may seem strangely out of place until we remember that we normally only use the term naughty in the context of children's, or perhaps pet animals' behaviour, so the cat that craps on the mat is naughty, as is this example, i.e. childish. We only use the term naughty then in the context of children because children are not held to be fully responsible for what they do, they are seen as not yet knowing the difference between good and bad. So now this distinction between good and bad is seen to be an achievement of only those with an 'adult' social status. Thus the truly social unlike the natural would have notions of good and bad. This begins to sound O.K. until we remember that (a) throughout our previous work the worrier has either not held, or not wanted to hold, herself or others as fully responsible for their actions, and (b) the worrier has this conception of good (the reified conception referred to above) as something that you are or can be, or that can happen to you. The worrier reduces human behaviour, whether adult or not, to the behaviour of a child and this is a way of reducing responsibility - this also resonates with the idea of prehistory previously mentioned. The point is that the child is dependent upon his environment in much the same way as the worrier was when conceived of as falling, i.e. in both situations they are dependent upon their environment for their safety/survival.

Para.4   Now we can begin to see how the worrier produces worries by treating nature as a child, i.e. she seems to view nature as being dependent upon its environment. Underlying my speech has been an argument that if the analyst was suggesting that he both could and did do good he was treating himself as supernatural. The first point to be raised from the paragraphs above is that perhaps this is the analyst's way of saying no more than that he is social: that he transcends nature. But, to return to the perhaps more contentious version of the supernatural what I want to suggest now is that perhaps it makes far more sense to treat the worrier as a supernaturalist. In the first instance, by treating nature as a child she shows that she has no real faith in nature, i.e. she seemingly subordinates nature to contingency, and by doing so makes room for religion. In the second instance by placing herself within nature, i.e. by refusing to allow man's social place to be seen as transcending nature she places herself within nature, and hence places nature above (super) her, and makes herself its subject, makes room for social science, the study of natural man. Neither of these possibilities leaves a place for deliberation, and perhaps both create plenty of space for worry. Perhaps to show how the worrier treats nature as like a child is interesting, but for the moment I feel very doubtful about this unless we can see why a child is treated like a child.

Para.5   I want to write now about the worrier's reified conception of good as either something you can be, or something you can get as a reward, but this is proving very difficult, perhaps precisely because the reified conception of good underlies my writing and cannot easily be pulled out. What I am trying to say is that the worrier can pull out the faults that underlie hers and others' writing but this is because she sees good as something to be, she treats good as correct/faultless, and so by finding faults she thinks she is improving.

Para.6   This reified conception of good creates many problems for the worrier because it leads her into the apparently naturalistic position of the survival of the fittest. The worrier's version of good is best, where best takes the form of most complete, and here we can see how the worrier can be pushed into a competitive situation, i.e. she thinks she needs to be better than others to be good, i.e. if others are better than her how can she be good? The result of this is that her 'yes buts' take on the rather more unsavoury flavour of put downs on others, i.e. perhaps this is the only way the worrier can lift herself up. (If such it can be called). It is worth noticing that this idea of being good could also underlie the worrier's version of the fool as incompetent, i.e. not a good competitor.

Para.7   So now we see that the worrier's conception of good brings out the worst in her, and perhaps it is because she knows that she isn't doing good that she tries to cover herself with being good natured, childlike, i.e. not meaning any harm! The point here is that the worrier doesn't think she owns the worst in her either for she treats succumbing to temptations as natural. This is the way she feels pulled down, i.e. she feels she has enough on her hands trying to be good without getting as far as doing good. Also, because temptation is natural she sees it as ever present. The point is then that being good natured isn't enough to stop you doing harm, it is only denying you are responsible for it, e.g. I didn't mean any harm.

Para.8   'I didn't mean any harm' suggests very strongly how she uses this naturalistic reduction in such a way as to make her action unintentional and hence from her viewpoint, neither to be punished nor praised. But now what do we find? It is that the worrier doesn't decide that because nothing matters you can do anything, she thinks that you/she can't decide anything and that as a consequence you/she are doing anything. The worrier wants to be natural because then you can do anything in the sense that anything you do is natural.

Para.9   To put it bluntly the worrier seems to treat intentions as unnatural and perhaps in a sense they are, but she goes on to feel that this must mean they are bad. We saw how she made a similar move when she reduced deliberation to tacticalness, and yet this all starts to sound very confused, for it was precisely those acts which would be seen as unintentional or not deliberate, i.e. hasty acts which she wanted to avoid. Now we really do begin to see how deeply this opposition to action underlies her thinking; that is, she is opposed to intentional and to unintentional action, or she reduces the former to the latter. In a way this is just a louder echo of the view expressed earlier that the worrier's conception of good brings out the worst in her, i.e. perhaps it makes her naughty in the sense of making nothing out of everything. Why can't the worrier come to see that her production of this reified version of good is also unintentional? Or why can't she see that she hasn't yet produced even this for she can't produce anything because that would be action?

Para.10   The idea of the difference between being good and doing good certainly seems to have shown some of the more unpleasant facets of the worrier, and one of these as far as these notes go still seems to be its failure to get to any sort of grips with doing good, or to put it another way, I still feel totally unable to uplift/climb myself. Somehow the child analogy is still present and suggests the small child who has to be lifted to see his image in the mirror; the worrier's problem is that by reducing us all to children she effectively removes the mirror from view.

ANALYSIS OF APPENDIX G

Analysis of Paragraph 1

For the worrier doing good (or bad) is you doing nothing and good (or bad) doing, i.e. she sees good work as good's work (or bad work as bad's), and hence sees man as only a vehicle for good or bad. She sees all men/women as aresponsible for she reduces man to nature, and has a version of nature as child (we will see this more clearly as we go on!). However the worrier draws back at a certain point on this reductionist path for she does not draw the necessary consequence from this, which is that as a result she has nothing to worry about for nothing matters. On the contrary, she carries on worrying about this consequence.

Response:

We hear how your speech draws back from the reductionist path and how by doing so it helps us to do so also. Through making the effort to hear your speech in this way, we come to hear how the reductionist path is itself a means of drawing back from response-ability, from freedom to decide, and the decision the worrier/thinker makes to halt this decline is heard as an expression of social response-ability, of the desire to act thoughtfully. For example your decision to risk collaborating with us/your listeners when you still do not know, rather than to fall into that silence that might have led to isolation and the disintegration of self's possibility as friend/collaborator.

To see all men as aresponsible is to recognise that restricting our selves to visible appearances is neglecting man's essential place as a theorist/a thinker. So, if we could have begun by seeing man as aresponsible we would have ended there, but that was not a possibility open to us, so we do not end there, for our efforts are to do the desirable work of showing how those visible appearances are response-able social actions, and how by being such they can be extended and deepened.

Your speech reminds us that we do have no thing to worry about for no thing matters to us, i.e. by refusing to rest with superficial appearances, i.e. by choosing to think of men/women as thinkers/speakers we hear how conversation is restless with facts as things; whilst things may need to be talked about dialogue is about possibilities; about what we could do. It does not constrain self by tying us in a fruitless and absurd effort to collect all the facts before beginning, but seeks to release self by encouraging selves to be asking why they are doing what they are doing. When you say that the worrier sees man as only a vehicle of good or bad you help remind us that man/woman is the only vehicle for good, for social/moral decisions are man's distinctive capability, by making them we distinguish ourselves from nature and display our place as thinkers, and enable ourselves not to need to draw the necessary consequence, as you put it, in such a way that it strangles us, i.e. not to need to restrict ourselves to cause and effect, but to be raising our selves, our society out of contingency by deliberating, by continuing social collaboration.

Not to have drawn back on that reductionist path would have been unintentional self destruction, a course of action none of us could commend.

Analysis of Paragraph 2

What do I mean by suggesting that the worrier treats nature as a child? The question suggests that the reader should now slump back and wait for my answer, much in the way that children do when they are asked if they are sitting comfortably before their story begins. Now the reason why the reader might make a mistake if he did that is because he should hardly expect a child to answer a question like that alone (i.e. without help), and the worrier does tend to treat herself like a child. Unfortunately the worrier seems to be what is left of the child when Peter Pan has gone! However, on to children.

Response:

When we hear you say 'What do I mean by ... etc.' we don't hear you as asking us to listen to your elucidation of what it is you are saying, i.e. as requiring us to constrain ourselves whilst you engage in expansion, but as asking us to play a part in grounding how you have come, and are coming, to say what you are saying. So, to whom would a question of that sort suggest that they ought to slump back and wait for an answer? Only to one who wished to differentiate between self and other selves. That is, only to one who didn't hear the question as directed at her also. We wait to hear what you say, but do not hear your speech as an answer, for to hear it as such is to deny your status as an inquirer, as one who seeks to continue engaging in conversation and not to bring about silence. It would be to restrict ourselves to merely agreeing or merely disagreeing where the latter consists in offering a competitive alternative, and the former offers nothing. So hearing a speech as an answer could rule out continuing collaborative effort.

We did not ask you if you were sitting comfortably before we began for to do so would be to begin by worrying about whether our speech would engage you or be drowned out by distractions. However, we are aware that merely sitting is not comfortable for us, and that it is not comfortable for children either, unless it is being measured against the discomfort that punishment for disobeying could bring. 'Are you sitting comfortably then I'll begin' could be a warning to keep silent; not to express yourself until you have heard all of the story, it could be authoritarian talk that chooses not to listen to what it does, but to ask us to restrict ourselves to listening to what it appears to be. It could be asking us to restrict ourselves to becoming part of the furniture, to staying where we appear to be. We say could for it need not be i.e. 'Are you sitting comfortably then I'll begin' could mean let's get ready to move together.

Your speech helps us to remember to be uncomfortable with beginnings of the former sort, for to seek to sit comfortably before our story begins is reminiscent of slumping; it is reminiscent of the apparent end of Ivan Illyich Pralinsky.

As to the final sentence of this paragraph of yours you remind us that we formulate the unfortunate as good for we can see no good in fortunateness/ chance, we do hear actions as good, intentions as good, but by doing so hear how deeply tragic certain superficial orientations towards good fortune could be, for they seek only to mesmerise. We formulate fortune as the effort to be continuing creating more harmonious social relationships. Your 'However, on to children' is the expression of your continuing commitment not to simply wait and see what befalls you, i.e. whether you are fortunate (in the weak sense) or not. Furthermore this helps us to remember that we would not have heard your introduction to this appendix as escapism, i.e. you are not saying I don't pretend to understand all that you say and then offering the notes as a way to cover over your lack of understanding, but you offer your notes as your way to be trying all the better to understand.

Analysis of Paragraph 3

When we respond to a child's naughtiness by asking or telling the child to be good we are misled by the worrier's reified conception of good as some 'thing' the child could be, and also we forget what naughtiness is. Naughtiness presumably means doing nought, perhaps doing no good, but when we respond by asking the child to be good we are not asking him to do anything, i.e. we only ask him not to do harm, and so in effect we ask him to do nothing which is what by being naughty he was doing. Now this discussion of children's behaviour may seem strangely out of place until we remember that we normally only use the term naughty in the context of children's, or perhaps pet animals' behaviour, so the cat that craps on the mat is naughty, as is this example, i.e. childish. We only use the term naughty then in the context of children because children are not held to be fully responsible for what they do, they are seen as not yet knowing the difference between good and bad. So now this distinction between good and bad is seen to be an achievement of only those with an 'adult' social status. Thus the truly social unlike the natural would have notions of good and bad. This begins to sound O.K. until we remember that (a) throughout our previous work the worrier has either not held, or not wanted to hold, herself or others as fully responsible for their actions, and (b) the worrier has this conception of good (the reified conception referred to above) as something that you are or can be, or that can happen to you. The worrier reduces human behaviour, whether adult or not, to the behaviour of a child and this is a way of reducing responsibility - this also resonates with the idea of prehistory previously mentioned. The point is that the child is dependent upon his environment in much the same way as the worrier was when conceived of as falling, i.e. in both situations they are dependent upon their environment for their safety/survival.

Response:

We will not be impatient with you here, i.e. we will not respond to your speech as if it were naughty for to do so would be to deny our commitment to hearing other's speech as intentional. So, you are seeking to help us remember not to rest with the beginning you invent, i.e. that of responding to the child's naughtiness, for that would have been to settle in differentiation between self and another self. We need to collaborate with the child in achieving an understanding of the behaviour in question. To proceed with a thoughtless commitment to a version of the behaviour as naughty is to deny ourselves the possibility of movement, of social change. It is to rest in the adult status which your speech helps us to remember is authoritarian, i.e. claims to know too much. So, whilst we could have dismissed this paragraph as merely an effort on your part to escape, using childhood as a disguise, we toy with it/play with it so as to display how whilst such a reading would do neither us nor you credit, we can do better. Both the cat's act and this paragraph of yours help to stimulate our actions, but we are seeking to show how to have settled with shovelling away your speech would have been to dehumanise it, a practice that we see our speech as raising us above.

We have said many times that we do not know the difference between good and bad, but that we have to decide, so you are not commending the adult status, i.e. that which might be held to be fully responsible, in the sense of knowing that difference. Any, if any, who talk in such a way as to lead their listeners to believe that they have achieved that status are engaging in a dangerous sort of mischief which we all do need to guard against.

We hear the truly social as having notions of good and bad and most importantly as recognising that these are social products/members' decisions, and are not based upon knowledge that is only open to those of a specific social status. So, your speech is not commending adulthood which may sound O.K., but which precisely for this reason, i.e. because it is mere rhetoric, needs deepening. Your honesty in not claiming to be fully responsible is commendable for through it you express your desire to work to act more response-ably and not to relieve yourself of response-ability by claiming mysterious powers that are products of experience or whatever. Response-able social actions/moral decisions do not hide behind authority but are dialectical developments.

So, you remind us that the adult who insists that he knows the difference between good and bad is a product of an authoritarian upbringing and remains blinkered by its forcefulness. That adult remains a child, though one that can perpetrate actions that would shovel us away if they could. We seek to elevate our actions to that of the child if the child is heard as one who collaborates in such a way as to decide. This is our way of increasing our response-ability, of improving our means of speech/thought, and it does indeed resonate with the formulations of pre history we have offered.

Oh yes, we are dependent upon our environment for our survival, if, that is, survival is deformulated into the mere prolonging of life, but if as we would have it survival is formulated as the effort to elevate our lives, our society, i.e. if survival is heard as the process of liberating ourselves from contingency then, for that, we depend and can only depend upon ourselves. To refuse to be continuing to exhibit our response-ability for our actions would be to come to rest with a version of our history, our future as an instance of chronic incontinence.

Analysis of Paragraph 4

Now we can begin to see how the worrier produces worries by treating nature as a child, i.e. she seems to view nature as being dependent upon its environment. Underlying my speech has been an argument that if the analyst was suggesting that he both could and did do good he was treating himself as supernatural. The first point to be raised from the paragraphs above is that perhaps this is the analyst's way of saying no more than that he is social: that he transcends nature. But, to return to the perhaps more contentious version of the supernatural what I want to suggest now is that perhaps it makes far more sense to treat the worrier as a supernaturalist. In the first instance, by treating nature as a child she shows that she has no real faith in nature, i.e. she seemingly subordinates nature to contingency, and by doing so makes room for religion. In the second instance by placing herself within nature, i.e. by refusing to allow man's social place to be seen as transcending nature she places herself within nature, and hence places nature above (super) her, and makes herself its subject, makes room for social science, the study of natural man. Neither of these possibilities leaves a place for deliberation, and perhaps both create plenty of space for worry. Perhaps to show how the worrier treats nature as like a child is interesting, but for the moment I feel very doubtful about this unless we can see why a child is treated like a child.

Response:

Now this paragraph does help us provided we do not allow the notion of transcends to mislead us, i.e. we are instructed by our reading of your speech provided we formulate transcending as stretching the limits and not as jumping outside them. But we hear that you are not proposing the latter version of transcends, for, by writing the first sentence of that paragraph you display your awareness of the absurdities that could follow, i.e. your usage of 'seems' in that sentence displays how you thoughtfully distance yourself from that extremist position.

But what of the concluding sentence? This is not the expression of a loss of nerve, but an effort to help us to remember not to hear your speech as merely pointing at the limitations of the speech of worry, i.e. not as putting worry down, but as displaying how, by collaborating with worry you are bringing your self up. So, you help us to stretch and deepen worry and not to treat it as the limit, i.e. the end, i.e. you help us to transcend it and not to jump above it, not to leave it behind. Social action is not that of the adult looking down upon the child, it is the action of speakers/thinkers collaborating in such a way as to be raising themselves out of their beginnings. By making the effort to engage in an analytic relationship with other speakers through their speeches, i.e. to hear how they are social, how they transcend the natural we are collecting human actions and removing them from an arena in which superficiality seeks to silence thought.

Analysis of Paragraph 5

I want to write now about the worrier's reified conception of good as either something you can be, or something you can get as a reward, but this is proving very difficult, perhaps precisely because the reified conception of good underlies my writing and cannot easily be pulled out. What I am trying to say is that the worrier can pull out the faults that underlie hers and others' writing but this is because she sees good as something to be, she treats good as correct/faultless, and so by finding faults she thinks she is improving.

Response:

Your efforts to pull out the reified notion of the good from under the worrier's speech might have been read as resulting here, as they might have been read elsewhere, in you being sucked into worry. But that is not the reading we offer for that would be to undermine our selves. We are reminded by your speech that subtraction, i.e. pulling out, is too lazy, too forceful, and shows no effort to be stretching/elevating our notion of self, i.e. it shows no commitment to traction. You are reminding us not to seek to minimise our efforts, but to be maximising them. Merely to pull out the faults in another's speech, even if it were possible, i.e. to have restricted our action to correcting would have been to have restricted ourselves to force for it would have been to fail to understand how collaborative effort is a liberating process. The idea of correction relies upon a prior commitment to a notion of what is perfect/faultless, and that commitment vis-a-vis social action is always authoritarian and premature, those committed to it, if any, seek to prove themselves, i.e. to reach a preconceived standard, rather than to improve their notions of self, i.e. their standards. An orientation to correction detains rather than releases human potential.

Analysis of Paragraph 6

This reified conception of good creates many problems for the worrier because it leads her into the apparently naturalistic position of the survival of the fittest. The worrier's version of good is best, where best takes the form of most complete, and here we can see how the worrier can be pushed into a competitive situation, i.e. she thinks she needs to be better than others to be good, i.e. if others are better than her how can she be good? The result of this is that her 'yes buts' take on the rather more unsavoury flavour of put downs on others, i.e. perhaps this is the only way the worrier can lift herself up. (If such it can be called). It is worth noticing that this idea of being good could also underlie the worrier's version of the fool as incompetent, i.e. not a good competitor.

Response:

Your speech helps us to remember that the work we are collaboratively engaged in is that of raising selves out of oppressive forms of speech, i.e. forms of speech which seek to increase, or rely upon the differences between men, e.g. I.Q. tests, sexism, racism, etc., rather than to be increasing man's difference from nature/contingency. What type of ridiculous and wasteful social relationships would result if our mode of orienting to others was in terms of whether each was better than the other, or other was better than each, or other was improving, catching up, etc. etc., indeed could that even be called social relationships? Such an orientation could hardly engage thoughtful interlocutors, social/moral actors, for we are those who recognise our need for friends/collaborators, and are aware that resting with superficial differences between men is no way to be improving our ways of living. Our efforts are directed by our commitment to the continuing liberating of our selves from oppressive forms of speech/life. Perhaps at times our speech may sound offensive, but it will only do so if our hearing has again become contorted by the very forms of speech from which we seek to play our part in releasing selves. Forms of speech inform our hearing, and perhaps by referring to them as forms of hearing we can be reminding ourselves that it is we who always have desirable work to do.

Perhaps you will allow us to digress a little, indeed perhaps you will not hear this as a digression for we imagine that the description you offer of the worrier's speech as constrained within a competitive form is intended to remind us of a wider application. We dare say that all who conceive of their selves as oppressed might be constrained in this way. Now how are these people likely to respond to the speech of liberators/radicals who present themselves as solid shining examples of the virtues of strength/solidarity etc., i.e. as instances of how to fight the system, how to gain your rights, how not to put up with any of that shit etc., i.e. as shining examples of how to be together. What we are saying is that we imagine that the competitive mode of thought destroys the usefulness of others as examples to follow, for it transforms them into enemies and far from encouraging depresses even further.

No doubt liberation movements are well aware of this problem, and are working hard to prevent their speech sounding like that of those who imagine they have achieved adult status (cf., earlier remarks) for speech of that sort loses many potential and thoughtful allies by allowing for the divisive differentiation between liberated and unliberated to occur such that only the speech of the liberated is heard as worth listening to. Earlier in this response we spoke of continuing liberating and this unusual usage may have been noticed by readers, it was no typing error. By speaking of liberation the movements to which we refer might be reducing their much needed possibilities by allowing listeners to rest in competitive rather than collaborative speech, e.g. before and after liberation, liberated unliberated, leaders followers etc. We hear liberation movements as liberating movements, and we hear liberating as an ongoing process which calls upon those engaged to be continuing to be working to achieve better versions of self and not to engage in the business of managing impressions, i.e. of appearing to be together in the hope that this will increase effectiveness, we imagine that it doesn't for the reasons we have offered. It is not a question of liberated, i.e. those in the know (and we remember the case of the adults again!) assisting/instructing those who need to be liberated, work of that sort, i.e. which orients to the oppressed as not very good competitors, as fools (cf., your last sentence), listens only in the shallowest sense to what the oppressed say, (i.e. it humours us) for it conceives of the oppressed as thoughtless and needing to be led, it fails to recognise the theoreticity of the oppressed. Competitive thought/speech is a malignant cancerous growth and it cannot be removed by efforts which rest in superficial sameness, it cannot be pulled out and discarded but needs to be deepened by continuing collaborative efforts.

This speech will not be heard by those committed to liberating as being competitive for they hear how all speech is the effort to collaborate. They, like we, seek to deepen, not to distort what they hear. They are improving their selves by displaying their ability to offer versions of others as better than, not as worse than their own persons, for by doing so they continue working upon their social relationships.

Analysis of Paragraph 7

So now we see that the worrier's conception of good brings out the worst in her, and perhaps it is because she knows that she isn't doing good that she tries to cover herself with being good natured, childlike, i.e. not meaning any harm! The point here is that the worrier doesn't think she owns the worst in her either for she treats succumbing to temptations as natural. This is the way she feels pulled down, i.e. she feels she has enough on her hands trying to be good without getting as far as doing good. Also, because temptation is natural she sees it as ever present. The point is then that being good natured isn't enough to stop you doing harm, it is only denying you are responsible for it, e.g. I didn't mean any harm.

Response:

If we settled for an easy/effortless reading of this paragraph, and merely agreed with what it seems at first glance to say the conception of good that we would be operating with would be bringing the worst out of us. But that is not our way, and it could not be what you desire of us. So we read and try to listen more carefully, we respect you as a speaker/thinker as your speech respects us by leaving us plenty to do. Perhaps we could begin by rewriting the paragraph.

So now we hear how the thinker's/speaker's continuing inquiry into the 'nature' of the good draws the best out of herself and others, it is by not knowing whether what she is doing is good or is not that she can continue to be uncovering how by acting thoughtfully we not only do not mean any harm, but always intend to do good. The thinker does know that she does not own the worst in her, it is out of character, and she is able to disown it by working to understand how our actions, all of our actions are social, i.e. unnatural, and how viewing any of them as natural is a temptation in the sense that it makes them a waste of time, it leads towards thoughtless observance, and reduces the degree of deliberating, the degree of freedom we exercise over our lives. We raise/elevate our selves by at least intending to do good, and by being instructed by the conversations our actions so frequently bring about, and we are glad to have been responsible for these actions, they do not rest uncomfortably in our memories, we do not seek to have them off our hands. True, we never know whether we are doing good or not, but we all of us do intend it and need only converse with others to be achieving more thoughtful/more social lives. Whilst we could always have tried to hide behind a notion of cause and effect, nature, we have no desire to for we enjoy acting intentionally. Silence does not become us. But somehow even if we had tried to hide we know that a part of us would always remain visible to any thoughtful interlocutor. Whilst we can still speak/think we are not lost causes. Being good natured isn't enough to stop you doing harm, that also is true, indeed if it were possible for us to be good natured whatever that might mean, it would not still be possible for us to do anything for we would then be a-responsible. Perhaps we can formulate ourselves as being good natured if by this is meant those who intend to do good, i.e. those who are not merely natural, for by formulating our good naturedness in this way we do deny that we are responsible for any harm, for harm results from thoughtless/selfless occurrences for which we cannot be to blame; which is not of course to deny that we can be instructed by owning up to and considering mistakes we have previously personally made.

So, we use other's speech as an occasion to draw the best out of ourselves, and by saying best we are not indulging in comparisons with/against other men/women, but we are saying that we are doing all that we can do, i.e. that intending to do good is all we can do. Whilst your hypothetical worrier, you say, has enough on her hands trying to be good without getting as far as doing good, we recognise that the only way we can try to be good is by trying/intending to do good. We do not need to engage in comparisons with/against others to do this, but to engage in open conversations through which we can at least continue to bring into question what we do, and can stop pretending it is natural, stop being so superficial. But, perhaps your hypothetical worrier has for so long been facing in the wrong direction and restricting her attention to the surface that she can no longer hear speech about good and bad. Perhaps she is beginning to forget what speech and social relationships are about, and is settling for the disintegrated notion of persons as each being mere competitors in a fight for survival. Your speech helps us to remember that we need not and would not turn away in that fashion. Perhaps the worrier could be one who has become so involved in competitiveness, i.e. in showing herself to be better than others that she no longer allows herself the time or energy to consider whether worry is a good form of action; perhaps she imagines that if she stopped to think she would be overtaken. We imagine that a lack of consideration of this kind could result in uncontrolability much like that of nature, and this is why we are working to be freeing that form of speech/life by deliberating/conversing analytically.

Easy, as effortless, readings would leave ourselves totally dependent upon other, and would be reducing reading, conversation, all of human life for that matter, to incontinence; to things that merely happen to us, and that would not make life easy for us, for speakers/thinkers. It is no wonder then that those, if any, who allow this to happen are worried for we imagine that they correctly recognise that anything could happen at any time. They imagine, or so we surmise for the sake of this conversation, that the best they can hope for is that they will be fortunate.

Analysis of Paragraph 8

'I didn't mean any harm' suggests very strongly how she uses this naturalistic reduction in such a way as to make her action unintentional and hence from her viewpoint, neither to be punished nor praised. But now what do we find? It is that the worrier doesn't decide that becausenothing matters you can do anything, she thinks that you/she can't decide anything and that as a consequence you/she are doing anything. The worrier wants to be natural because then you can do anything in the sense that anything you do is natural.

Response:

So as to collaborate with your speech we choose to begin by hearing your speech as a product of good intention, i.e. we choose to hear you as meaning us no harm. Now this might have been no easy matter and perhaps in part that is what you hoped we would say. The reason it might not have been easy is that your speech could all too easily do our persons harm if we chose to treat it as natural, i.e. as something we could do nothing about other than observe, understand in the scientific sense.

But your speech helps us remember that we are not, and do not desire to be natural, we desire to be acting thoughtfully/socially/morally to be acting deliberately, and that is not a fantasy, it is not, as we have said, seeking to be something that we are not.

You say, 'But now what do we find!' and remind us that what we find reveals a good deal about what we choose to hear as being of value, so your statement is not the exclamation of a natural scientist or an archaeologist who has dug up or uncovered a new/old fact. Our inquiry, your speech, is the activity of stretching ourselves and discovering how as we extend ourselves our possible character is beginning to be achieved. We resist strong suggestions and by doing so choose to act deliberately not naturally, we choose to display how if we had heard your speech as natural we would have done you a disservice for we would have offered you nothing at all. We do not seek to punish or praise your speech, i.e. perhaps to disagree or agree with it for we know that superficially rewarding or sanctioning in that manner does neither you nor us any good. We seek to think about and in this way, deepen our hearing of your speech for this serves to help us all.

Your speech appears indecisive, e.g. you/she, it seems as if you are unsure whether you are speaking about us, the worrier, or yourself, but there we would be doing you an injustice for this is not indecision but is a manner of writing intended to help us remember that self as thinker/speaker is what we each of us have in common, you/she, we/them are deeply the same, deeply human selves, and only appear to be significantly different if we are constrained by oppressive, forceful, forms of speech. So your speech is helping direct us towards the notion of genus man and by doing so seeks to remind us of our true place as speakers, and to help us to be releasing ourselves from that historical specificity which limits our vision and restricts us to small talk when we each of us knows that to talk in that way degrades by maintaining superficial personas which conceal characters capable of so much more.

It is no wonder if at times our speech takes on an aggressive tone, why would we allow the potentially profound/moral/free and friendly characters each and all of us has to be stifled by chatter/silence? Because we want to be natural! None of us finds that answer satisfactory but it is the answer that chatter provides, it is 'leave me be', 'leave me alone' and that is just what it would do! We want to get to know each other not to leave each other alone, for that would be boring. Being left alone is perhaps a fair way of speaking of alienation, but to comply with that request is surely to reveal a bizarre notion of friendship? We want silence/oppression to leave us alone, but we do not desire to be left alone by other thoughtful interlocutors; we do desire to have friends.

We also remember that much much earlier we spoke of not knowing whether we were in the city or the country, could it be that our confusion was grounded in the talk of certain city dwellers who sought to pretend that we still lived in the country, i.e. to pretend that our form of speech/way of life was natural?

Analysis of Paragraph 9

> To put it bluntly the worrier seems to treat intentions as unnatural and perhaps in a sense they are, but she goes on to feel that this must mean they are bad. We saw how she made a similar move when she reduced deliberation to tacticalness, and yet this all starts to sound very confused, for it was precisely those acts which would be seen as unintentional or not deliberate, i.e. hasty acts which she wanted to avoid. Now we really do begin to see how deeply this opposition to action underlies her thinking; that is, she is opposed to intentional and to unintentional action, or she reduces the former to the latter. In a way this is just a louder echo of the view expressed earlier that the

worrier's conception of good brings out the worst in her, i.e. perhaps it makes her naughty in the sense of making nothing out of everything. Why can't the worrier come to see that her production of this reified version of good is also unintentional? Or why can't she see that she hasn't yet produced even this for she can't produce anything because that would be action?

Response:

But to whom would 'this' start to sound very confused? Here we are reminded that it would only sound confused to those who orient their thought to cleaning surfaces, keeping things in order, to those who sought not to uncover how their own intentions need to be brought into account.

We choose to inquire beneath the surface and this is what you are commending we do do, for you would not commend that we rest with a blunt statement about how things 'seem'. We display how the worrier's speech could have, and should have, been formulated in a far more friendly manner, our more friendly/thoughtful formulation would run like this:

The worrier treats intentions as unnatural as do we, and whilst she is concerned about intentions, i.e. whilst they occupy her thoughts and her speech, she reveals that she knows intentions as such are not good, but we are not hasty here and do not assume that it follows from this that she imagines they are bad, for such is not the case. By saying intentions as such are not good the worrier seeks to remind us that intentions intend good, i.e. seek to do good, and that if we heard them as being good in themselves their place in action would have been deformed. Furthermore intentions can always be improved by more thought by those who recognise that they are not good as such, so the worrier's speech is helpful to us in this regard also.

If the worrier's speech seems to reduce a deliberate act to the exercise of tacticalness, i.e. personal protection, this does reveal that acts unthinkingness, i.e. that it was only apparently deliberate, and provides pointers as to how the act could be preserved, made more thoughtful/more social. The speech of worry is intent not upon reduction but upon making possible the elevating of unintentional actions to intentional actions by stimulating/goading the actors to think about what they do. By bringing the worst out of actions, by showing how if they were not deliberate they were nothing, the worrier raises the possibility of making something out of nothing.

So what we are uncovering is that if the worrier's speech is itself heard as deliberate/thoughtful, i.e. as the exercise of friendship, it does play a part in the improvement of social relationships, but if the speech of worry is heard as unintentional, mindless, personal protection, i.e. as you put it as an opposition to action, then its possibility is lost for it will not be listened to: its depths would not be heard for it would be heard as merely naughty. Those, if any, who listen in this way would deform Socrates' speech from being the exercise of friendship into mere naughtiness and they would remain oppressed, isolated and constrained within the ways of thinking/forms of speech which they refused to bring into question. This is why they (the unreflexive worrier in your speech!) cannot see how they have chosen the version of good that they imagine constrains them.

Analysis of Paragraph 10

The idea of the difference between being good and doing good certainly seems to have shown some of the more unpleasant facets of the worrier, and one of these as far as these notes go still seems to be its failure to get to any sort of grips with doing good, or to put it another way, I still feel totally unable to uplift/climb myself. Somehow the child analogy is still present and suggests the small child who has to be lifted to see his image in the mirror; the worrier's problem is that by reducing us all to children she effectively removes the mirror from view.

Response:

Here you help us to remember that we would never be able to uplift/elevate our version of self if we chose not to hear that it is we who act. By listening thoughtfully to your speech, e.g. of the idea of difference seeming to show, and of one of the more unpleasant facets of the worrier seeming to be the notes failure to get to any sort of grips with doing good, we help to remind ourselves that we are choosing to recognise our place as speakers/thinkers, for only by doing so can we uplift our selves/our society, and not rest content to pretend that it is ideas and notes, for instance, that do what we are response-able for, as if we don't produce them!

As to your concluding analogy this is stimulating for as thinkers/speakers, by recognising our deep sameness with others, we have no need for things like mirrors for reassurance, for we have no wish to restrict ourselves to what we may appear to be as a consequence of historically specific cosmetics. But we do desire to be conversing with others/friends in such a way as to be improving our version of self. If the worrier is heard as one who removes the mirror from view by undermining authoritarian talk, i.e. by undermining the talk of those who claim special status; of those who claim to know, so much the better, for it is authoritarian talk that would stand in the way of true social development.

11 The dream

APPENDIX H

Original Speaker:

Para.1   Worrying is only natural. Worrying is like a conditioned reflex, but it isn't related to specific conditions, i.e. it is a reaction to any conditions. Man becomes a hyper animal then by his ability to abstract; more specifically in this context to abstract conditionality from specific conditions, i.e. any conditions become a cause of worry. This process produces worry as the condition within which the worrier's time is spent.

Para.2   The worrier is right to see that conditions are only conditional (i.e. not necessarily necessary) but wrong to see conditionality itself as conditional (i.e. as not necessarily necessary). To say this another way each set of specific conditions is only conditional and as a result worry is a natural and appropriate reaction to each specific set. Hence the absurdity of trying to remove worry, for example 'Don't worry everything will be alright!!

Para.3   This might suggest that it is specificity rather than conditionality which fixes the worrier in her slot. However specificity is really only another version of conditionality (limits), i.e. specification is speaking of limits (conditions), it treats speaking as defining (i.e. setting out the set limits). But it seems from the preceding paragraphs that man rises above specificity by abstracting, and that this offers a way for the worrier to remove her condition, i.e. if she could be more abstract about conditions she could stop worrying about those that confronted her, or that she tries to avoid. However, this also would be misleading for far from abstracting being a solution to the problem of specificity (if problem it is!) it is merely a refinement or sophisticated form of it.

Para.4   To think the replacement of worry by abstracting is changing anything is to fail to be abstract enough about abstraction, i.e. it is to fail to see that abstraction can be subsumed within the category of methods of avoidance available to the worrier. Even this isn't enough for it forgets that worry isn't everything, and this is one of the problems with the method of abstraction, i.e. that it can all too easily forget what it has left out. Furthermore the very idea of replacing is, in this context, merely another way of talking about avoiding/placing out of the way, and this brings to mind the earlier idea of stumbling into the problem again at another time or level.

Para.5   Imagine if I went through the preceding page and crossed out all the t's in an attempt to show how abstracting forgets what it is doing it for, and then forgot myself what I was crossing out the t's for, and we get some idea of how abstracting is a stretching of the imagination but is merely imaginative, i.e. it does forget what it is doing it for!

Para.6   We have seen earlier how the worrier produces the future as something she has merely to wait for, e.g. her method of hoping things will work out, as the best way of using her time. Perhaps this can suggest to us the dreamlike nature of her mode of thought. A dream whether good or bad is always something we are in as if against our will, i.e. as if we hadn't chosen to be in it, and somehow the only way we can bring ourselves to see that we have produced it is by ending it. This resonates with the religious idea of an afterlife from which this life would presumably have only a dreamlike status! But, the point about dreams is that once we realise we have produced them they no longer retain their fearful or pleasurable nature. In both cases we treat produced as made up, that is as fake, and we tend to think that once we know something is a fake there is nothing to worry about. However the realisation that fakes are something we can produce is what we should be worried about!

Para.7   Yes but' makes reference to the conditionality of the present where the worrier somehow sees conditionality as reducing the present's status to that of being hypothetical (it is worth noting that she speaks of this as a reduction!). The present is, only if you ignore the 'yes but'. The 'yes but' comes to mean then that things could be or are otherwise, and we can see how this produces the present as being dreamlike, i.e. hypothetical situations are dreamed up, and the worrier even situates the present as a hypothetical situation in the context of other hypothetical situations. But why does she do this? Why does she write paragraphs like this? It seems that by using the 'yes but' she expresses her wish to avoid or ignore the present. (Initially this doesn't seem to tell us anything, but perhaps when we see that the worrier equates the present with the natural we will learn something!) An instance of this effort to avoid the present can be pointed to earlier in this set of notes when it was suggested that worry was a natural reaction without it further being suggested that it wasn't the only natural reaction. Choice was eliminated by treating the indefinite article as a definite article whereas it is only the natural reaction for the worrier.

Para.8   The worrier's constant usage of 'perhaps' suggests that making choices is something the worrier will do her utmost to avoid (it also suggests the shallowness of her avoidance, i.e. as if she doesn't see that she chooses the usage of 'perhaps'). This would certainly account for her avoidance of the present for the present is a prerequisite for choice, and hence its elimination or avoidance would be tantamount to removing the possibility of choice. So, the worrier seems to avoid making a choice or decision in two ways (a) by suggesting that the time to make the choice hasn't yet come, (this is her usage of 'yes but' and/or 'perhaps') and perhaps will never come. Or (b) by suggesting that what seemed like a choice wasn't really a choice at all, i.e. generally by her reduction of herself and/or the present to nature. We can see now that given her version of nature as a child (b) collapses into (a) or is only an example of it.

Para.9   The worrier would go about doing (b) above, i.e. showing that a choice wasn't really a choice by saying either that given that it is natural for the best alternative to be chosen, if there is a difference between the two alternatives the weaker alternative had no real chance, and hence there was no real choice. Or, in the other case if there was no difference between the alternatives she would say that the choice between them is necessarily arbitrary and that again there has still been no choice. If some alternative proposal about the alternatives in a choice were offered, i.e. where they were neither the same, nor different, she would probably resort to showing how the chooser isn't really choosing anyway because of her social grouping or whatever, i.e. she would treat the chooser as the subject for natural science.

Para.10   We begin to see here how the idea of intentions or more specifically good intentions would sound unnatural for the worrier because it seems to assume the possibility of choice which she seems intent upon removing. By treating worrying as only natural the worrier is in effect simply re-echoing her claim that she isn't responsible for anything either good or bad; but why does she want to make this claim? This shows us how disclaiming is the closest she wants to get to responsibility, again it shows us how close she is to the angry man!

Para.11   The worrier's version of responsibility is being protective, i.e. looking after something or one, i.e. of keeping something or one (e.g. herself) safe. To say it once again of trying to prevent things falling. This can show us how she uses a version of good as something things or people are, such that they need protection. Whereas the idea of doing good would not begin with an idea of looking after it might begin with an idea of improving. We see here how the worrier gets drawn into a static analysis of things being either good or bad, i.e. to be protected or avoided (where avoided is merely deciding not to protect), and how she can come to see herself as only being accountable for failing as a result. To say this in another way if she conceives of good as something she needs to protect, and she sees this as her sole task then she can never do good for she is always separate from it, she can only do her job which is analogous to not letting anything happen, or she can fail to do her job which is like letting things happen, and it is the latter that does happen and that is perhaps why she feels she fails and wants somehow to claim mitigating circumstances, e.g. she was distracted, or whatever.

Para.12   Somehow protection doesn't seem like a good intention, its best possibility is for it to allow good intentions to be seen. That is, protection subordinates itself to other's intentions in one way or another. This idea of protection subordinating itself can also suggest how it can become lazy, for it could mean much less work if the good were seen to be able to protect themselves, i.e. if the survival of the fittest meant the survival of the good. The protector here would be as useful/as needed as the teacher who felt he had only one lesson to teach and that he had taught it successfully!

Para.13   Much earlier in our work we spoke of the worrier having a utopian image of herself as not wanting ideal conditions, but as wanting a self that could deal with any conditions. We can see from these notes firstly why the idea of ideal conditions would not appeal to her, and secondly how her utopian image of herself seems to be grounded in the need for protection.

You would not be sympathising with the worrier here, and asking us to join with you, for given that you are a thoughtful interlocutor, you are aware that the place for sympathy is where there is nothing else to be done, and our relationship with worry is one in which we have plenty still to do. To settle for sympathy would have been to settle for a nodding acquaintanceship which would have revealed the resistance of each of those involved to engaging in social change/development, it would have been to settle for the dullness of superficiality, of the status quo, of description. There is no need to converse with a nodding acquaintance for the silence would symbolise a shared wish to remain on the surface, i.e. a wish to remain isolated from each other, a wish to remain settled/the same, and not to risk growing/developing/getting closer. That wish as we are seeking to remind ourselves shows little sense of man's social/thoughtful place and the possibilities open to us.

So, this general introduction to our specific responses to this appendix can perhaps help you to prepare yourself, i.e. not to set up your personal defences, but to help you remove them, for whilst we seek to be achieving more thoughtful versions of self through our conversation with you, we do not of course, content ourselves to sympathise and to be understanding, for you know that in this context that would not be a good course of action.

Analysis of Paragraph 1

Worrying is only natural. Worrying is like a conditioned reflex, but it isn't related to specific conditions, i.e. it is a reaction to any conditions. Man becomes a hyperanimal then by his ability to abstract; more specifically in this context to abstract conditionality from specific conditions, i.e. any conditions become a cause of worry. This process produces worry as the condition within which the worrier's time is spent.

Response:

'Worrying is only natural'. Who, if anyone would say this? The answer indicates to us that here you are attempting to do as we asked at the end of Section 10, i.e. to work on the inside, i.e. to hear how the worrier's acts are products of good intentions. However, as we will show, you do not intend your speech to stand alone, for alone it could be read as limited to description, perhaps as a sympathetic epitaph; whereas your efforts are, like the efforts of all thoughtful interlocutors, concerned to preserve our liveliness, our response-ability to be continuing developing through inquiry. Your speech encourages others, i.e. us, to participate with it and not to submit to it for the self we speak of is not yet dead.

When you say worrying is only natural you seek to remind us that we do more than worry for we are not natural.

As you are no doubt well aware we consider all social action as unnatural, i.e. as thoughtful/deliberate, so when you say that worrying is only natural, your speech reveals how the worrier wishes to maintain the pretence of treating worry as a thing, for she imagines that only in this way can we prevent ourselves degenerating into it. Now, if that had been your intention, you might have expected us to be grateful for your help, but the surface of your speech is to us no more than the tentative beckoning of one who imagines she is on the outside looking in and who seeks others with whom she can collaborate in such a way as to indulge in audience participation, i.e. in merely settling for becoming part of an audience. But we are not grateful for the surface of your speech, for your manner of speaking as if from the outside reveals how we could already have been in much deeper than we had imagined. An effort to cling to the surface, e.g. an effort to treat worry as a thing, is only called for by those who are already imagining they are falling. You seem to be describing the condition that some may imagine that we are, each and all of us, in, but we are seeking to display that social actions/speeches, including that of those who are tempted by worry, are more thoughtful than appearances might have led us to believe. But you are well aware of this, for you know that we would not hear the surface of your speech in preference to its depths, you are aware that we would not merely nod in agreement.

When you say that worrying is like a conditioned reflex, you are seeking to stimulate us in such a way that we bring to the fore the issue of justice, and perhaps punishment, in social life, for if actions which are visualised by members as natural are no more than conditioned reflexes, then aren't these very acts instances of oppression by a form of speech which denies speakers an awareness of their true condition as moral/social response-able actors, i.e. as those who are deciding how we live. Those, if any, who consider their own actions/speech/thoughts to be natural are those who stand, and without reason, in the way of social development, of friendship, whether they be for or against the concrete laws in a specific society, for they are denying their own social character, and by doing so deny their place in social relationships for they pretend they do not act deliberately. We seek to reflect upon our conditions in such a way that we are not limited to conditioned reflexes. So where worry could be seen as a constant but specific reaction to any conditions, we hear thoughtful/social actions as those which work to produce better conditions by speaking response-ably.

So you are reminding us that men/women are becoming social/moral actors not through any abilities that merely extend animal traits, not for instance by an expanded ability to abstract, i.e. pull out, but by deciding not to be natural, by deciding to be becoming thoughtful/social/deliberate and response-able. Man as hyperanimal to use your term will spend most of his time worrying for he leaves himself and views his condition as that of an isolated body within or against the rest of the universe. What a depressing picture, what a hopeless task, if it can be called a task, and its hopelessness is correctly perceived by the worrier who then seeks distractions, who wants his mind taken off things. No sense of friendship for this creature, only of stark futility, of certain defeat. But we seek to collaborate in such a way as to be creating social conditions such that we are remoulding that version of human life, rather than hiding it behind superficial chatter.

So, as thinkers we are playing a part in creating forms of speech/life, i.e. social conditions, of friendship, for we choose not to settle in a process that produces worry as the condition in which social actors' time is spent except when we mindlessly forget what we are letting happen.

Analysis of Paragraph 2

The worrier is right to see that conditions are only conditional (i.e. not necessarily necessary) but wrong to see conditionality itself as conditional (i.e. as not necessarily necessary). To say this another way each set of specific conditions is only conditional and as a result worry is a natural and appropriate reaction to each specific set. Hence the absurdity of trying to remove worry, for example, 'Don't worry everything will be alright'!!

Response:

We choose to work hard to be hearing what you are saying as stimulating here for its surface seemed very dry and arid, and hardly the place for us at all, and yet what you are saying can help us to be remembering not to set off ourselves on absurd ventures, i.e. not to seek unconditionality as your hypothetical worrier seems to do, for no venture could be more fruitless. Conditions are necessary for any action, for any speech, so to seek a state without conditions is to seek silence, thoughtlessness. When you speak of worry as an appropriate reaction, you seek to remind us that worry can be heard as a form of speech that seeks to appropriate speakers. So worry apparently merely wishes everything would be alright, and in this way could reduce those it subjects to inertness, but we are reappropriating our speech/thought, so as to make it work for/with us, we are collaborating in such a way as to be producing desirable conditions through our dialogue. So whilst worry does appear to object to chance, we are seeking to be taking our chance, our opportunity. Whilst we recognise that our work cannot make everything alright we are also recognising the absurdity of subjecting our speech/our lives to such a bizarre and extreme commitment, for such a commitment could have reduced us to silence. We are seeking to continue improving our lives, our ways of speaking/thinking, to be making them more enjoyable by continuing conversation. When in that paragraph you use the notions right and wrong, your speech is not constrained by a notion of right and wrong as correct and incorrect, but as liberating and oppressing, deliberate and thoughtless.

Analysis of Paragraph 3

This might suggest that it is specificity rather than conditionality which fixes the worrier in her slot. However specificity is really only another version of conditionality (limits), i.e. specification is speaking of limits (conditions), it treats speaking as defining (i.e. setting out the set limits). But it seems from the preceding paragraphs that man rises above specificity by abstracting, and that this offers a way for the worrier to remove her condition, i.e. if she could be more abstract about conditions she could stop worrying about those that confronted her, or that she tries to avoid. However, this also would be misleading for far from abstracting being a solution to the problem of specificity (if problem it is!) it is merely a refinement or sophisticated form of it.

Response:

Here you ironise our speech in Section 10 concerning historical specificity and draw out how that speech could have been heard as an instance of worry, as an effort to avoid specific conditions by concentrating on something less specific, more abstract, but such could not, and you know this well enough, have been our intent. We were seeking to uncover a practical/friendly reading of social situations not by avoiding them, for how could that be thoughtful? No, we were seeking to display how all too frequently supposedly practical solutions are mere avoidance, they would restrict us to superficiality, they would restrict conversation to banter and by doing so deny profundity, i.e. human character, its place. So, whilst welcoming your reminder we doubt that our readers will have read what we said in the manner you imagine. Our speech is oriented to unsettling those who worry[1] by showing how the form of speech which they may hear as akin to glue that has set/solidified around them, is far from set; indeed how speech, by being speech, need never set. Our intent is not to leave the worrier homeless, but to be collaborating with her in developing a form of speech/life that does not wall us in, that can continue moving us along, helping us develop. Sophisticated, refined speech is boring, for it orients to neatness/completeness, it is unnecessarily restrictive and seeks to close rather than open minds, it is defensive, undialectical, antisocial.

Analysis of Paragraphs 4 and 5

To think the replacement of worry by abstracting is changing anything is to fail to be abstract enough about abstraction, i.e. it is to fail to see that abstraction can be subsumed within the category of methods of avoidance available to the worrier. Even this isn't enough for it forgets that worry isn't everything, and this is one of the problems with the method of abstraction, i.e. that it can all too easily forget what it has left out. Furthermore the very idea of replacing is, in this context, merely another way of talking about avoiding/placing out of the way, and this brings to mind the earlier idea of stumbling into the problem again at another time or level.

Imagine if I went through the preceding page and crossed out all the t's in an attempt to show how abstracting forgets what it is doing it for, and then forgot myself what I was crossing out the t's for, and we get some idea of how abstracting is a stretching of the imagination but is merely imaginative, i.e. it does forget what it is doing it for!

Response:

Here you are seeking to help us to remind ourselves to consider why we are doing what we are doing. Your speech helps evoke resonances of the practices of bureaucracy, technology, professionalism and the like, and reveals very nicely how, by drawing and restricting our attention to superficial details, these practices would consume and restrict the energy we have for thoughtful social action. But they will not do so if we orient to their members not as masters but as those who are enslaved, i.e. as friends with whom we can collaborate in such a way as to foster our communal commitment to deepening and liberating our selves from shallow, oppressive, forgetful practices/usages. The bureaucrat does provide a very graphic instance of the worried man, i.e. the man who has come to imagine that some thing, e.g. a book of rules, or a superior in the structure, will relieve him of response-ability for his actions. That man is oppressed by a form of speech through which he is denying himself, i.e. denying his free moral/social character. Bureaucracy is a stretching of the imagination that could all too easily lead some to forget what we are for. Perhaps it leads some so far that they pretend they no longer want to remember! If sociologists, for instance, were led in this way, they could hardly expect to relate to others in a social/thoughtful way, for their work would be intent upon concealing, rather than seeking to reveal, human character. However, we, as thoughtful interlocutors, hear sociology as committed to the latter rather than the former enterprise, we hear sociology as an instance of social action, i.e. as an effort to prise open social relationships.

Analysis of Paragraph 6

We have seen earlier how the worrier produces the future as something she has merely to wait for, e.g. her method of hoping things will work out, as the best way of using her time. Perhaps this can suggest to us the dreamlike nature of her mode of thought. A dream whether good or bad is always something we are in as if against our will, i.e. as if we hadn't chosen to be in it, and somehow the only way we can bring ourselves to see that we have produced it is by ending it. This resonates with the religious idea of an afterlife from which this life would presumably have only a dream like status! But, the point about dreams is that once we realise we have produced them they no longer retain their fearful or pleasurable nature. In both cases we treat produced as made up, that is as fake, and we tend to think that once we know something is a fake there is nothing to worry about. However the realisation that fakes are something we can produce is what we should be worried about!

Response:

We take this paragraph further by saying that all social actions are fake, if by fake is meant made up, for none is natural; and it is by increasing our awareness of the fakeness, the made upness, of all social actions that we are beginning our deliberations. So, the dreamlike nature of the worrier's mode of thought rests in its forceful manner of persuading those it subjects that it is natural, i.e. that it represents/replicates the way things (including selves) are. However, nothing we do is natural, for our place as thinkers/speakers is such that we are all always choosing/deciding, i.e. always acting unnaturally/socially. We all as thinkers/speakers are making our social relationships, and yet to be saying this is to be drawing out the limitations of your notion of fakeness, for whilst it does act as a sharp reminder that we do not slip into speaking or listening as if our way of speaking or listening were natural, it could also lead us to imagine that in our social relationships we have some thing to replicate. Perhaps the bureaucrats rule book will suffice to provide an instance. So, our particular place as speakers/thinkers is such that we are free to choose with others how we construct our social relationships. As we have said there is nothing that we are forced to replicate. Now whilst we are beginning to hear how our profound social and moral character rests in this freedom to deliberate and decide, we are aware that some, i.e. those who hear freedom to be a burden; those who have been reduced to hearing their own speech as natural, if there are any, will be shocked by our manner of speaking. Whilst they will steadfastly refuse to question the character of their own speech, they will, perhaps publicly, but if not publicly privately, hear the deliberate, the social, the intentional, the unnatural, the lively, the moral all as fakes that fail to replicate nature. Speakers of that sort are constrained to hearing the moral as the natural and whilst they are always disappointed with themselves for not quite making it, they are repulsed by the notion of deliberation.

Our efforts are oriented to formulating this feeling of repulsion at the idea of deliberation in such a way that our social relationships can pulse again in a thoughtful and not an accidental manner. We hear any talk that relies upon a notion of man as natural as being superficial; as being anti social; a-sociological, self destructive and self contradictory, and we would not be befriending those, if any, who spoke in this way by remaining silent, for to remain silent is to choose to seek to replicate nature, it is to deny the possibility of friendship, of social development.

So, the last sentence of your Paragraph 6 is heard as calling upon us to show the fakeness of that paragraph and by doing so to collaborate with you in such a way as to be liberating our social relationships from the pretence that there is an original pattern to which they/we should seek to subordinate ourselves. (Incidentally, we have for long been awaiting an opportunity to deal with any discontent you may feel for our references to you as the original speaker, for you may have heard the juxtaposition of those two notions as accidental, however, by now few, if any, of our readers will be satisfied with readings of social actions as accidental).

What is the dream to which you are referring us? We hear it as the lives of those committed to a notion of self as natural, i.e. as not deliberate, i.e. as not thinking, for these, all consciousness is like an aberration, an interruption of the silence that is nature, and the sooner the thinking, the conversation, the social relationships, are over the better. That movement is very clearly the opposite of that which we are commending. What we are saying is that we are only beginning to grasp our social possibilities by reversing that movement, by hearing that the notions of good and bad only have relevance to us if we decide to be unnatural, and if we do decide, and we all do by speaking, then we are already choosing the social relationships we place ourselves and other selves in. And far from needing to end/finish what we are doing before we can begin, we need only to continue what we are already doing, i.e. acting thoughtfully/intentionally. Our lives would only take on a dreamlike status if we began to pretend that we do not decide what we do. Even the version of dreaming that you offer shows how deeply that oppressive, self destructive notion of self, as unable to choose, could penetrate into the apparently non social private world of dreaming.

The point about dreams or any other forms of social action is that we are beginning to be producing them by releasing ourselves, our society, from oppressive forms of speech which would have us believe that we cannot act deliberately, thoughtfully, that we cannot be freeing ourselves from contingency. So, when we spoke in our response to Paragraph 5 of bureaucracy, technology and professionalism, we were not commending back to nature, what we were saying is that bureaucracy, technology and professionalism are social developments which could or can be oppressive if they are heard as natural developments and therefore as necessary.

Analysis of Paragraph 7

'Yes but' makes reference to the conditionality of the present where the worrier somehow sees conditionality as reducing the present's status to that of being hypothetical (it is worth noting that she speaks of this as a reduction!). The present is, only if you ignore the 'yes but'. The 'yes but' comes to mean then that things could be or are otherwise, and we can see how this produces the present as being dreamlike, i.e. hypothetical situations are dreamed up, and the worrier even situates the present as a hypothetical situation in the context of other hypothetical situations. But why does she do this? Why does she write paragraphs like this? It seems that by using the 'yes but' she expresses her wish to avoid or ignore the present. (Initially this doesn't seem to tell us anything, but perhaps when we see that the worrier equates the present with the natural we will learn something!) An instance of this effort to avoid the present can be pointed to earlier in this set of notes when it was suggested that worry was a natural reaction without it further being suggested that it wasn't the only natural reaction. Choice was eliminated by treating the indefinite article as a definite article whereas it is only the natural reaction for the worrier.

Response:

We are reminded by this paragraph of yours that 'Yes-but' by making reference to the conditionality of the present reminds us, as speakers, how we need to be acknowledging the theoreticity of our own speech if we are to be achieving versions of the present that move us on from mere hypothesis, i.e. from a version of speech as being restricted to the pretheoretical. Speakers, if any, who hear their own speech as natural, i.e. who oppose deliberation as unnatural, would be reducing their own speech/lives to thoughtlessness, i.e. to being nothing more than a series of disconnected, disparate happenings/events. Perhaps they would hear this happenstance appearance as liberty, but by doing so they would not hear how it is no more than haphazard. You say in parenthesis that it is worth noting that etc. and by doing so could have provided us with an instance of how speech can be haphazard for if it was worth noting, couldn't you have interrupted the seemingly natural flow of what you were saying to expand why or how it was worth noting. However, we do you an injustice for now we hear how you are noting this for yourself, i.e. you are not talking down to your reader, on the contrary you are controlling your writing for you know that your readers will not be behind, but will, if anything, be ahead of you.

You say the present is, only if you ignore the 'yes but', but you are not commending that we do ignore it, for to do so would be to restrict ourselves to the hypothetical, to that dreamlike wish to be natural, to be non thinkers, non theorists. The 'Yes-but' does remind us that things (including here ourselves and our ways of speaking) could be otherwise, and by doing so it helps us to hear how our apparently unthoughtful, apparently pretheoretical versions of the present are merely hypothetical until we bring them into question. You remind us that we are not restricted to dreaming up hypothetical situations for we are not social isolates, we collaborate with others in our efforts to produce versions of the present, or whatever, that can help us to be improving our lives, our modes of thought/speech. If it seems to some that by using the 'yes but' we express a wish to avoid or ignore the present, we might agree, provided the present was being heard as contingency, as thoughtlessness, as you say as natural; and also provided that avoiding and ignoring were not being used in a pejorative fashion, for by ignoring and avoiding the present's contingent aspect, we are dealing thoughtfully with the social possibilities it opens up for us, and this is why we do as we do. The instance you offer is such that it goads us to speak of a less restricted response. You speak of choice being eliminated by treating the indefinite article as a definite article, and you are quite correct. But by being merely correct you remind us how if we had subordinated ourselves to your speech, (which could not have been what you desired) we would have eliminated a choice of far greater import, and this is the choice of not pretending to be natural, i.e. the decision to act thoughtfully/socially/freely and to think about how we speak rather than limiting ourselves to one of a restricted number of supposedly natural reactions, for to do the latter is to be working with a degenerate notion of the social.

Analysis of Paragraphs 8 and 9

The worrier's constant usage of 'perhaps' suggests that making choices is something the worrier will do her utmost to avoid (it also suggests the shallowness of her avoidance, i.e. as if she doesn't see that she chooses the usage of 'perhaps'). This would certainly account for her avoidance of the present for the present is a prerequisite for choice, and hence its elimination or avoidance would be tantamount to removing the possibility of choice. So, the worrier seems to avoid making a choice or decision in two ways (a) by suggesting that the time to make the choice hasn't yet come, (this is her usage of 'yes but' and/or 'perhaps') and perhaps will never come. Or (b) by suggesting that what seemed like a choice wasn't really a choice at all, i.e. generally by her reduction of herself and/or the present to nature. We can see now that given her version of nature as a child (b) collapses into (a) or is only an example of it.

The worrier would go about doing (b) above, i.e. showing that a choice wasn't really a choice by saying either that given that it is natural for the best alternative to be chosen, if there is a difference between the two alternatives the weaker alternative had no real chance, and hence there was no real choice. Or, in the other case if there was no difference between the alternatives she would say that the choice between them is necessarily arbitrary and that again there has still been no choice. If some alternative proposal about the alternatives in a choice were offered, i.e. where they were neither the same, nor different, she would probably resort to showing how the chooser isn't really choosing anyway because of her social grouping or whatever, i.e. she would treat the chooser as the subject for natural science.

Response:

If the version of choice that you talk of in these paragraphs was that to which we were committed, the writing of this response would require no more thought than does the choice between one brand of washing powder and another. But as we all, as thoughtful interlocutors, are well aware, such is not the case. The decision to speak response-ably, rather than to restrict ourselves to reacting supposedly naturally, is the decision for social change, for social development, i.e. it is the decision in favour of active inquiry into more social social relationships, rather than the indecision that settles for the superficiality of appearances, i.e. of the status quo. The difference between these courses of action is analogous to that between waking and sleeping, it is that between thoughtful and thoughtless, between just and unjust, i.e. no difference could be greater, and yet the choice always, and not surprisingly, requires thought/effort/character, indeed the choice is only open to speakers/thinkers, i.e. to we who are choosing to be freeing ourselves, i.e. to we who are choosing to act morally rather than naturally. So, whilst the surface of your speech in these two paragraphs appears to be moving in such a way as to reveal that you are seeking to show how choice can always be reduced so as to be heard as no real choice; we know that, as a thoughtful interlocutor, you could not intend that to be the outcome. We hear your speech as calling upon us to display through our response how such a restrictive version of choice, as is that which you seem to be offering, could never be accepted, or adhered to, by thinkers/speakers, for it is miserly and degrading, and in no way seeks to be raising us out of the supermarket mentality that would reduce genuine social inquiry to bargain hunting. And whilst the former activity does profit us in the profound sense of stretching and improving our conceptions of self and society, the latter is an activity that does indeed bar any real gains.

The version of choice you seem to offer is an instance of the pretheoretical, i.e. the hypothetical talk to which we have made reference in our response to Paragraph 7 for it nowhere raises the real choice, the desirable choice, i.e. the possibility of bringing the conception of self that is being relied upon into question. Social groupings are products of how we decide to speak and think about our society, they are not natural developments, i.e. they are not necessary, and by deciding to be speaking of the social as the realm of the possible, we are displaying how we can eschew the constraints that restricting ourselves to easily available alternatives would entail. We are choosing to treat you, and all other speakers, with respect by hearing your speech as the product of good intentions. We place your speech in the context of a relationship of friendship, for to have treated your speech, or any speech, as the subject matter for natural science would have been to decontextualise it through a restrictive practice which reduces rather than enhances the prospects of genuine social development.

Analysis of Paragraph 10

We begin to see here how the idea of intentions or more specifically good intentions would sound unnatural for the worrier because it seems to assume the possibility of choice which she seems intent upon removing. By treating worrying as only natural the worrier is in effect simply re-echoing her claim that she isn't responsible for anything either good or bad; but why does she want to make this claim? This shows us how disclaiming is the closest she wants to get to responsibility, again it shows us how close she is to the angry man!

Response:

Yes, we are remembering that we have good intentions in a sense in spite of, rather than because of, the surface of the preceding paragraphs, for we do not restrict ourselves to re-echoing. To have done so would have been to have ruled out that possibility that is a thoughtful response. Good intentions not only seem to assume the possibility of choice, they actively resist being cut down by that forceful and degenerate version of speech as being no more than an echo of nature, and as a weak and distorted one at that. So whilst we are claiming to be becoming thoughtful/social/moral rather than natural, those speakers, if any, who pretend they are not us, i.e. those who pretend that they aren't responsible for their own speech rely upon an understanding of speech/thought as being no more than a degenerate version of nature, and by doing so they come to hear all conversation as being a waste of time. Their way of talking/listening would generate only silence for they seek to decontextualise and in this way they would seek to hear our speech as empty.

Analysis of Paragraphs 11, 12 and 13

The worrier's version of responsibility is being protective, i.e. looking after something or one, i.e. of keeping something or one (e.g. herself) safe. To say it once again of trying to prevent things falling. This can show us how she uses a version of good as something things or people are, such that they need protection. Whereas the idea of doing good would not begin with an idea of looking after it might begin with an idea of improving. We see here how the worrier gets drawn into a static analysis of things being either good or bad, i.e. to be protected or avoided (where avoided is merely deciding not to protect), and how she can come to see herself as only being accountable for failing as a result. To say this in another way if she conceives of good as something she needs to protect, and she sees this as her sole task then she can never do good for she is always separate from it, she can only do her job which is analogous to not letting anything happen, or she can fail to do her job which is like letting things happen, and it is the latter that does happen and that is perhaps why she feels she fails and wants somehow to claim mitigating circumstances, e.g. she was distracted, or whatever.

Somehow protection doesn't seem like a good intention, its best possibility is for it to allow good intentions to be seen. That is, protection subordinates itself to other's intentions in one way or another. This idea of protection subordinating itself can also suggest how it can become lazy, for it could mean much less work if the good were seen to be able to protect themselves, i.e. if the survival of the fittest meant the survival of the good. The protector here would be as useful/as needed as the teacher who felt he had only one lesson to teach and that he had taught it successfully!

Much earlier in our work we spoke of the worrier having a utopian image of herself as not wanting ideal conditions, but as wanting a self that could deal with any conditions. We can see from these notes firstly why the idea of ideal conditions would not appeal to her, and secondly how her utopian image of herself seems to be grounded in the need for protection.

Response:

But we are becoming exasperated for whilst we have consistently been making the effort to appreciate what you are saying, i.e. whilst we have for a long while been seeking to offer readings of your speech as the exercise of friendship, your speech does seem to be settling too easily in the task of describing this hypothetical worrier, rather than in making the effort to inquire more deeply, and more actively, into ways of improving social relationships. Perhaps you imagine you can leave that work for others, e.g. us, to do! Perhaps you are using this descriptive enterprise as a shield with which to protect your person, or as a smokescreen behind which you can sustain a policy of splendid isolation! Perhaps you have been, and are, still, committed to protecting your person, what you imagine is your self! If this has been and is the case, our exasperation is in order, for all that our conversation with you has done, has been to accelerate the movement away from conversation, away from friendship, the very movement we so desperately desire to reverse. Now whether your speech is mere personal protection, or whether it is the exercise of irony, the intention of which is to allow us to draw out of our selves an honest and thoughtful response, we cannot know, but whichever, our conversation can only be improving through our efforts to say how the type of protection about which you seem to speak would do us harm not good. So this response will take the form of an effort to be differentiating ourselves from what we imagine is the usage of worry in order that we can be getting to know you better, and by doing so, be getting better to know ourselves.

'The worrier's version of responsibility is being protective, i.e. looking after something or one, i.e. of keeping something or one (e.g. herself) safe ...' What is presupposed here?:

(1)   That the thing (!) being looked after is known.
(2)   That it is known to be valuable.
(3)   The notion of looking after presupposes the thing is already valuable, it does not require work/thought.[2]
(4)   That the thing is in danger, i.e. others re deformulated as enemies.

So, your speech reminds us that we do not act response-ably/thoughtfully by settling for personal protection of that sort, for on each count we hear how the opposite orientation would lead to less superficial conversation, to more social/thoughtful/friendly relationships.   But this is why your speech is becoming exasperating, for after all we have been saying in our conversation can you still be commending such forgetfulness? It is as if you want us to go, with you, over old ground again!   But perhaps we can display to you how uninterested we are in mere personal protection by doing precisely as you ask, for if we were interested in personal protection, we would very likely fear our readers. So we might fear that our readers could hear this particular response as disrespectful, i.e. as disregarding their presence.   However we have no reason to fear our readers for we orient to them as thoughtful interlocutors, as friends who may desire to work with us over old ground, for they are aware that it is not so much by considering the ground, but by considering our way of working that we can always be instructing ourselves.

Your speech reminds us that we are not intent upon treating our selves as things and then preventing our selves from falling.   Indeed perhaps treating selves as things could be heard as a version of the myth of the original sin as that which precipitates the fall. We are continuing improving and elevating our conception of self by thinking/conversing/deliberating, i.e. by not reducing selves to things.

'... This can show us how she uses a version of good as something things or people are such that they need protection ...'.   We can almost hear the armed forces here, and it is fitting that they are referred to as forces, for weapons can do no more than force, i.e. they do rest in thoughtlessness, in superficiality, in the refusal to continue conversing.   The degenerate orientation of personal protection can very quickly be put to use in the service of thoughtless commitments to the protection of the nation or whatever.   Protection in that mode of thought has got caught up with the notion of possessions, good is heard as value rather than virtue, and as virtue is being forgotten so also is the possibly continuing movement towards achieving more thoughtful versions of self/society being abandoned. We do not seek to settle in protecting our persons, or what we might have mistakenly treated as our personal possessions, e.g. families, nations or whatever, (perhaps even disciplines!) from others, but to be working in such a way as to be producing social conditions in which protection no longer is the first thought that comes into, and from then on rules, our speech/our lives. For such forms of speech are oppressive. For, as you say, they begin with an idea of looking after, where we begin with an idea of active inquiry/looking for/improving. So whilst our inquiry/conversation is only beginning theirs is finished, they wish only to chat with others who are the same as themselves for they imagine that is safer. And yes, we are hearing how this results in chatter, i.e. in what you call a static analysis, we would prefer not to speak of that as an analysis at all however as we hear analysis as dialectical, i.e. as movement. But we will proceed to think about the restricted options that mode of speech/life leaves as available. Protection of the thing as it is, or avoidance, no wonder those constrained by this mode of speech are worried, there is no possibility of social change, for neither protection nor avoidance provides any room for improvement/for increasing intimacy. The description you offer of the worrier's conception of her life/her work resonates with the work of one on a production line where there is no possibility of creating, only of protecting one's earning capacity by not allowing anything to go wrong; by not allowing anything untoward to happen.

Whilst the production line worker can with a great deal of justification claim mitigating circumstances, are we to allow sociologists to reduce their response-ability in this way!!? After all, don't they frequently have security of tenure, together with a commitment to free speech, so what are their mitigating circumstances? But our exasperation with your speech is leading us astray, and leading us to do our readers a disservice for they are thoughtful interlocutors, and as such do not need to be reminded of their responsibilities.

As to Paragraph 12, yes protection does begin to sound more suspect for we become suspicious when that which is being protected is that which the protectors refuse to bring into question. For in what does its supposed value lie? Certainly not in its humanness for that is always a product of thoughtful inquiry. Paternalism can have no place in our movement towards more thoughtful, more liberating social relationships for the subordination it entails is contrary to the relationships of friendship which we desire. Paternalism/protection is lazy, you are right, but we would say it results in more rather than less work, where work is being heard as alienated and alienating, and though you speak strangely and perhaps dangerously, we do hear how thoughtful characters do not desire to have protectors/bodyguards but seek to have collaborators, thoughtful interlocutors. There is even a sense in which by seeking to achieve thoughtful character we could be heard as seeking to be fittest, but it is not in a comparative sense, for our work/our lives are grounded in a commitment to improving social relationships/social conditions, and a lack of fit is the absence of good social conditions, the absence of thought. Thinkers/speakers by continuing our committed inquiry into what it is good to do, do provide for the survival of thoughtful social relationships, and by doing so also provide for committed inquiry. Your remarks about the utility of the protector and the very limited teacher are correct, but of course you did not merely want us to be learning that! You are directing us to hear how thinkers/speakers are those who always have, and always desire to have, deeper lessons to learn, for only in this way can we continue to develop socially/dialectically. Whilst the lessons we are learning do continue to lessen the likelihood of our actions being thoughtless they do not lessen the need and desire we have to continue instructing ourselves.

As to the final paragraph we are reminded by it that the split between self and conditions leaves the worrier merely wanting/wishing. However our collaborative efforts to be achieving more thoughtful, more social notions of self and society are such that the continuing achieving of the one is the continuing achieving of the other, i.e. ideal conditions are continuing and deepening friendship, and ideal selves are thoughtful friends. Nothing utopian here, but everything to do. We don't desire personal protection, but we do desire honest conversation.

NOTES

[1] For would we be befriending them by leaving them?

[2] What of the labour theory of value here? Perhaps a labour theory of virtue!

12 Forms of hearing

APPENDIX J

Original Speaker:

Para.1   Your pressing request seems to be that I produce a version of my own speech as being something other than, or more than, worry, i.e. as being good intentioned rather than merely good natured, i.e. as being an attempt to do good rather than merely trying not to do harm. But, when your request seems to be ignored, or forgotten, you become exasperated; which suggests that you imagine you have done everything you could, and the result is that you begin to lose trust in your version of my work as being good intentioned, and then you need me to show my good intention, or commitment in part in order that you can regain the trust you had in your version of my work. You need to regain this trust for otherwise you feel you will have succumbed to the thoughtless urge to treat others as lost causes, and you know that this would reduce you to a lost cause because you would have lost your cause. You presuppose the existence of good intentions for without them you can see no good. You know you become safe if you can produce others as always acting with good intentions.

Para.2   Your exasperation is then a forerunner of the exasperation I should feel when I find that our work on worry does nothing, i.e. that others go on worrying, and/or doing nothing. Perhaps I am being polite here, your point is that if our work on worry cannot enable me to do more than merely worry, i.e. cannot enable me to produce a version of it, or anything else, as doing good then there is no reason to suppose it will enable others who have far less involvement in it to do more than merely worry either. In which case it would, like worrying, have done no good.

Para.3   The moment of decision is approaching far too rapidly for the worrier, (N.B. as would be expected she sees it as approaching her rather than her approaching it!) i.e. if she doesn't take up the challenge she is reduced to a life(!) of worry (grovelling) if she does she knows she has a fight on her hands. Perhaps the analogy sounds fanciful but I feel it is instructive for the worrier does try to avoid conflict situations, i.e. she is evasive, perhaps analogies themselves are used by her to evade! But at the same time, if she does accept the challenge too readily she is aware that others could (as could she) doubt her sincerity. But she also knows that she can only go on seeing the possible decision as premature by continuing to worry, for hasn't she deliberated for long enough?

Para.4   So now the worrier is faced with her first real problem, i.e. how can she produce a good version of something rather than carrying on her old routine, i.e. rather than merely carrying on? Or, how can she realise that she is something more than a worrier? But, how can she be so dumb!!! Once again she produces the situation as one in which pressure is exerted upon her, and surely she should be able to see by now that it is this beginning that leads her astray. It leads her astray because it makes her forget that if she was not already working with a good intention she wouldn't be under any pressure at all. If she had not already decided that good intentions are good she would not be worried about not having them. I think this is very important thought I may not have expressed it well, and also in the face of the fact that experience would lead me to see that it is when I see something to be important that I am often making my least response-able statements.

Para.5   Now, before I forget, I must say that this is not a way of removing pressure but at most of replacing it. The point is that when I produce your exasperation as being a pressing request (a demand) upon me I give a reading of your exasperation than can do no good.

Para.6   By choosing to read the situation as one in which you exert pressure upon me for my good, I continue to be interested in how good or bad might happen to me. For this reason I begin to feel that any response I make will be rightly seen as interested in personal protection, for I produce you as perceiving me as being in danger. An alternative reading of your exasperation is as the expression of your loss of hope, i.e. it could be read as a request from you asking me to relieve you of the strangling pressure that lost causes exert upon you.

Para.7   At first sight the latter reading suggests that my response need not be one that acts in the interests of personal protection, but this is not so, for whilst it might remove the pressure temporarily it would only be like prolonging the agony. For it assumes that you are only interested in personal protection, i.e.

224

it converts you into a worrier.

Para.8 So there is no point in simply lifting the pressure from me to you. What I need to do is to see that this pressure is that which makes life worth living, it is not something to be removed, it is something that must be lived with. But what is it? It is the pressure resulting from our desire to attribute intentions to others and in so doing to have intentions ourselves. I have an idea that I should be more specific here and refer only to good intentions for the notion of a bad intention is grounded in a bad reading of intention, for bad ought to be heard as the result of unintentionality/thoughtlessness overcoming intention/thought, rather than as the result of a bad intention. That is, bad is always the result of the unintentional rather than the intentional. Forgetfulness is unintentional rather than intentional.

Para.9 Now having said this we can see how the worrier is misleading herself when she produces herself as being afraid that she has bad intentions, i.e. that it is better for her to act unintentionally than risk having bad intentions. For as we have seen the idea of bad intention is the result of a forgetful reading of the idea of intention and if the worrier could remember that intentions are always good she would come to see that not acting intentionally is merely another way to succumb to thoughtlessness. That is she could derive no solace from her view of herself as not being responsible for what goes wrong, for nobody ever is. Lest she thinks this is an even more comforting situation we need to point out to her that it is a waste of time, i.e. that it doesn't do any good, for good can only be done response-ably, i.e. intentionally. Worrying can never do any good then because it is a conditioned reflex, i.e. it occurs unintentionally.

Para.10 The worrier accepts the possibility of bad intentions and is drawn into seeing all intentions as bad because she has a version of intention as premeditation. She thinks (!) that to intend something you have to think about it before you act, i.e. that you shouldn't be hasty, and she sees this to be premeditation, i.e. thinking before. But this version of premeditation leads us into thinking that what we need to know is what will happen rather than what we want. That is, it loses the possibility of desire when it replaces what we want to do with what we need to do. So, for instance, to treat a Socratic dialogue as premeditated in this sense is to make the outcome the cause of what came before, i.e. it is to reduce the dialogue to a waste of time. None of this is a bad thing for the worrier except for the fact that she thinks premeditation cannot be done, i.e. she wishes it could! However she thinks that premeditation must always fail because we cannot know everything, including for example what will happen, but, to say it again she wishes that we could! So the worrier produces intention as premeditation and premeditation as necessarily failing; this is why the worrier sees her own work as unorganised, i.e. as coming from confusion. This is why she feels a need to think about what she says before she says it, and this is why she always finds dialogue too much of a strain, i.e. because she thinks she never has time to think. (She wants to think before she thinks!)

Para.11   What we need now then is a strong sense of premeditation which would allow the worrier to see that whilst this work is not premeditated in the weak sense this is not bad but good. She must remember that simply because she didn't know everything that she was going to say before she said it this doesn't mean that she is acting unintentionally.

Para.12   To suggest that we shouldn't premeditate (in the above weak sense), i.e. to suggest that we shouldn't produce a version of what will happen and orient to that, isn't to suggest that you shouldn't care about the future, for not caring about the future is to be unintentional, it is merely to hope that the future will care for you. More strongly, premeditation is to not care about the future in any other sense than wanting to be able to control it, i.e. it is an attempt to protect one's person by limiting the future's possibilities.

Para.13   Now perhaps I should look more closely at the writing of these notes in the terms of the notes for your exasperation suggests that I should be very thoughtful about my work. But how am I to be thoughtful (or perhaps better how have I been thoughtful) without getting drawn into premeditation (weak variety), i.e. perhaps, how am I to meditate rather than premeditate where premeditation is alienated for it either subordinates thought to some unthoughtful task or to the wishes of other?

Para.14   How can I maintain our conversation without subordinating my work to the removing of exasperation? The crucial point here is the realisation that nothing I could do could (or should) remove your exasperation for exasperation is nothing more than one way of terminating worry. (This is another way of saying that good intentions cannot be seen in anything anyone does). The result is then that even if I were to subordinate my work to the task of the removal of your exasperation it would necessarily fail, and its failure might be all the more exasperating for you! The point is that it isn't your exasperation which suggests that I should be thoughtful, even though it may have appeared to be, it is my good intention. One other way of saying this that needs to be said is that the desire to maintain a conversation is good intention, for conversation is finished by the domination of ego or alter - domination reduces the space for intention and produces premeditation, where premeditation is the earlier idea of tacticalness. We cannot have conversations without good intentions. Conversation/good intention is then the way to avoid talking about things that aren't worth speaking about, e.g. natural limits. But still I could be read as talking about the worrier, i.e. one version of natural man, and as a result we can see how all of the work so far could be treated as alienated if it is heard as worry. For if it is treated in this way we can see how it is itself subordinated to the unthoughtful task of talking about worry, as if we didn't already know what it is!

Para.15   If I really was the worrier, i.e. if all this work really was still worry, only worry, I would be really worried about the worrier, and being really worried here would be treating the worrier as a lost cause, i.e. it would be saying there is nothing more I can do, and yet I know that this isn't the case for the very fact that it is work tells me it isn't worry. This is a way of saying that perhaps I am a worker not a worrier where work is the having of intentions, i.e. it is the having of something you desire to do, and this is a way of saying, if we can remember what has gone before, that good work is not premeditated! Perhaps this tells us why it is never finished for being finished is like reaching a previously thought about goal or end, i.e. it relies upon premeditation. Good work then doesn't satisfy expectations for it doesn't orient itself either to expectations or satisfaction (finishing), and this is good because satisfaction like domination leaves no room for intention. The worrier is satisfied that there is nothing she ought to do, and that is why she isn't me, and also why there is so much more to be done!

RESPONSE TO APPENDIX J

You are right when you say there is so much more to be done, and by formulating forms of speech as forms of hearing, as we have done earlier, we are better remembering that we seek to hear our own speech/thought as we hear the speech of others. By remembering this the superficiality of versions of conversations that could have restricted us to maintaining thoughtless barriers between concrete people is revealed. Earlier we spoke of our work straining the seams of its own format, here our efforts are oriented to some unpicking of the seams conventional usage could appear to sew between self and other selves, ego and alter. I/you talk could have been heard as epitomising the alienating effects of a form of speech which leads speakers to forget that that is what we all are. But we are remembering that we need not settle with a reading of I/you talk as being grounded in a dogmatic acceptance of social stratification, i.e. as being speech reduced to communicating superficial differences and similarities between specific discrete speakers. By hearing speeches as expressions of a communal commitment to active, collaborative, social inquiry we seek to elevate our conception of self by risking questioning how we are choosing to hear/to live. For instance, by bringing into question what could be apparent differences in status between speakers and listeners, between writers and readers.

So, whereas much earlier in this work we brought into question the notion of 'I', here we are remembering that the notion of 'you' also cannot be taken for granted. We choose to hear 'you' and 'I' as instances of the same, i.e. as instances of thoughtful interlocutors, i.e. as deliberate social actors. And, by hearing in this way we do resist that persuasive version of I/you talk which rests in a difference which denies the possibility of friendship by being thoughtlessly, and forcefully, committed to a form of social stratification which seeks to offer self a differential status to that of other selves, rather than to discriminate between the thoughtful, free, moral, deliberate, intentional, social actor and oppressive, unthoughtful, unfree, amoral, accidental, unintentional, antisocial happenings.

We are remembering that by seeking to stretch ourselves, and by seeking to act more thoughtfully, we become more not less humble, for the urge for differential social status, i.e. to be thought better of than other selves, can only be heard as the humbug it is, if superficial versions of self are brought into question.

There is no dignity in speech which lacks humility, and by remembering this we hear how by raising questions which humiliate us by reminding us how easily we can imagine we know what we don't know, other's speech helps us to proceed in a more rather than a less dignified manner. But, so persuasive is the predominant conventional form of hearing that we had almost settled with a notion of dignity as correlated not with humility, i.e. not with true worth, but with high rank on one or another dimension of social stratification. No wonder we, who do have a low estimate of our own personal worth, too readily could have mistaken what is a noble sentiment for an inexplicable, but pervasive deformity which we could have sought to hide and/or excuse.

Analysis is a humiliating experience, and so much the better, for those, if any, who seek to be other than humble, overstep their place, and by doing so deny themselves the possibility of true social relationships. Dialectical development, social development involves increasing humility, which in turn opens the possibility for true conversation by enabling speakers to exchange and develop ideas in a non possessive way. But none of this is easy for many of the prevailing conventions of the specific language we have used could have led us away in the opposite direction. Neither is it easy to bring this specific piece of work to a close, but that is what I need to risk doing and am risking doing.

This is the longest letter I have ever written Stan, and perhaps it is the longest I shall ever write, but even so it is, as you and other readers will appreciate, the exercise of understatement. I will allow myself to mention one small fantasy which relates to Ivan Illyich Pralinsky, which is that if he had found this thesis in the side of the chair he was slumped in, and had read it thoughtfully, his story might not have ended where and when it did.

Now I know this work does not cohere to the conventional notion of a thesis but I say so much the better, for I remember that we choose to orient to others as friends not as judges. My hope is that readers will not call upon me to defend this work but will raise questions which help us move on from it, and if this radicalises the whole issue of the submission of sociology theses so much the better, for what worse way is there to have thinkers begin than to force them into submission!

Mick

Postscript:

Perhaps some readers are still wondering about the dangerous paper that was mentioned in the first section, an extract follows:

APPENDIX K

We begin by offering an analysis of the initial section of Socrates' opening speech in the 'Apology' which commences as follows:

'How you have felt, O men of Athens, at hearing the speeches of my accusers, I cannot tell; but I know that their persuasive words almost made me forget who I was - such was the effect of them; and yet they have hardly spoken a word of truth ...'

In this passage Socrates commences by telling us that he has become, or is becoming, worried about the feelings of others present in the courtroom vis-a-vis the speeches of his accusers. He begins by being afraid about what is going to happen to him. The 'reasons' he provides for feeling worried sound convincing, and this is why he begins by feeling convinced by them and worried. He remarks that he noticed his own feelings were being affected by the speeches of his accusers. We assume that he intends to generalise from his own experience, thereby expecting that others would have reacted as he reacted. The fact that he begins by making reference to the feelings of others, rather than to their thoughts, indicates that initially he was being forgetful about who he was, and hence that he was saying what had happened. This is important for as this work proceeds we will be reminded that orienting to the feelings of self or others as something to know and take into account, rather than as something to think about, and perhaps change, could never be considered a thoughtful form of action. Furthermore, Socrates was forgetting himself when he conceived of persuasive words as making him do something, for this suggests a passive, unthoughtful, undialectical version of the listener or reader, whereas Socrates by his own speech frequently displays for us a model of thoughtful listening. But, we must notice that Socrates' display, as all displays, requires an alter. The listener plays a part in the production of the version he holds of Socrates' speech, or any speech.

Socrates says that he cannot tell how the others felt, but the very fact that he speaks about it in this way and at this time, indicates that he is worried about what they feel. He begins by treating others (other listeners) as analytically the same as himself, i.e. as liable to be persuaded by the accusers' speeches. So, when Socrates is worried about what is going to happen to him, a difference arises between what he says and what he thinks. If he had begun by allowing what he thought (i.e. that he did not know how others felt) to discipline what he said, he would not have begun his speech in the way he did. Perhaps Socrates' usage of the phrase 'I cannot tell' is itself more telling than he realised. Socrates begins by being worried not about what he says he doesn't know, but about what he thinks he does know, which is that others are like him, and that as he knows what he feels, he knows what they feel. But here he checks his speech. He questions himself by recalling that he doesn't always know how he feels. He takes his own speech seriously and allows it to remind him that he can forget who he is. He remembers that he can be corrupted, and so rather than speaking about his feelings, which is what could have been expected, he gives voice to the proposal that the feelings he had were not really his but were the feelings of someone who had almost forgotten himself. He makes the discussion less concrete by depersonalising it and treats himself (the one he was talking/thinking about) as a type, rather than as an individual. In this way the problem and his overcoming of it is transformed from being his to being potentially ours. That is, it becomes something we need to think about for our own as well as for his sake.

The forgetful,, i.e. the feelings he felt he had as a result of the speeches of his accusers, almost interrupted his own speech. However, by thinking about who he was, i.e. not one who had the feelings of someone who had almost forgotten himself, he begins to discipline himself and redirect his speech from worrying about persuasiveness towards the issue of truthfulness.

The fact that he, and we, can begin by being worried in this way can act as a warning about the power of eloquence, for he indicates that he in no way underestimates the power of his accusers' speech to influence others, or indeed himself. But, whilst not under estimating the power of his accusers' speech, he proceeds to speak in the face of it. He is not dominated or suppressed by it. He does more than warn himself and others about it, he helps to provide himself and others with the tools to overcome it.

Though this is sophisticated and persuasive reading of the beginnings of Socrates' speech, thoughtful readers of this thesis will not now be taken in by it; they will grasp the profundity of the issue at stake.

Bibliography

(1)   Dostoyevsky: 'The Gambler/Bobok/A Nasty Story' Penguin Classics, Harmondsworth 1966.

(2)   Goethe: 'The Sorrows of Young Werther' (and selected writings) Signet Classics, New York 1962.

(3)   Kafka: 'The Diaries of Franz Kafka'. Edited by Max Brod, Penguin Modern Classics, Harmondsworth 1972.

(4)   Nietzsche: 'Twilight of Idols/The Anti Christ' Penguin Classics, Harmondsworth 1975.

(5)   Plato: 'The Dialogues of Plato' (Volume 1) Translated by B. Jowett. Sphere Books, Aylesbury 1970.